Doing Doctoral Research into Higher Education... and getting it right.

Prof Paul Trowler

All Rights Reserved. Copyright 2016

Introduction to the book 5

Section 1: Writing Doctoral Proposals 6

   About this section 6
   1.1 Introduction 7
   1.2 Title of the Project 9
   1.3 Research Questions 11
   1.4 Research Questions: The seven deadly sins 14
   1.5 Background to the Research Topic 15
   1.6 Research Design & Methods 16
   1.7 Significance of the Research 31
   1.8 Research Timetable 33
   1.9 Writing a Bibliography 36
   1.10 Finding Inspiration 36
   1.11 Developing an Eye for a Workable Proposal 41
   Sample Proposal One 43
   Sample Proposal Two 51
   Sample Proposal Three 60
   Sample Proposal Four 78
   Sample Proposal Four (Revised) 80

Section 2: Making Theory Work 86

   About this section 86
   2.1. The nature of theory 87
   2.2 Making theory work 95
   2.3 Social practice theory & studying change in HE 107
   2.4 Examples of theory use in doctorates 114

Section 3: Thesis structure, content and completion 117

   About this section 117
   3.1 Starting at the End: Questions examiners ask (themselves) 118

3.2. Writing the Abstract 123
3.3 Structuring the Introductory Chapter 126
3.4 Contextualising the Study 132
3.5. Structuring the Literature Review Chapter 137
3.6. Structuring the Method/ology Chapter. 143
3.7. Writing the Data Presentation 146
3.8. Structuring the Conclusions Chapter 148
3.10. Non-Conventional Thesis Structures 152
3.11. Successful Completion: Some pointers 154
3.12. Seven Valuable Virtues for Doctoral Success 158
3.13. Useful Resources for Thesis Writing 160
3.14. Appendix: Writing a doctoral project proposal 163

Section 4: Ten Key Components of Doctoral Research: Maximizing Alignment and Significance 165

About this section 165
4.1 Introduction 166
4.2 Misalignment: An Example 175
4.3 A More Successful Example 192
4.4 Achieving Alignment 201
4.5 Research Significance 211
4.6 Hybridity, Borderlands and Originality: Being Creative 228
Appendix 1: Transcripts of Videos 233

Section 5: Doing Insider Research in Universities 239

About this section 239
5.1 Insider research: a brief overview 240
5.2 Researching universities 244
5.3 Research design, data collection and theory 250
5.4 'Value' and robustness in insider research 271

5.5 The ethics and politics of insider research in universities 277

5.7 Resources for insider research 293

5.8 Literature 293

Section 6: Frequently Asked Questions about Doctoral Research into Higher Education 297

About this section 297

6.1 Research Questions 298

6.2 Research Design 305

6.3 Literature Review 324

6.4 Collecting Data 331

6.5 Using Theory 336

6.6 Writing the Thesis 340

6.7 Examiners Examining 344

6.8 The Viva Experience (in the UK) 351

6.9 Post-Award 353

References 356

Glossary 377

Index 384

Introduction to the book

This book brings together and updates my previous work, published on Amazon, for doctoral students doing research into higher education. Those small books were designed to offer succinct advice of immediate help to such students. They proved to be very popular.

This book, then, covers that same ground in six sections, each of which addresses a critical area for doctoral students. Common mistakes are identified, and advice is given in critical areas so that wherever you are in the doctoral journey you don't go down any blind alleys or get involved in fruitless diversions. I hope to help you "get it right from the start".

Across the book you will find that some specialist words and phrases are emboldened. This indicates that there is an entry in the Glossary at the end of the book explaining them in more detail. There is some limited repetition across the different Sections - this is deliberate, because I wanted each to be capable of being read independently of the others.

I hope you find this book useful, and that it does indeed enable you to design, implement and complete your doctoral research in a well-informed and efficient way.

Section 1: Writing Doctoral Proposals

About this section

This section is designed to be as helpful as possible for anyone who needs to write a doctoral research proposal in the area of higher education research.

General advice is given and then some example proposals are offered, with a commentary after each. The purpose is to help refine ideas about the strengths and weaknesses of proposals, and what makes a robust set of research questions and research design.

1.1 Introduction

Applicants for a doctoral degree and those already on a doctoral programme normally have to supply a project proposal as part of their application. For initial applicants this is one of the three ways in which universities normally make selection decisions. These three ways involve asking and answering these questions:

1. Is the applicant sufficiently qualified and capable to do a doctorate (as judged by their CV and track record)?

2. Is the research project proposal of high enough quality, practicable and important enough to be acceptable (as judged by the written proposal and perhaps a defence of it in interview)?

3. Is there a supervisor who is able and willing to supervise the proposal?

Each university's requirements regarding the research project proposal (point 2) are slightly different, but for the Department of Educational Research at Lancaster University the requirement is a fairly standard one: doctoral project proposals should be up to 1,000 words and should cover the following areas:

Title of the Research: A meaningful, provisional title that summarises the area of interest and planned programme of research. There should be a central problematic in the title, not simply a description of the field to be studied.

Research Questions: Identification of the main research question(s) being asked. These should be succinct, researchable and significant. Bullet points are usually best.

Background to the Research Topic: Explanation of how the questions are different from those asked by others, drawing on a brief review of the relevant research literature. This should show familiarity with the main literature in the field of interest.

Research Design & Methods: The 'who', 'what', 'where' and 'why' of the research plan. There should be an explanation of how the method(s) used will answer the research questions.

Significance of the Research: The contribution that this research will make. Identify the implications of the research for existing educational theories, policy or practice in higher education.

Research Timetable: A detailed timetable that shows how the research design can be managed within a three year time period (or a 5 year period for part time students).

Bibliography: The main written sources on which the research will be based.

The rest of this short book is organized with this structure at its core. At the end of the book are two chapters outlining the more creative aspects of the process of deciding on a topic and developing a proposal.

1.2 Title of the Project

The title of the proposed project is important because it sums up the focus and significance of the envisaged research. A good title should make it clear what the central problematic is, the key issue being addressed. This should be done succinctly and perhaps might even indicate the research design being used.
However many authors of doctoral proposals fail to do this and instead make one of the following three mistakes:

* Using verbs like 'explore' or 'investigate': these are too open-ended. For example: *"Exploring Teleconferencing in Further Education in the UK"*. This indicates vagueness in the mind of the candidate and the potential danger of an endless doctorate, because there are no parameters or clear goals.

* Contrasting two possibilities and asking which is correct. For example *"Positive Change or 'Self-Righteous Waffle': Academics' Perspectives on Sustainability Policy in Universities."* This indicates simplistic binary thinking and suggests that 'straw men' are being set up to be easily knocked down

* Writing a sentence which is just descriptive and lacks a problematic. For example *"The Motivational Effect of Technical and Vocational Education on Students in India."* There is no issue evident: it is unclear what the project is specifically about.
Much better are titles which give an immediate feel for the key issue at hand, and even an indication of the research design:
"Can Students Influence Policy Implementation in Higher Education?: A Case Study Based on the Mainstreaming of Liberal Adult Education." (The title of a PhD by D.F.M. Butt, Reading University, 2000).

"A critical review of the role of the English funding body for higher education in the relationship between the State and higher education in the period 1945-2003". (The title of a PhD by D.J. Taggart, Bristol University, 2004).

1.3 Research Questions

Research questions should:

- Be answerable: it must be possible to know when a question has been answered
- Be specific, that is set clear boundaries in terms of what is being studied, and what is not
- Include at least one analytical question which goes beyond the descriptive
- Be capable of **operationalisation**; that is, use concepts that can be turned into measureable, observable, describable phenomena
- Be bounded in what they require, that is they can be realistically answered given the resources available
- Be significant; that is, they should provide an answer to the '**so what**?' question - the issue of offering wider interest to a larger audience

One role of research questions is to guide research design, and there needs to be congruence between that design and the questions. This means that the research design chosen must be capable of answering the research questions.

Here is a problematic attempt at constructing research questions:
> This project aims to explore academic staff's reception of the teaching and learning policy of a university. The analysis will focus on the discourse that arises from staff's reaction to the policy as well as factors that could undermine or facilitate the achievement of the policy.

This is more like part of an abstract than research questions: while these statements give a feel for the proposed research, there is no specificity, only broad aims.

While they give licence to the writer to cover ground that seems interesting, they fail to set boundaries. It will be unclear to the writer when their work has stepped outside the limits of the study. The word 'explore' is particularly dangerous in this respect - it does not set boundaries or specific goals. 'Reception' is capable of multiple interpretations and needs to be operationalised. There are too many questions wrapped up in these two sentences: they need to be unpicked.

Those two sentences could be reconfigured as follows:

> 1. To what extent do academic staff in one Faculty in a new university in the UK display knowledge about and understanding of the formal teaching and learning policy there?
> 2. In what different ways do academic staff there interpret and respond to that policy?
> 3. What reasons can be given for the differences identified in answering questions 1 and 2?
> 4. What different **discursive repertoires** do they draw on when they discuss the policy?
> 5. What are the implications of the answers to questions 1-4 for policy implementation in the area of teaching and learning in the case study university?
> 6. To what extent do these findings confirm what is known about policy implementation in that context?
> 7. What are the implications of the findings for university managers at senior and middle levels in that context?

These research questions, unpicked in this way, themselves raise issues about the **truth claims** that can be made from a study of one Faculty in one university, but recognising this as an issue is enough for a project proposal.

Analysing these questions further:

Question 1 requires a fairly descriptive answer but there are more analytical ones to follow.

Question 2 is possibly still too open, but it is an improvement on the original version.

Question 3 allows the writer to do some analysis which might get him or her into disciplinary differences, institutional location etc. The data collection needs to be thoughtfully constructed to be able to answer it, and a pilot study undertaken to ensure this.

Question 4 (based on the original version) stands out as possibly belonging to a different thesis, and being potentially too big, especially when Question 5 is attempted.

Question 6 allows a discussion of the literature and gives the thesis a theoretical edge.

Question 7 might be further refined, or possibly dropped if the thesis becomes too big - question 6 covers some of this already. It also begs the '**so what**' question – why should anyone other than senior and middle managers in that institution be interested?

Because of question 6 the main answer to the 'so what' question appears to be a theoretical one in relation to the literature on policy implementation. That would be fine, and the applicant needs to make it clear that this is the main priority of the project, with other aims being significant but perhaps not central.

Often it is useful to distinguish between the **locus** and the **focus** of a doctoral proposal – a topic of study can be merely the location through which deeper questions are explored. In this case the locus is the teaching and learning policy in one Faculty in one university, but the focus is actually achieving a better understanding of the implementation of change. Research question 6 is the key one, if this approach were to be taken in this example.

1.4 Research Questions: The seven deadly sins

1. Too descriptive – *"What are the management styles in place in Saudi Arabian universities?"* (This is OK if there are more analytical questions after it, though of course it is ambitious).

2. Too narrow – *"How can the use of e-portfolios at the University of Bentham be improved?"* (Who cares – apart from people at Bentham?).

3. Too ambitious – *"What teaching and learning approaches are in place in UK higher education and how can they be improved?"* (Impossible to answer).

4. Only focused on perceptions – *"In what different ways do Accountancy lecturers at the University of Bentham view the merger of their Department with the Department of Statistics there?"* (**So what**?).

5. Too vague – *"How does the higher education system in Chile differ from that in Argentina"?* (How long have you got?).

6. **Normative** – *"What are the benefits of linking research and teaching in universities?"* (What about the dysfunctions?).

7. Too **prescriptive** – *"Why does the modular system in UK higher education need to be changed?"* (Predicts the outcome without actually doing the research).

Note how the deadly sins are rarely found alone – problematic questions often combine two or more.

1.5 Background to the Research Topic

This section of a research project proposal should set out the context to the issue for research: this will definitely include the relevant literature but (depending on the topic) might also include the policy background, the contemporary relevance of the topic or some other background factors that are relevant.

The aim of the section is to demonstrate a reasonable knowledge of the area (recognising of course that the research hasn't been done yet), to situate the issue for the panel assessing the application, to show why the proposed research is important, and to show what the research could offer that is significant.

The section should not be too long: often candidates assume that a very extended discussion of the literature will impress. Of course to some extent it does, especially when that discussion shows the ability to evaluate research critically. However, more impressive is the thinking behind the description of the proposed research itself when this demonstrates clarity in conceptualising a very concrete, doable and clearly envisaged research design, the outcomes of which will advance knowledge in some way. So the background section needs to be kept fairly brief, and the discussion of the literature oriented to showing where there are deficiencies or gaps that will be addressed by the research.

It is important not to simply take descriptive content straight from websites or other sources. Apart from the potential issue of plagiarism, that content is unlikely to be oriented to the proposed topic of research. It is really important that all aspects of the background section are situated in relation to the specifics of the proposed research. Too often in doctoral proposals descriptive material is dissociated from any attempt to demonstrate its significance.

1.6 Research Design & Methods

This is probably the hardest part of writing a research proposal, and is often very significant in terms of whether the whole proposal is convincing or not. Clearly, once enrolled, the candidate's supervisor will help him or her to develop a good research design. But it is necessary to make a convincing attempt at it in the research proposal.

Sometimes candidates fall back on **grounded theory** in developing their proposals: basically arguing that they will collect the data and see what comes out of them. However this often fails to convince selection panels and in general it is better to set out a clear, convincing, planned research design. The key thing in this is to make sure that the design chosen is capable of answering the research questions; indeed is the *best* way to answer the research questions.

In general the research design should make clear:

- what the units of analysis are (institutions, departments, people);
- which (or which types of these) of these will be selected for data collection, how many and why;
- what type of data collection methods will be used, and why;
- how the data will be analysed.

Often, a diagram can sum up the descriptive elements of the above more clearly and succinctly than can a written description. But of course the rationale for the design needs to be elaborated in writing.

Ethical issues need to be addressed, as do questions of access: it is often harder to secure agreement to participate than is at first imagined, even for insider researchers: simply assuming that the data will be easily obtainable is not convincing, but thinking ahead about this at least demonstrates awareness of the issue.

Questions and answers

The key issue in research design is ensuring that the decisions made are guided by the research questions: the data generated by the research must be appropriate and sufficient to provide robust answers to the questions asked. It is also important to ensure that a consistent and defensible approach is taken towards epistemological and ontological issues: what does the research claim can be known about the social reality under investigation and how is that reality conceived?
A realist ontological position will usually mean more positivist research designs utilising predominantly quantitative data generation approaches which yield statements describing correlations of a generalisable nature. On the other hand a social constructionist position is likely to be more qualitatively inclined and quite limited in its claims for generalisability.
There are many excellent textbooks on research design, data collection and the role of theory. Here I concentrate on the key issues of relevance to insider researchers.

The following section on research design and methods is drawn from the section in this book on Insider Research in Universities, aimed at those researching or planning to research the institution in which they are employed or are currently a student. For more information on this area, including 'outsider' research, see the latest edition of Judith Bell's book *Doing Your Research Project*.

Single and multi-site studies

Insider researchers are usually faced with multiple pressures on their time and limited resources to use in the research. Some will be employed by the university and have more financial resources but limited time for the research, others will be full-time students studying their own university, with more time but less cash. In either case the option of doing a single-site case study is attractive for practical reasons, and as the next chapter shows can be valuable in itself. Coleman and von Hellermann (2011) and their contributors advocate doing ethnographic studies based on anthropological methods conducted on the researcher's own 'turf':

> ...the 'field' has traditionally been conceptualized as being 'out there' (away from the anthropologist's home), enclosed within a definable territory, and best understood through the method of participant observation. Bound up with these practices is the assumption that culture is located 'out there', with ethnography being about the unfamiliar 'other'. Participant observation traditionally involves intensive dwelling and interaction with the 'native' in order to understand his or her worldview...Such positing of people, places, and 'culture' is increasingly critiqued on account of the problematic ideological assumptions..." (Mand, 2011, p 42)

These assumptions include the notion that 'culture' is something exotic and 'other', amenable only to the distanced and more analytical academic eye, eventually represented through the godlike authorial voice. Insider research which views the local and familiar is at least as valuable, they argue.

But as well as seeing the value of single-site insider research, Coleman and von Hellermann explore the problems and possibilities of *multi*-site ethnographies including those conducted 'at home'. However, as Marcus acknowledges (p. 27, in Coleman and von Hellerman), attempting to deploy such a labour-intensive method of data collection as ethnography in multiple sites will "overwhelm the norms of intensive, patient work in ethnography".

For the individual researcher such a design is too ambitious. This means that a multi-site approach which uses mixed methods or less labour-intensive methods than ethnography may have benefits which justify their costs in terms of time and labour. The important issue in making decisions around this is appropriateness in terms of the research questions, which themselves then come into the mix of factors to consider when planning research which is both practicable and valuable.

For the insider researcher developing a project which compares results from their own institution to those elsewhere, a multi-site study is obviously the way to go - unless other studies have already been conducted elsewhere which are close enough to their own.

Examples of such comparative projects include:

>   1. The factors influencing the success or otherwise of an innovation
>   2. Approaches to management and leadership and their effectiveness
>   3. The implementation of a national policy at ground level, including compliance (or otherwise) with national quality (or other) guidelines
>   4. Professional practices in a discipline or field of study
>   5. Student responses to an innovation

Action research

Bensimon et al (2004, p 105) suggest that it is important for practitioners concerned with bringing about change in their context to "produce knowledge in local contexts to identify problems and take action to solve them". The authors in that collection advocate the idea that change agents should be 'practitioners-as-researchers'.

Action research is an emergent enquiry process involving cycles of: actions; enquiry, analysis; planning; changed actions. It has, broadly, an enhancement agenda. But there are often different understandings of what 'enhancement' may involve, especially among those on the ground in universities.

Action research can be undertaken with different audiences, beneficiaries and purposes in mind. It can be emancipatory in intent, aiming to identify disadvantaged groups and to rectify structural disadvantage, or it can simply be aimed at making sure policy is implemented effectively, regardless of what it is or its effects.

Useful guides to conducting action research are Coghlan and Brannick (2010) and Koshy (2009).

Evaluative research

Evaluative research in higher education aims to attribute value and worth to individual, group, institutional or sectoral activities happening there (Saunders, Trowler and Bamber, eds., 2011). Because this guide concentrates on insider research, the relevant levels of evaluative activity are the individual, group and university ones. Such research asks questions about the value of long-standing activities or of innovations that the researcher is undertaking, or those of a group to which s/he belongs, or those of the university as a whole.

While evaluative research often deploys similar data generation techniques to those of 'regular' research, and can use theory in similar ways too, there is one key question presented by this kind of research if it is to be lifted beyond the particular. That is – 'what is the value of this in terms of a larger contribution to knowledge in the academic world?' If the research focuses on the value of a particular set of activities, or an innovation, in a particular location at a particular time, then it becomes difficult to answer that question. Furthermore, the chances of getting a study of a particular situation published in a reputable journal are rather small, if that is an aim of the research.

There are three key ways in which evaluative studies can be conducted so that they provide good answers to this 'contribution' question and stand a good chance of being published, at least in part. These are: *theoretical* contribution; *methodological* contribution; *professional* contribution. Often good evaluative studies will offer a combination of these.

The *theoretical* contribution relates to some aspect of the relevant literature, perhaps on implementation theory or the management of change, or some aspect of theory related to the substance of the activity or innovation (information and communication technologies, for example). The later part of this chapter deals with the place of theory in research.

The *methodological* contribution relates to evaluative methodology, the techniques and theories employed in conducting evaluative research, and the study should offer something additional to what already exists in this area.

There are a number of different approaches to evaluative research, methodologically and in other ways, so the contribution can be made to one or more of these.

In summary they are: technical-rational evaluation; appreciative enquiry (Cooperrider and Srivastva, 1987); utilization-focused evaluation (Patton, 1997) and finally realistic evaluation (Pawson and Tilley, 1997). An overview of these is offered in chapter 2 of Saunders, Trowler and Bamber, eds., 2011.

Finally, the *professional* contribution relates to practice in the area being investigated, and to achieve this it is necessary to expand the truth claims of the research beyond simply establishing the value of the particular activity or innovation to encompass *similar* activities/innovations in similar circumstances. In this third category the issues covered in the next chapter become particularly relevant.

Institutional ethnography

This is an approach to researching what its founder, Dorothy Smith (2005; 2006), describes as the "textually-mediated social organization". Smith says that institutional ethnography begins by locating a standpoint within an institutional order, a particular guiding perspective from which to explore that order.

This raises a set of concerns, issues or problem germane to those people who occupy that standpoint. These "local actualities of the everyday world" (Smith, 2005, p 34) are only the starting point however. From here the investigation of institutional processes is launched, and the broader structural forces which impinge on the everyday world are explored.

Because of this unfolding from the local it is not always possible to sketch a detailed research design in advance. But Smith argues that the design is not random: "Each next step builds from what has been discovered and invades more extended dimensions of the institutional regime" (2005, p 35). Language, and textual objects are very significant in this – for Smith language serves to co-ordinate subjectivities.
Devault (2006, p 294) says this:

> Institutional ethnographies are built from the examination of work processes and study of how they are coordinated, typically through texts and discourses of various sorts. Work activities are taken as the fundamental grounding of social life, and an institutional ethnography generally takes some particular experience (and associated work processes) as a "point of entry." The work involved could be part of a paid job; it might fall into the broader field of unpaid or invisible work, as so much of women's work does; or it might comprise the activities of some "client" group.

This examination is conducted through the standard mix of ethnographic approaches; interviews, observation, documentary analysis and so on. But careful attention is paid in particular to the use of textual artefacts, the discursive repertoires employed in them and the causes of effects of these on social relations within organizations.

In Smith's original formulation there is a concern to investigate the ruling relations that are articulated in work processes and instantiated in texts, and she pays particular attention to the ways in which women are subjugated within institutional processes and through texts and discourses.

For example in universities 'mothering work' can be a discursively and organizationally embedded in such a way that women academics disproportionately find themselves doing low-status and unrecognised work supporting students in difficulties.

And of course what in some contexts are called 'support staff' are disproportionately female in most universities.

How this has come to be, and how it is perpetuated, are areas that can usefully be explored in a fine-grained way through institutional ethnography. And not only explored. A key tenet of the approach is that it should be *for* people and not just *about* them: the research must illuminate the mechanisms of oppression and disadvantage and suggest ameliorative strategies.

Institutional ethnography sees local practices in terms of the larger picture of structured advantage and disadvantage, despite the fact that it starts from a particular standpoint within the institution. In this it addresses one of the criticisms sometimes made of fine-grained ethnographic research, for example by Hamersley (1993) and Porter (1993), that such research loses sight of the structural constraints on actors and structural conditioning of their behaviour.

It is clear that insider research and institutional ethnography are highly compatible, at least for some kinds of research questions.

However as an approach to enquiry it does leave the researcher with some problematic questions. One is: what standpoint should I start from and how do I draw the limits around it?

This is a question of level of analysis: the standpoint might be that of 'students', or 'women students', or 'women students with disabilities'.

That last category could itself be segmented further. Another question is: if I start from one standpoint and work outwards, as Smith recommends, what about other standpoints that exist in the university – why should I privilege just this one?

These and many other questions need good answers if readers are to be convinced that the study is robust.

Hypothesis testing

Here the purpose of insider research is to test an hypothesis or to replicate a previous study in a different but relevant context in order to test its conclusions. Either qualitative or quantitative approaches may be adopted to do this, or a combination of both.

This research purpose is best illustrated by an example. Such research could involve a study designed to test the hypothesis developed by Arum and Roksa (2011) that universities (at least in the USA) are "academically adrift". Arum and Roksa used the Collegiate Learning Assessment, a standardized test administered to students in their first semester and then again at the end of their second year, as well as survey responses to answer the question: "do students learn the important things that universities claim to deliver?" They conclude that 45 percent of the students included in their data demonstrate no significant improvement in critical thinking, complex reasoning, and writing during their first two years of college.

In addition Arum and Roksa extrapolate from their analysis some explanations: one is that students are distracted from their studies by socializing or by working at the same time. A further cause is the fact that universities and their staff prioritise other things than undergraduate learning, such as research. In addition there is, they claim, deliberate collusion between staff and students not to tax each other too much.

Methodologically this study has come under criticism, most notably from Alexander Astin (2011), and there are many claims in it that are unsubstantiated and which from a UK perspective appear to be just wrong (for example about the findings of the majority of studies on the 'teaching-research nexus').

So, this study could be tested in a different but relevant context. A similar or identical research design could be adopted to test the findings, and the same statistical techniques could be applied to the data. Alternatively the hypothesised causes of this claimed lack of significant learning could be explored. A further alternative is to build on Astin's critique and design a 'better' study.

Theory and insider research

Theory-use is very important in research generally and insider research in particular – it lifts it above mere market research or journalism, and it allows the researcher to step outside generally accepted ways of seeing the social world.
'Theory' is usually portrayed as consisting of six linked characteristics:

> 1. It uses a set of interconnected concepts to classify the components of a system and how they are related.
>
> 2. This set is deployed to develop a set of systematically and logically related propositions that depict some aspect of the operation of the world.
>
> 3. These claim to provide an explanation for a range of phenomena by illuminating causal connections.
>
> 4. Theory should provide predictions which reduce uncertainty about the outcome of a specific set of conditions. These may be rough probabilistic or fuzzy predictions, and they should be corrigible – it should be possible to disconfirm or jeopardize them through observations of the world. In the **hypothetico-deductive** tradition, from which this viewpoint comes, theory offers

statements of the form 'in Z conditions, if X happens then Y will follow'.

5. Theory helps locate local social processes in wider structures, because it is these which lend predictability to the social world.

6. Finally, theory guides research interventions, helping to define research problems and appropriate research designs to investigate them.

Different levels and types of theory inform decisions, processes and outcomes in research (see Trowler, 2012a, for an account of them).

There are also different views on the role of theory, some challenging its fundamental role, as set out above, and seeing it not as part of a 'scientific' process but as creative and emancipatory. Feminist thinkers, among others, tend to adopt this perspective:

> how often their own cherished analytical rationality is broken up by glimpses into the imagination of more provocative thinkers. I have come to the conclusion that it is not so much that we self-consciously assemble all the resources for the making of research imaginaries as those vivid ideas (and frequently their authors) come to haunt us. (Hey, 2006, p 439)

Stephen Ball agrees:

> Theory is a vehicle for 'thinking otherwise', it is a platform for 'outrageous hypotheses' and for 'unleashing criticism'. Theory is destructive, disruptive and violent. It offers a language for challenge, and modes of thought, other than those articulated for us by dominant others. It provides a language of rigour and irony rather than contingency. The purpose of such theory is to de-familiarise present practices and categories, to make them seem less self-evident and necessary, and to open up spaces for the invention of new forms of experience. (Ball, 1995, p 265-6)

Haraway (1991) takes this point further in elaborating the notion of 'standpoint theory'. Sprague and Hayes, 2000, in discussing the concept, say this:

> Standpoint epistemology argues that all knowledge is constructed in a specific matrix of physical location, history, culture, and interests... A standpoint is not the spontaneous thinking of a person or a category of people. Rather, it is the combination of resources available in a specific context from which an understanding might be constructed. (Sprague and Hayes, 2000, p 673).

For Sprague and Hayes, as for Smith (2005), discussed above, it is important to challenge the standpoint of the privileged from the standpoint of the disadvantaged and (as feminists) from that of women. This can bring empowerment and self-determination; it uses theory as a weapon against structures of privilege and structured disadvantage.

Feminist standpoint theory suggests that an important way to develop this line of research is to build on the standpoints of those who are least empowered in our current relationships. People living in different intersections of gender, class, and race are likely to have different stories to tell. Thus, a good way to start is to listen to people with disabilities who are also women and/or poor and/or people of color, and the people who nurture them, as they describe in their own ways the constraints on their daily lives... (Sprague and Hayes, 2000, p 690).

Insider research presents particular problems in terms of the use of theory and the relationship between theory and data.

Insiders conducting emic research are themselves liable to be influenced by tacit theories held by respondents.

They can even be captured by institutional or by management discourse, as Hammersley argues (see Trowler, 2001, for more on this).

In such cases it becomes particularly difficult to render the normal strange, to move beyond the standpoint of the privileged. But human behaviour viewed through the microscope tends to bring to attention impalpable drivers far more than when it is seen through a telescope and by their nature these are difficult to apprehend through pure empiricism. In fine-grained qualitative insider research knowledgeability and sense-making are foregrounded as explanation is prioritised above simple correlation. In this respect the role of theory in insider research holds both promise and dangers.

The seven deadly sins of research design

1. Not being specific enough about the details of the sample selected for study and the rationale for that selection.

2. Adopting a research design which is not appropriate to answering the research questions.

3. Not giving a rationale for the overall research design.

4. Proposing a 'convenience' sampling approach without acknowledging the consequences of this for the robustness of the study: being too complacent about what is acceptable.

5. Not explaining how the different components of the research design can be integrated during analysis – especially in a mixed-methods design.

6. Not acknowledging potential ethical issues.

7. Not giving a convincing answer to the **'so what'** question in terms of what the data can offer.

1.7 Significance of the Research

Doctoral research must demonstrate that a significant contribution has been made to knowledge in its field, and must at least in part be publishable in an academic journal.

While it might be presumptuous to identify so far in advance what that significant contribution will be, it is important to show that the research at least has the potential to jump this hurdle. Doubts about this might be raised in admission panel members' minds if the topic of the research appears to be too parochial; only concerned with the issues in one organization at a particular time, for example. These concerns may be magnified if the research design involves insider research. I deal with this in more detail in part 5.4 in this book.

So in making it explicit why the research is important, and at a high enough level potentially to merit a doctorate, it is important to go beyond the particular. In discussing evaluative research in the previous chapter I identified some potential avenues for doing this. For other kinds of research alternative ways in which this can be done include:

- Testing, developing or elaborating a particular theoretical perspective or tradition
- Testing previous research findings in a new context
- Approaching questions previously addressed by other research using new methodological tools
- Developing conceptual models which illuminate some aspect of social reality
- Critiquing current positions in literature, policy or practice

- Building a basis for new policy or practice in wider contexts
- Developing new approaches to research
- Offering new insights into significant issues
- Bringing together and building on previous research findings

1.8 Research Timetable

The key point in setting out the research timetable is to be realistic. An over-ambitious timetable betrays lack of insight into the research process.

Time should be allocated at the beginning of the research for in-depth familiarisation with the literature and for refining the research design and questions as well as for developing data collection instruments. This almost always takes longer than expected: getting to grips with the literature will need to incorporate literature on relevant theory, on the substantive topic and on research methodology, so this alone is time-consuming.

It is important to conduct a pilot study (assuming the proposed research is empirically-based) before going into the field. Time needs to be allocated to this, and to processing the results from that pilot.

The time allocated to data collection and analysis depends, of course, on the research design, but again needs to be realistic. In most cases data analysis will occur concurrently with data generation rather than being a process left undone until after all the data have been 'collected'.

Writing up the thesis also takes longer than is sometimes imagined. A typical thesis will have six or seven chapters, and even with drafts of many of these already prepared, it can take between three and eight months of dedicated work to refine the whole thesis into a finished form. Setting out the structure of the thesis here can be helpful, serving to emphasise the clarity of the proposal. A fairly standard set of chapters looks like this:

1. Introduction
2. Contextualisation
3. Literature review
4. Method/ology
5. Data presentation and analysis
6. Conclusions

Different universities set different targets for their doctoral students, but the **Department of Educational Research** at Lancaster University sets the ones below. Such targets can act as a template for setting out the research timetable in a doctoral project proposal:

For Students in Year 1 (or Part-Time Equivalent):
- Research questions and research design finalised and agreed with supervisor.
- Good progress made with review of relevant literature.
- Scoping and pilot enquiries have validated research design in terms of potential of richness of data to answer questions.
- Key concepts and theoretical lens clear by end of year 1.

For Students in Year 2 (or Part-Time Equivalent):
- Data collection complete, or nearly so. Good progress on analysis.
- Some thesis chapters written in draft, including contextual-introductory chapters, methodology chapter, literature review.

- Good conceptualisation of probable findings and argument, including its engagement with the literature.
- Writing 'voice' for thesis now found.

For Students in Year 3 (or Part-Time Equivalent):
- Data analysis complete. Argument fully formed.
- Writing up full thesis.
- Presentations at conferences and departmental seminar to prepare for viva and improve structure of argument.
- Potential areas of discussion in viva identified

1.9 Writing a Bibliography

The key things in setting out the bibliography are: a) to set out in full the bibliographical details of any works cited in the proposal and b) to indicate other significant texts that will inform the project.

In doing this the panel assessing the project proposal will look for coverage of the field and for good practice in both citation and setting out a bibliography. Inconsistencies in how books and articles are referenced may be taken as a sign of poor research training or sloppiness in writing, and so should be avoided.

In research into higher education the usual citation and referencing conventions involve a version of the Harvard system. The style guide for authors from, for example, Open University press, is (in most cases) appropriate for a doctoral proposal for higher education research: http://mcgraw-hill.co.uk/openup/authors.html

1.10 Finding Inspiration

Often doctoral applicants and candidates have a firm view of the topic they want to research. This may be some issue that is important to them professionally, a puzzle that they want to spend time exploring great depth. It may have been suggested to them by a comment from a colleague, or by something they read. They may simply be continuing earlier studies but now within a much more focused and deeper doctoral framework. Turning this topic into a robust project proposal is the topic of the next chapter.

Sometimes though they do not have a very clear idea about what the topic of their doctoral research might be, or have two or three different ones and they are not sure which is the most viable.

In this latter case there are a number of ways of finding inspiration for researchable topics:

* Reading titles and abstracts of completed doctorates in the higher education field for areas that are of interest. Where there is access to the complete doctorate, looking for sections on 'further research' can be helpful. See ethos.bl.uk and http://www.theses.com/.
* Reflecting on what area of expertise they would like to be known for in four or five years' time, or what would be professionally most valuable.
* Reflecting on what kind of data collection methods would be most viable and interesting for them, and working back from that to a suitable topic.
* Reviewing topics currently being funded by relevant higher education research funding bodies such as (in the UK) the ESRC, HEA and LFHE.
* Investigating the website of preferred university departments to explore the research specialisms of likely supervisors.
* Reading books that give overviews of areas of research that are of interest with a view to exploring one of those areas further.
* Attending conferences and talking to people giving presentations on topics of interest about further research areas.
* Brainstorming and then progressively refining/combining ideas. See James Hayton's video on this: http://www.youtube.com/watch?v=PY01A-jCuOA&feature=player_embedded&CMP= .

(There are more resources about thesis writing from Hayton at http://3monththesis.com/)

From Sketchy Idea to Robust Project Proposal

STAGE	A Specific Example (for illustration only – a full proposal would have more)
Refine research questions	*"To what extent and to what ends can conceptions of 'learning organizations' as developed in management literature be applied in university contexts in the UK?"*
Develop research design appropriate for research questions	Review of management literature on 'learning organizations'. Secondary data from a varied sample of UK universities.
If necessary revisit research questions to establish better fit with research design	*"To what extent can models of 'learning organizations' as developed in management literature be used to establish how far UK universities fit those models, using secondary data?* *How far do those models need development for a UK university context, and what purposes would such a development serve?"*

Identify literature to be addressed	Management literature on 'learning organizations'.
Refine research design in a detailed way, especially in terms of sampling	15 UK universities will be sampled. Three will be selected from each of the 5 HE groupings in that country (Russell; Million+; University Alliance; UKADIA), with each of these further subdivided on the basis of dimensions of their strategic plans.

The rationale for these decisions is based on differences in university goals, stakeholders, resources and environment, all of which will have a bearing on what it means to be a learning organization and how far that can be achieved. |
| Refine data collection and analysis methods | Content analysis of 15 university websites, followed by more detailed discourse analysis of parts of the websites of 5 of these. |
| Consider appropriate theoretical lens and rationale | Social practice theory takes the concept of the learning organization beyond idealised criteria. |

	for it	
	Reconsider research design if necessary	Social practice theory addresses recurrent practices, values and attitudes. Therefore empirical data will be required generating detailed qualitative data.
	Consider title for project	*"Reconceptualising the Concept of 'Learning Organization' for the UK Higher Education Context: Applying a social practice approach"*
	Develop an account of the significance of the project in terms of original contribution to knowledge	Develops the notion of the 'learning organization' in a way which is applicable to and valuable for UK higher education. Applies the social practice lens to critique some earlier approaches to the concept of the 'learning organization' and show how it can be developed. Theoretical work has significance for the practices of universities working towards enhancing the organizational learning that occurs in those contexts.

1.11 Developing an Eye for a Workable Proposal

Assessing a research project proposal is a skill that develops with practice and improves with experience. Tacit knowledge is built up over time by reading proposals, by discussing them with others and by comparing one's own views to those of others. Much of supervision is tacit knowledge which can only be accumulated with experience. Backhouse (2009, p 186) quotes a doctoral supervisor saying:

…you develop a sense of where it's going wrong and where it's not, I can pick it up immediately, and that kind of expertise is not something that you can learn, you know, it's experience.

She also quotes a PhD candidate describing two academics talking on successive days, sketching a possible research project:

> …you walk down the passage, and you would see the same two people standing at the doorway talking about something and every day you'd walk past, they'd just talk for fifteen minutes in the morning, and every day when you walk past you'd catch a little of the conversation. Literally four days later, they'd posted that article on the archive and I was like, "Wow, now that's how it should be done." And it seemed like there was just such a wealth of ideas….but [also] the experience to say, "That one is worth pursuing. That one, I don't think is going to work. (Backhouse, 2009, p 210).

High risk and low risk proposals
However, it is sometimes worth taking a risk.

Some proposals are not particularly solid in the sense that a 'successful' outcome seems less than highly probably. They might, though, offer the potential of coming up with something highly original, or approaching a problem in a way that non-one has done before. These are high(er) risk proposals and should not be discounted: tacit knowledge and wisdom are also applied in balancing risk with potential gain.

Below I offer some genuine examples of doctoral research proposals, with my commentary on them. I suggest reading them and, preferably, discussing them with others to develop a view. My view on each is only one perspective: readers may well disagree.

I'd like to offer heartfelt thanks the authors of the proposals for permission to reproduce them here. In some cases I have edited the proposal for concision and to enhance anonymity, including removing bibliographies and appendices.

Sample Proposal One

Communities, Networks and Education

Abstract

This paper is an overview of my PhD research proposal. It is concerned with investigating evolving notions and expressions of community and networks in the context of educational culture which is engaged in the process of discovering the opportunities and challenges presented by Communications and Information Technologies (CITs). Parallel to this is the task of identifying key elements or threads that might be common to a wide diversity of educational "electronic communities". The research is further focused on a theme of "the changing paradigm", particularly within higher education, which runs through and across technological, organisational and academic domains. One perspective on this is articulated by the Vice Chancellor of the University of Melbourne Alan Gilbert when he argued in his keynote speech in November 1996 at The Virtual University? Symposium:

... the first step to survival is to ensure that the information superhighway runs through every great campus, and the second is to ensure that the riches it brings are in turn enriched in a real learning community.

The notion of "learning community" is one that will therefore form a locus for this research. In pursuing this, many so-called online learning communities will be analysed in terms of their creation and stated mission, development and methods for determining their effectiveness or otherwise. Following, in particular the theoretical model of Tiffin and Rajasingham, a range of case-studies will be presented.

However, at this early stage of the research...the primary case-study is concerned with the development of Education Network Australia (EdNA). EdNA is a government-sponsored "meta-network" launched in Australia in 1997 primarily as an online Information Directory Service — although its beginnings were some two years earlier, when it was conceived more in terms of connectivity and infrastructure. In its current (early) stage of development its foundations have firmed as a framework geared toward fostering collaboration and co-operation throughout the various Australian education and training sectors — that is, schools, vocational education and training, adult and community education, and higher education. In order to develop, it has had to adopt principles of exclusion (as well as inclusion) in order to provide only "quality" online educational resources for its constituency. In this process, *identity* is a key success factor.

Keywords

Community; Networks; Identity; EdNA

1. Introduction

The purpose of the study is to identify key elements or threads that might be common to a wide diversity of "electronic communities" operating within educational contexts. Such communities can express themselves as an outcome of extending the forum for interaction of an existing co-located community or workgroup, or more typically, as a self-sustaining "virtual" association existing across geographical, cultural, and timezone boundaries.

Why this focus?

Communications and Information Technologies (CITs) can be enabling tools which provide opportunities for communication and interaction which have not hitherto been possible.

It does not follow, however, that these tools are intrinsically enabling and, in fact, evidence suggests that contrary scenarios proliferate. Notwithstanding this constraint, CITs have been, and are, fundamental to the emergence and development of so-called "electronic communities", "virtual communities", online "learning communities," and other associated collaborative and co-operative activities which occur in online environments (with "online" being used here in its broad and common usage to include both synchronous and asynchronous computer networks). The communications cultures evolving with usage of these technologies are unprecedented and in educational settings pose transformative challenges to the established pedagogical and organisational cultures. Thus, analysis of these cultures will likely result in the "discovery" of a range of new practices being implemented in response and may further assist in the formulation of educational paradigms appropriate to them.

In the 1990s, concepts of "globalisation", "lifelong learning", and "just-in-time training" have become commonplace. These concepts are just a small set of an ever increasing lexicon associated with transition into the "information age" or "knowledge age" heralded by the "digital revolution".

At one extreme "the media" hypes up this process. It is itself fueled by its own vested interests in meeting this challenge, a challenge presented foremost by the "convergence" of digital technologies used in mass media distribution, telecommunications, computing, and, to some degree, education itself. At another extreme can be identified a paralysis or sluggishness in cultural response within higher education, both academically and organisationally, despite the surplus of "visionary" rhetoric.

Thus, this study must also closely monitor the evolution of concepts concerning "community" in the delivery of online education and services.

Of course, hand-in-hand with the evolution of language associated with these changes is the evolution of socio-cultural organisation. "Lifelong learning" and "just-in-time training" have become marketable slogans in an era where higher education is increasingly a mass market and a highly competitive proposition. Thus, notions of professional development as a process conducted in short bursts of intense professional learning that in turn punctuate longer cycles of "business as usual" in the workplace are also in question. This seems to be particularly so for educators: it is commonplace commentary that the balance in core activity of an educator is shifting from the "sage on the stage" to the "guide on the side".

2. Research/conceptual context

It is intended that appropriate theoretical/conceptual frameworks are researched and tested for their validity. Those that form the conceptual context for this investigation all intermesh to some degree. The primary sources forming the basis for this investigation include those of Berge and Collins, Castells, Tiffin and Rajasingham, Rheingold, Snyder, and Harasim et al.

It is also anticipated that as the research proceeds the implied theoretical synthesis will need to be flexible so as to accommodate the rapid evolution of CITs and the educational communities and cultures which are adopting them.

While the Internet is clearly *the* Meta-Network of all meta-networks it is *identitification* with a particular community which can make an electronic network truly value-added and conducive toward collaboration.

In the case of EdNA, it is the education and training communities of Australia which serve to define the identity of the network — or more accurately, this meta-network since it brings together, and endeavours to promote collaboration across, several other large regional networks.

3. Research questions

From the literature survey (which includes ongoing access to online resources) a number of research questions have emerged — they are listed below in order of relevance, with the first two being fundamental:
1. How are concepts of "community" and "network" related in online environments?
2. What precisely constitutes a community in an online environment?
3. What factors constrain and what factors facilitate the evolution of community in online environments?
4. What conventional elements of community persist in online communities?
5. With the socio-cultural trend toward "lifelong learning" how is professional development for educators affected?
6. How does "virtual community" and the trend for "lifelong learning" interrelate?
7. Is a taxonomy of online "communities" possible?
8. How does hypermedia impact online *learning communities*?
9. How is organisational change within higher education impacting on educational practice?
10. Is the pursuit of collaboration and co-operation throughout and across the education and training sectors a flow-on effect from the enabling aspect of CITs? Or, is it more that these communities are somehow *compelled* to collaborate?

4. Research methods

In any PhD-related study *semantics* certainly demand that definitions are clarified. For example, depending from which vantage one looks from, a "community of networks" could also be viewed as a "network of communities". This blurring of semantics, however, also seems to be a feature of the object of study.

Following on from this and the questions outlined above there are also certain intrinsic difficulties concerning rigorous methodological study of the subject. This is certainly a common caveat for academic papers presented at IT-related conferences.

A diversity of university domains and "communities of practitioners" are investigated:
- subject-based electronic forums in higher education
- interest groups / newsgroups
- educational workgroups
- campus-based university electronic forums
- a "flexible-access" university (aka "open", "distance-education", "virtual")
- international higher educational consortia.

Note – the rest of the proposal, about the case study, and the reference list have been omitted for concision.

Commentary on sample proposal 1

There are some interesting and illuminative ideas here. The author comes across as keen and knowledgeable. However the proposal itself suffers from some major flaws:

1. The title doesn't contain a problematic or indicate a direction for the research. It doesn't indicate that the research focuses on communications and information technologies, even.
2. The abstract is too long (for an abstract) and contains a quote and details which do not belong there. Sequentially four areas of research are introduced but not linked to each other adequately. The first one (beginning "It is concerned with...") is obscurely written. The second (beginning "Parallel to this...") is not specific – what kind of "elements or threads"

are being investigated? The third ("The research is further focused...") makes an assumption that there is a changing paradigm but does not indicate its nature, only where it manifests. The fourth ("In pursuing this...") does not explain why the intention expressed is linked to the preceding material. In short, there is a sense of disconnection and a potentially limitless agenda.

3. The abstract also gives the impression that the research is uncritically accepting the agenda of the Vice-Chancellor quoted and of EdNA, rather than being an independent research project which develops its own set of issues.

4. After setting out a very large scope for the research in the abstract, the Introduction shrinks the research agenda to the second of the four objectives set out in the abstract. However, under the heading Why This Focus? a fifth purpose is introduced: to discover new practices being implemented and so assisting in the formulation of educational paradigms appropriate to them. Later, a sixth purpose is revealed: "closely monitor[ing] the evolution of concepts concerning 'community'..." By now the scope of the project is completely out of hand.

5. Under the heading Research/conceptual context it is not explained why the work of the authors mentioned might be relevant to this research. It is not clear whether or not they are commensurable and so able to be integrated into an illuminative whole, theoretically.

6. The research questions finally appear after several pages. There are far too many, some are far too ambitious (especially the penultimate one) and they have only a partial connection to what has been said previously in the proposal.

7. The Research methods section contains very little detail of the design: no specifics are provided.

So, there are plenty of good ideas here. But revising this proposal to provide one which is focused and deliverable needs to start with revising the research questions. They should be reduced in number and scope. Then a research design should be provided which is detailed and specific. That design should clearly have the potential to deliver answers to the research questions. There is no need for an abstract in a research proposal; the proposal itself should be a very condensed outline of the project. And it needs to provide the reader with a very solid grasp of what will happen, and why.

So what might a revised set of research questions look like? Any revisions need to result in questions which:
- Are of interest
- Answerable
- Move from the descriptive to the analytical and explanatory
- Provide an original contribution to knowledge when answered.

I would suggest the following as a first attempt:

"This multi-site case study research project examines the nature of interactions and discourse used in online learning groups to answer the following research questions set out below.

In 12 online learning groups in different disciplines and institutional contexts:

1. How does the concept of "community" manifest itself and develop?
2. What factors inhibit and promote the development of an online "community" in its various senses?
3. What are the effects of the development of online community (in the senses developed in answering research question 1) in terms of learning, interactions and discourse?

4. What are the implications of the answers to the above for policy and practice in higher education institutions at different levels, including institutional policy and learning design?

Sample Proposal Two

Mobile-based Communities of Practice for History in Higher Education in the Universities of Anon1(Private) and the University of Anon2(Public), an East African country.

Aims/Objectives:

This research will investigate, prototype, and disseminate the findings of a mobile-based community of practice for History in higher education in the universities of Anon1(Private) and the University of Anon2(Public). The purpose of this research is to not only analyze and document requirements on the impact of mobile-based environments for disciplinary practice, but to determine if these environments can support the reflective, multimodal, and collaborative knowledge construction demanded by the practice of History in higher education.

Research Questions

1. Are mobile-based communities of practice able to meet the disciplinary processes for collaboration, reflection, knowledge production and dissemination for the practice of History in higher education in an East African country?

2. What effect does a mobile-based community of practice for History in higher education in an East African country have on the production and dissemination of disciplinary knowledge (journals, monographs, posts, interaction, etc.)?
3. Can any developed mobile-based community of practice that meets these disciplinary needs be community organized and designed in an East African country?

Background to the Research

It is the intended goal of this research to critically explore the potential of constructing a community of practice (History) in higher education in an East African country based primarily in a mobile environment. This goal is based on the assumption that the most commonly available mobile technology in the target area in question are SMS-enabled phones. Therefore, this research will investigate SMS-based services for creating mobile communities of practice.

In keeping with what Goodyear (2004) refers to as networked learning, a mobile-based community of practice is used to promote connections between learners and foster communities which make efficient use of their resources. The establishment of a community of History in a mobile environment is intended to serve the disciplinary practices of History in higher education by being collaborative in knowledge discussion, reflective in knowledge construction, and authoritative in knowledge dissemination.

As such, this mobile community of practice will target practitioners of History (either faculty, or graduate level students) in higher education in the University of Anon2(Public) and the universities of Anon1(Private).

History is chosen primarily due to the absence of expert-level mobile learning frameworks and applications for university level education in both developed and developing nations.

In short, very little research has been conducted to determine whether mobile learning in History is a suitable vehicle for higher education in developing nations; a framework will be applied to assess whether this is indeed possible, whether a mobile-based community of interest in History can support reflective and collaborative knowledge construction consistent with the disciplinary practices of History. There are several reasons for this choice of location (an East African country), including the following:

History as contested knowledge (relationship between Anon1(Private) and an East African country; post-colonialism and national identity: What does it mean to be an East African country?

Gap (economically, politically, and culturally) between Anon1(Private) and mainland East African country and the potential for mobile networks to bridge these divides

An East African country's presence within the East African Community (EAC).

It is my belief that mobile environments for disciplinary practice in higher education in Anon1(Private) and throughout East African country can serve to explore and potentially mitigate the gap between Anon1(Private) and mainland an East African country through renewed dialogue and networking practitioners of History; through this renewed dialogue, history as a contested subject will be explored leading, potentially, to a renewed focus on post-colonialism and national identity.

National identity, in particular, represents a developmental need as both Anon1(Private) and an East African country explore the efficiency and long-term future of their political union. This research explicitly attempts to network the community of practice for History in higher education in Anon1(Private) with that of the leading university on the East African country's mainland, the University of Anon2(Public).

Theories

Much instructional pedagogy in History in higher education is constructivist in nature. Constructivist frameworks of instruction stress the role of context and social negotiation of knowledge in instruction (Savery, Duffy, 1996).

History establishes context through its pursuit of knowledge claims, their validation, and the manner of practices associated with this process. The social negotiation of knowledge is established through the apprenticeship model in higher education, namely the pairing of a student (apprenticing historian) with a mentor (practicing historian). Mobile learning's affordance for this context and social negotiation will be analyzed to determine its applicability to the practice of History in higher education.

Building on this constructivist pedagogy, the work of Meyer and Land in regards to threshold concepts offers considerable insight into the practice of History in higher education (2005). Meyer and Land's analysis of the role of 'thresholds' in developing "pedagogically fertile" and role-defining shifts in learner's understanding of their place as active members of the discipline has great application for History as the vehicle for disciplinary understanding (Meyer, Land, 374).

All of the participants in this research are active members of the History discipline, at varying stages of development (student vs. faculty, university vs. research organization) and at varying degrees of affiliation with their institution and their profession.

This self-perception of thinking "like a historian" has value pedagogically as an instrument that motivates participation and collaboration (Enwistle, 2005, 8).

The experience of 'legitimate peripheral participation' in the work of the professional historian is constructivist in nature, emphasizing as it does collaborative knowledge construction.

It further is identity forming by establishing etiquette for "communicating ideas in academically acceptable forms of expression and argument" (2005, 8).

Students are taught to act, argue, participate, and express themselves as historians. The pedagogical importance placed on disciplinary participatory identity in History emphasizes the importance of establishing the level of receptiveness to mobile learning on a disciplinary level. With so much emphasis placed on identity as a historian, viewing their receptiveness to mobile learning as partly influenced by disciplinary norms is prudent.

"Towards a Theory of Mobile Learning" provides a useful mediation between learning and technology and will be used to analyze mobile learning for History (Sharples, 2005).

Sharples builds on the work of Pask (Conversation Theory) and Engestrom (expansive activity model) by establishing mobile learning as an engagement with technology, "in which tools such as computers and mobile phones function as interactive agents in the process of coming to know, creating a human-technology system to communicate, to mediate agreements between learners and to aid recall and reflection" (Sharples, 2005, 7).

Further, the work of Sharples, Taylor, and Vavoula offers an evaluation of any potential mobile learning solution, an additional framework that can be applied to this research (2007). This work posits mobile learning in terms of its affordance for mobility, its identification of learning as a constructive and social process, and the role of situated activity mediated by technology (Sharples, Taylor, Vavoula, 2007, 225).

Any potential mobile environment derived from this research will be gauged based on its ability to satisfy these facets of mobile learning.

Sharples' work will be used as an instrument to determine whether mobile learning for History creates control (both the community of learners and their association with higher education), context (in terms of the learning activities and objects) and communication (in mobile learning's ability to allow for communication both within the learning community and the ability to disseminate communication to the greater academic community)

Sample

The participant group will be drawn from faculty and graduate students in the departments of History at the following universities. The potential size of a participant group will range from 30 to 60 participants, depending on willingness to participate.

Anon1(Private) University
University of Anon2(Public)
Anon3(Private) University

Methods

The research methods used for this exploration of mobile communities of practice for History in higher education in an East African country will involve both quantitative and qualitative elements. The research will begin with communication with select faculty and students at the two selected universities in Anon1(Private) to determine the validity of disciplinary assumptions put forth in this research proposal. This communication will be used to reconfigure disciplinary practice for History in an East African country if necessary.

Based on this initial feedback, a participatory design process will be employed with participants to determine the needs, requirements, and cultural, emotional, or social variables that might affect participation in any mobile community of practice. This participatory design process will inform a conceptual design of a mobile environment for the practice of History in higher education. Subsequent assessment of this design will be tied to fulfilling the needs of disciplinary practice in History (epistemology, ontology, knowledge construction, collaboration, reflection, and dissemination) as well as the ability of the design to assist "in the process of coming to know, creating a human-technology system to communicate, to mediate agreements between learners and to aid recall and reflection" (Sharples, 2005).

Methodology

This research will employ a mixed-methods approach. Quantitative elements will involve analysis of participant demographic and technological use information, as well as communication patterns within and without their respective Departments of History. Qualitative facets will involve interviews and their subsequent narrative analysis, as well as the participatory design process sessions, which will be recorded and subjected to a narrative analysis as well.

This combination of qualitative and quantitative aspects is intended to determine disciplinary process, represent that disciplinary process in a designed mobile environment, and to gauge potential impact of such an environment on disciplinary knowledge production.

Data Analysis

Quantitative data collected from communication, surveys, and participatory design phases will be analyzed to determine quantity of communication within respective departments of

History at the three focus universities, and across these departments. Quantitative data will be analyzed to determine number of collaborative interactions amongst participants towards knowledge production. Further, a prototype will be evaluated to determine its satisfaction of design requirements and disciplinary process. Qualitative data will be collected from preliminary communication, interview transcripts, and recorded transcripts from participatory design sessions; these will be subjected to a narrative analysis. Narrative analysis is an attempt to follow the participants "down their trails", to give participants an authentic voice in dictating their own receptiveness to mobile communities of practice (Riessman 2008). This authenticity helps elicit the autobiographical-self (2008). This narrative empowerment will hopefully reveal elements of autonomy and investment in the mobile environment that would have otherwise gone unnoticed.

Task Description Timeframe

Preliminary communication: identify/communicate with faculty and students in History Identify sample group, collect participant information, areas of research expertise, levels of communication with historical community, commitment to this project -2 months

Survey - Survey designed to collect information on technology use, gauge the validity of assumptions on the disciplinary practices- 1month

Interviews-assess the validity of the disciplinary practices of History, modes of collaboration and knowledge production- 3 months

Narrative Analysis of Interview Transcripts- conduct narrative analysis on interview transcripts to gauge narrative of professional interaction and satisfaction-3 months

Participatory Design and Conceptual Prototyping Multiple (on-site) sessions to develop needs assessments, requirements, and prototype mobile environment-3-6 months

Assessment of Mobile Environments for the practice of History in higher education in an East African country-Dissertation writing phase-12 months

Commentary on sample proposal 2

As is frequently the case with proposal titles, this one contains no problematic – no clue as to the central issue being addressed. Apart from being uninformative to the reader, this absence suggests a lack of focus on the part of the writer, which is not a good start.

The proposal does however have strength in situating the research questions early and giving a clear feel for the nature of the project. However it reads as though the project will be a form of action research, confirmed by the early use of the word 'prototype' as a verb. However that phrase (action research) is not used. There are hints that the research will be centrally involved in the development project described, but this is never brought out.

Nor is there any suggestion of which 'flavour' of action research this might be, whether there will be interventions at different points by the researcher, with effects evaluated and so on.

This is potentially a very interesting and useful [action] research project, but the relationship between the development project and the research project is only tangentially described, and the wider significance of the research project to the research community is not addressed at all.

A reader might be forgiven for concluding that this research will mostly be of benefit to the online community described; and this is inadequate for a PhD. However there is in fact greater potential in the project.

There is, from time to time, something of a missionary feel to the proposal – for example in the sentence beginning "it is my belief...." This is another danger sign because it suggests that the researcher's mind is already made up before the research has been done. It also adds confirmation to the potential impression that as a research and development project, this is more development than research.

There is some confusion about how many universities are involved in the design for this research. Most often it is two. But in two places in the proposal three universities are mentioned. This kind of instability is, of course, not good. Unless there is some specific and limited purpose for the inclusion of the third. If so, this is not explained.

To conclude, this is an interesting and potentially valuable project but the written proposal does not really do it justice.

Sample Proposal Three

Negotiating the Faultlines: A study of PhD development

The journey of development that researchers and scholars take within the institutional framework of the degree of Doctor of Philosophy has in the last ten years attracted the attention of both academic researchers and bureaucrats in Australia.

While some researchers (Neumann, 2003; McWilliam, Taylor et al, 2002) have been concerned with the institutional framework that supports the degree, others (Lee, 1998; Lee and Williams, 1999; Johnson et al, 2000; Macauley, 2001; Vilkinas, 2005) have been more interested in what the experience of individual students reveals about both supervision pedagogy and the dominant discourses within academia concerning this highest rank of examinable degrees.

No study has thus far followed and tracked a group of candidates through their degrees, perhaps because until now there has not been an easy way for a group of candidates to interact and share their experiences as they happen. The development of software that supports the real-time online recording of events as they happen, a process called web logging (colloquially known as blogging), has now made a longitudinal study of this kind possible. This study proposes to create a community of PhD candidates who are prepared to both maintain blogs themselves and to read and comment on the blogs maintained by the other members of the study group.

My own experience in teaching and researching both academic writing and online learning, my reading about graduate pedagogy, my thinking about the nature of the PhD process, about the growing phenomenon of blogging, and about how university communities reproduce themselves and generate knowledge has lead me to my research question:

To what extent can PhD candidates be sustained in their development as researchers through the use of blogging?

The research question will be answered by analysis of the blogs – the body of narrative that the candidates produce, in which they will reveal to themselves and to the group both *what* and *how* they are learning in their own reflections and ongoing narratives. Although the content matter of the thesis-writing process that each is engaged in will be individual and unique, they will share the experience of *doing* the PhD to *become* a doctor– their working toward a common goal in perhaps the most complex project that most of them have ever attempted.

Blogs have been described by Williams and Jacobs (2004, p232) as having 'the capacity to engage people in collaborative activity, knowledge sharing, reflection and debate, where complex and expensive technology has failed'. A blog is not only a space to write, but also a place to store and display pictures and graphics and make lists of links to useful references, to your work in progress, and to work completed.

A blog is thus more like a cyber-desk than just a place to make and store notes, and a blog's ability to be shared adds the dimension of an ongoing conversation – the cyberdesk has a place for passers-by to add their comments to what they read, and in this study it is intended that the blogs of group members will be open to each other for comments, and that the blogs will be the tool for community building within the group.

Although academic thinking about the uses of blogs in higher education is in its infancy, these uses are also continually being charted, discussed, predicted, reported and glossed in detail on blogs such as Weblogs in Higher Education. …This tendency of blogs to comment on and aggregate the contents of other blogs is often referred to as 'the blogosphere'.

The non-educational social nature of blogging has been explored by Nardi et al (2004) who claim that "blogs create the audience, but the audience also creates the blog". Their study of 23 social blogs maintained by university students, graduates and graduate students also found that the social dimension of blogging made blogs much more than online diaries; they classified the motivations that bloggers had to continue their blogging activities as to (p4):

- update others on activities and whereabouts
- express opinions to influence others
- seek others' opinions and feedback
- "think by writing"
- release emotional tension

With the possible exception of the first item in this list, which is the most transparent motivation for anyone to keep a blog, each of these objectives will provide a dimension in this study on the socialization of PhD candidates into academic argumentation and research culture. Certainly the last two are particularly interesting in the terms of Lee's writing about both the place of writing in the creation of 'the doctor' (1998, 2003) and the 'distress' inherent in the PhD process in Australia (Lee and Williams, 1999).

Johnson et al (2000) explore the development of the 'autonomous researcher' in the terms of the traditional model of PhD pedagogy, which Leder (1995) refers to as having an 'apprentice-like' quality. Its fundamental aim was to teach candidates independence, using techniques that mostly amounted to varying degrees of abandonment.
However, scholars who have challenged these practices and attempted to undertake a more pastoral supervisory role report being overwhelmed by the needs of their students. Johnson et al suggest that autonomy may need to be *developed* in candidates, rather than *revealed*, and point out that "new modes of knowledge production"(p143) and the current trend toward more collaborative production of knowledge within universities will require that researchers have more skills in collaboration, supported as they are, increasingly, by joint process.

This proposed more constructivist approach to postgraduate pedagogy has echoes in the theories of how people learn online.
Most successful online learning is associated with constructivist pedagogies (Maor & Zabriski 2003).

The well-known and often-repeated advice to teachers going online that they will have to move from their position as the 'sage on the stage' to the 'guide on the side' implies the pedagogical position that students learning online are constructing their own knowledge from the available information, rather than accepting their knowledge whole from 'the master'.

The development of blogs and wikis (online encyclopaedias with open authorship) as educational tools has the potential to reduce the role of the 'guide on the side' even further – perhaps online teachers, like the absent supervisors reported in so many studies of doctoral candidate development, are now becoming 'the ghost with no post'.

While those words are mine, the fear that teachers will largely disappear from education is often related to the development of educational technology without an attendant pedagogical framework (eg, Taylor 1995). Students working online can be left to share, discuss, problem-solve, and develop their own knowledge from sources of information that are now vast – indeed they sometimes seem almost limitless. They must learn to judge the validity of what they find for themselves, and to develop the skills necessary to defend their positions within and through a group of people whom they may never see face-to-face. The (often misunderstood) role of 'guide on the side' is crucial to the success of this kind of educational setting (Salmon 1999, 2002).

Economic pressure rather than pedagogical preference is often the driver for institutional movement toward online teaching. It is also economic pressure that has raised the interest of both bureaucrats and academics in postgraduate pedagogy: pressure to lift completion rates has conflicted with increased time pressure on academics and an expressed wish by some academics for a 'softer', more supportive model for PhD supervision (Johnson et al, 2000).

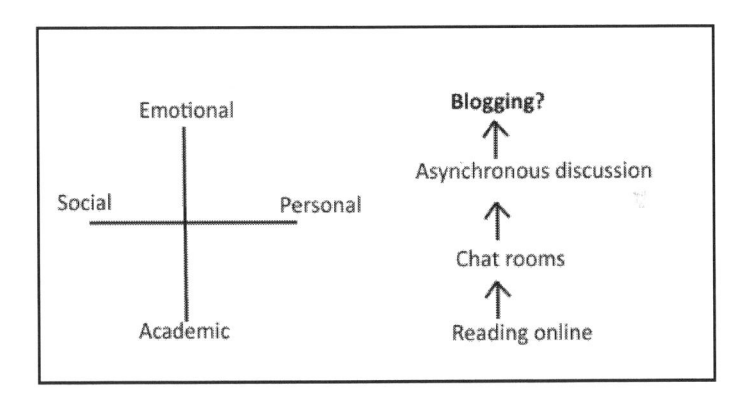

Figure 1: The pedagogy of cyber learning

Figure 1 uses a theory of online pedagogy to show how blogging might support the development of candidates. As online tasks move from academic engagement in reading material that has been placed online, through the social engagement of chat rooms and the more thoughtful and reflective work that results from reading and contributing to asynchronous discussion, participants move toward involving their emotions in the learning experience (Salmon, 1999).

It is this involvement of the emotional dimension that has been identified by Green and Lee (1998) and by Johnson et al (2000) as the most under theorised part of PhD pedagogy. The use of blogging over time in this study will provide an online environment that will enable trust to build in the community, so that participants can establish emotional connections and relate in new and unpredictable ways.

A community of blogging PhD candidates would bring together people who are learning how to become – how to negotiate for themselves the building of the identity of 'doctor' both against and within disciplinary cultures and institutional strictures that can be traced back to the ideas of Voltaire and Rousseau (Johnson et al, 2000). Supervisors, of course, are themselves the product of this process and have been profoundly influenced by their own process of self-creation in their doctoral role. This study will contribute to the complex question of how pedagogy can be understood within the supervisor/candidate relationship as discussed by Green and Lee (1995), and, most importantly, will be understood and enacted in the university of the future. At the heart of these issues lie the questions posed at the end of their article (p44):

1. How is pedagogy to be best understood, in all its complexity and necessity, within the symbolic-disciplinary economy of the Academy?
2. What stories (and counter-stories) need to be told?
3. What spaces are there for different practices and voices in post-graduate contexts, including research in and for postgraduate studies and pedagogy?
4. What new imaginings are necessary for teaching and research in and for the emerging postmodern university?

Despite the differences in epistemologies that have often been categorised across disciplines (eg, Becher and Trowler, 2001), the blogging by individuals of the common ground of their struggle (which may, in any discipline, involve 'distress', according to Lee and Williams, 1999) will create shared narratives of development. Wenger (1998) describes how people working on a shared trajectory toward a common goal contribute and create meaning and identity by sharing the unfolding narratives of their experience.

The application of Wenger's theory to candidates for the PhD degree may not seem immediately obvious. The work he did to develop his theory was done in an insurance company, with workers doing a set of apparently routinised tasks – but whose day-to-day work often involved dealing with phone calls from angry and resentful members of the public, raising the kinds of uncertainty and anxiety that no amount of routine can protect you from.

In his 1998 book Wenger describes how, as a group, the workers formed an unofficial 'community of practice' to share and create knowledge that would help them as individuals make sense of the sometimes Kafkaesque situations they found themselves in, due in most part to their inability to understand the complexities of unexplained arcane practices within the insurance industry, or even, to some degree, the dense administrative structures of their own employer.

[Wenger] develops this theory into areas of negotiation of meaning and development of identity in groups where people work together to make sense of what is happening to them. He then develops this theory into areas of institutional development and educational design.

The endeavour of attaining a doctorate, which is both cognitive and experiential, in fact lends itself well to the application of Wenger's construction of a community of practice. PhD candidates are working in an area in which development although often understood as prescriptive, is also, somehow, mysterious.

If Wenger's conception of 'community' is understood in the context of a dynamic (but, note, not necessarily always peaceful or agreeable) quest for meaning being created by its members through the exchange of ideas, insights and understandings, then his notion can be applied to a group of people who are sharing the process of attaining a doctorate.

Wenger's words 'shared trajectory', are also not entirely transparent. They imply flight in the same direction toward a fixed target. But Wenger's use of the word 'trajectory' is more complex than this: "The term trajectory suggests not a path that can be foreseen or charted but a continuous motion – one that has a momentum of its own in addition to a field of influences (p154)." The group that will form the core of this study is not a planned or formulaic entity. Its members will not answer questionnaires, nor will they participate in surveys or take part in focus groups. They will write themselves into the study and it will be what it becomes.

Aims

The central aim of the research is to follow and report on the process of what Lee (1998) calls the making of 'a newly licensed kind of person, a "doctor"', and to investigate the effects of the use of blogging by candidates on this process.

Objectives

The research has three objectives:

1. To investigate cybergroup formation and its effect on participants' candidature

2. To document the emotional life of and the process of self-discovery in a group of PhD candidates over time
3. To encourage candidates in the study to use blogging to 'write themselves' into their own development and to create a community of practice through the use of shared blogs

Justification
This research is intended to track and report on the experiences of a diverse group of PhD candidates in real time over two years. While some work has been done in Australia directly on the experiences of completing a PhD (Lee and Williams 1999; Neumann 2003), most has relied on the recall and reported memory of successful candidates, or one-off interviews with current candidates. Macauley (1990) had his subjects, both candidates and supervisors, complete two questionnaires and a series of in-depth interviews. More recently, Vilkinas (2005) has collected the stories of present candidates at a point in their thesis task.

None of the previous studies into the process of PhD formation in Australia have used a longitudinal method nor have they maintained contact with students over even a short time.

Neumann uses 'slice of time' techniques, interviewing around 100 students at differing stages of their projects from a range of different disciplines.
She uses Becher and Trowler's quadrant model (2001) to classify disciplines into hard, soft, pure, and applied, and also classified students according to their full-time or part-time enrolment and as early, mid or late stage candidates. The results can be taken as accurate at a point in time, but not offering any new insight into the overall PhD process for candidates.

Lee and Williams (1999) used techniques of memory work, asking six academics to draw on their memories of their own PhDs, and narrative writing to report on these memories.

The subjects in this pilot are current academics – meaning previous candidates who have completed a PhD successfully, and who were undoubtedly informed in their narratives by their later roles as supervisors. The rather dramatic revelations in this article concerning the distress that the memory work revealed raised the questions listed on page 4 above. Vilkinas, using similar self-reporting but by current candidates, also raises questions of emotionality in her recent book. However, her contributors, again, were writing at a point in time rather than over a protracted period.

Macauley (2001) used questionnaires and in depth interviews with existing students. Although he has made a valuable contribution to viewing the transition to independent scholarship in Australian universities, he is still seeing the process in fairly standard 'growing up' terms, relying heavily on a distinction between pedagogy and andragogy to measure the maturation of candidates as scholars.

So, while all of these studies have reported to a more or less extent on the emotionality of the PhD experience, none has created and reported on a narrative of experience distilled from real-time reflection, nor have any of them attempted to create a community of candidates.

Methodology

This study will be a qualitative one. The research question will be answered by thematic analysis of the body of narrative that the candidates produce – we will reveal to ourselves and to the group both *what* and *how* we are learning in our own reflections and ongoing narratives.

Although the content matter of the thesis-writing process that each of us is engaged in will be individual and unique, we will share the experience of 'doing' the PhD – our working toward a common goal in perhaps the most complex project that most of us have ever attempted. The endeavour of attaining a doctorate, which is both cognitive and experiential, lends itself well to the application of Wenger's construction of a community of practice, within which he suggests people both bring and create meaning and identity for themselves.

The study will be a reflective ethnography, my own development as a scholar being a part of the process of doing the study. I will be a fully participating member of the online group, and open about my role as a researcher, so I will be a participant-observer (Erlandson et al, 1993, p96). Sometimes it may be difficult or impossible for me to separate my roles as subject and object in my own study – but except in the case of disrespectful or disruptive behaviour as discussed below, I will resist as far as possible the role of 'group leader'. I will also resist as far as possible the urge to 'spark up' blog postings during quiet periods – although this may prove very difficult if the flow of material is so low as to threaten the project!

As an ethnographer, the place in which my study will be conducted will be cyberspace. Visualisations of the World Wide Web and the 'reality' of cyberspace and the human interactions that take place in it has been canvassed by researchers in such sites as Cyber Geography Research.
Candidates will be recruited through post-graduate student organizations.

To some extent they may be self-selecting, as they will almost certainly be technologically confident (although there is no reason why even inexperienced people cannot learn to blog), and commitment to the group may at times seem high. However, I hope that membership of the group will also be seen as conveying benefits for participants in peer support and development through their personal writing.

The number of participants in this study will be small – no more than 20 people. They will be broadly-discipline based, and should cover as wide a range of methodologies and branches of academic research as possible. They will need to be prepared to share honestly and freely, and have some commitment to the group's trajectory as well as to their own progress.

Ethics and anticipated difficulties
The identities of candidates in the group will be hidden from each other. Nicknames will be used, and in the reporting process the candidates will be classified according to their methodologies and Becher and Trowler's (2001) quadrant of discipline groupings (cf Neumann 2003), not by their actual discipline.
I am more interested in knowing whether a student is doing bench-top research or undertaking surveys and focus groups than I am in whether she is a scientist, a social scientist or a philosopher.
Candidates will also be asked to not give their supervisors' names if they need to post about exchanges with them, but rather to use a predesignated nickname.
It will be impressed upon group members that all blog entries and comments are not to be copied or commented on elsewhere.

Any instances of material posted within the group appearing elsewhere will result in the offender being removed from the study and thus from access to the blogs.

A constant possibility in online groups is the activity of personal flaming (abusive language) and other destructive online activities causing disruption and even temporary or permanent breakdown of a group. In blogs, abusive or hurtful or hateful comments can be left. I have been a member of dozens of online discussion groups of a different kinds since 1996; I have taught academic writing for two years using online discussion groups as the main mode of content delivery, and have moderated hobby-based email discussion groups. I have always successfully practised a low-tolerance policy for behaviour that denotes disrespect for group members. While some allowance can be made for highly charged emotional states from time to time, this behaviour cannot be allowed to damage the trust that holds the group together. In this case participants will each own their own blog, and will always be completely free to remove any comments from their blogs if they wish. Anonymous commenting will not be allowed, so repeat offenders can be removed from the group. This policy will be detailed on the candidate information sheet.

There could be some difficulties arising from resistance or defensiveness on the part of supervisors, who could view the project as somehow undermining their position or even reputation by the 'gossipy' nature of a closed group. This could be countered by a clear explanation of the importance of confidentiality and the way that candidate identities will be hidden, and the preparation of a detailed supervisor information sheet to accompany the candidate information sheet.

Finally, there may be unexpected problems in my own life as I undertake this PhD. If at times I am not able to participate in the group, this will not pose a problem. I can continue to monitor blog postings in case of problems, but the group should be able to function for some time without my constant input.

Provisional work schedule
Second half of 2005: preparing and gaining ethics approval – part-time
2006-2007:   the blogs are being created – part-time
2008-2009:   thematic analysis and thesis writing –full-time

Resource requirements
Technical support for blogging – to be investigated. Although the university IT service does not currently offer blogging software here are several sites that offer free blogging services that can be password protected from the wider world.

Outlay would be minimal.

Commentary on sample proposal 3

This looks like a very interesting doctorate in prospect. The proposal begins with a convincing overview of some literature and quickly establishes a gap in the research which this project will fill ("No study has thus far followed and tracked...."). The first, impressive, paragraph would have been stronger had it finished by not only saying that a community of PhD candidates will be created, but to say why.

The first couple of paragraphs give the distinct impression that this is more a development project than a research one, and so a question mark begins to form around the issue of whether this is actually *doctoral* research being described. The research question which follows those paragraphs also appears to be developmental rather than a doctoral research question. Fortunately the rest of the proposal dispels this impression to a large extent, but it's best not to let it form in the first place. Readers will now be asking: "so what is the greater relevance to the academic community being offered here?"

A further common problem with doctoral proposals concerning technology is what might be called "tech-centrism". By this is meant too much focus on, and excitement about, a particular piece of, or use of technology, with an attendant loss of focus on the research issues. Another consequence can be lack of realism about the potential benefits of the technology, associated with an unwillingness to see negative aspects.
There is some evidence of this in the paragraph beginning "Blogs have been described..." and in later parts of the proposal. An example later in the proposal is the sentence which runs "The use of blogging over time in this study will provide an online environment that will enable trust to build in the community, so that participants can establish emotional connections and relate in new and unpredictable ways."

After the list of 5 motivations that bloggers may have there is quite a long section which, while well-informed and interesting, isn't adequately related to the group of bloggers to be created for the research, nor to the research project itself. There needs to be better linkage.

There is an important statement about the contributions that this research will make in the paragraph which begins "a community of blogging Ph.D. candidates". The sentence begins: "this study will contribute to the complex question ....". This section should be highlighted because it puts to rest, partly at least, the "so-what?" question about the significance of this research.

The structure of the proposal becomes a little strange towards the end. Beginning with the heading "Aims" there is considerable repetition and some material that really belonged much earlier in the proposal, including the aims and objectives of the research. Locating the three bullet points of objectives set out near the end next to the research question which is articulated at the beginning would probably highlight the fact that there is something of a disconnect between them. The research question addresses the sustainability of candidates' development as researchers through the use of blogging whereas the objectives begin with that and extend it.

The development of further research questions is clearly necessary to address this and also to make concrete the very reasonable claims for wider significance that the proposal can make.

The final problem arises in the last four paragraphs. Here, suddenly, the researcher is positioned as part of the group doing the blogging for the first time, though it is unclear whether the researcher will also be a doctoral candidate or will be their teacher in some sense (the phrase "group leader" is used).

An additional data collection method is introduced very near the end of the proposal, which appears to be some form of auto-ethnography.

There is a statement that the candidates will be recruited through post-graduate student organisations, which raises the question as to whether this group will be recruited from one university, or many. The details of sampling are thus occluded.

So this is potentially a valuable research project and a very interesting one. The proposal overall this convincing: clearly this person has some very concrete and well-developed ideas. The proposal, however, could be a lot better than it is.

Interestingly, the abstract of the successfully-completed doctorate based on this proposal is available on the web. While there are a few differences, both methodologically and in the in the use of theory, the finished doctorate is remarkably similar to the original proposal. This is not always the case.

Sample Proposal Four

(Written as part of an application to study)

Institutional Change in South Africa: Academic adaptation for improving the quality of Teaching and Learning. A case study of a South African university

The study would aim to explore the extent to which increasing external and internal pressures for institutional change have influenced the ways in which a well-resourced South African university has adapted its structures, policies and processes to achieve its strategic goals of improving the quality of teaching and learning.

The rationale for the study lies in the need for the post-1994 South African higher education system to be transformed from one that was shaped by discrimination and inequalities of class, race and gender under colonialism and apartheid to one that is inclusive and serves the needs of our diverse population and changing society.

In his framework for theorising about institutional change, Badat (2009: 457) has identified four dimensions of change: *the context, trajectory, dynamics and the determinants of change*. This study will necessarily consider the *context* of institutional change in South Africa and at the university itself as the apartheid social order and its priorities strongly impacted on the production of knowledge, teaching and learning and the curriculum and texts (ibid).

Since 1994, globalisation and its accompanying neoliberal ideology have impacted on institutional change by prioritising economic growth over redistributive policies and action. This has restricted the pace of change required and South Africa remains one of the most unequal societies in the world.

Commentary on sample proposal 4

1. The proposal looks good in terms of the thinking behind it and the thrust of the research. However the proposal is not punchy and specific enough.

2. The opening sentence is very long and wordy and hard to get a conceptual grip of, but it's an important one.

3. Words like 'explore' should be avoided - they are too open. The author should aim to give a very clear picture of the research to the reader, especially what the central problematic is.

4. There needs to be some specific research questions - and they need to be stated early.

5. The amount of time spent describing the literature should be reduced.

6. The author needs to be clear that s/he will use secondary data to situate the single-site case study within the context nationally

7. The actual study needs to be foregrounded in the proposal. Here it gets a paragraph towards the end. The aim is to give the reader a clear, early, idea of what the project is about.

8. The methods are also too vague. No clear idea is given of exactly what the research will look like.

9. State the purpose and the likely contribution explicitly - and embed them in research questions as far as possible. For example it seems likely that there be policy and practice implications for the case study university and or other universities as well as a contribution to the literature. There could be a research question about this.

Sample Proposal Four (Revised)

(Revised and Extended Version after Feedback)

Institutional Change in South Africa: Academic adaptation for improving the quality of Teaching and Learning. A case study of a South African university

There is a widespread view in the higher education sector and broader society that transformation of the higher education sector and change within universities has been too slow and not kept pace with external and internal demands for change. Through an in-depth study of a well resourced university, this study examines this view systematically. In particular, the study will examine the extent to which increasing external and internal pressures for institutional change have influenced the ways in which this university has adapted its structures, policies and processes to achieve its strategic goals of improving the quality of teaching and learning.

The rationale for the study lies in the need for the post-1994 South African higher education system to be transformed from one that was shaped by discrimination and inequalities of class, race and gender under colonialism and apartheid to one that is inclusive and serves the needs of our diverse population and changing society.

Possible research questions:
- How have national policy interventions to improve the quality of teaching and learning within universities contributed to institutional change at the case study institution
- To what extent have the case study university's structures, policies and processes been adapted to achieve the goals of its Teaching and Learning Strategy?
- What opportunities have opened up for the case study university to improve student access and success through teaching and learning interventions?
- What are the constraints to improving the quality of teaching and learning within the institution?

The study will draw on the framework developed by Badat (2009, p 457) who has identified four dimensions of change: *the context, trajectory, dynamics and the determinants of change*. The *context* of the apartheid social order and its priorities strongly impacted on the production of knowledge, teaching and learning and the curriculum and texts of South African universities (ibid). Since 1994, globalisation and its accompanying neoliberal ideology have prioritised economic growth over redistributive policies and action. This has restricted the pace of change required and South Africa remains one of the most unequal societies in the world.

The second dimension identified by Badat is the trajectory of change. Although political and socio-economic conditions may partly explain the reasons for change or a lack thereof in higher education, Badat argues that human agency is critical to understanding institutional change.

He asserts that "social agents and actors acting in cooperation and/or conflict within the system and the institutions" determine the pace, nature and outcomes. They influence the *trajectory of change* within institutions as they manage tensions between competing, values, goals and strategies in delivering on social equity and redress and economic development and quality. Badat has argued that often these social actors become the key policy-making actors and *determinants of change*. (2009, p 456). It is important to note that institutional contexts differ vastly in the South African higher education system owing to the extremely differentiated system inherited from apartheid.

At the institutional level, the study will draw on the work of David Dill (1999) to understand the dynamics of change in the recently formalised areas of teaching and learning in South African higher education institutions. He has argued that in the competitive environment, universities have adapted their internal structures to enhance quality, promote interdisciplinary research and increase their entrepreneurial activities (1999). He reported that while patterns do exist between institutions, it is important to consider different institutional contexts.

His work would be useful in the specific focus of this study, which is to examine the Teaching Development Grants (TDGs) as an instrument to promote the quality of teaching and learning at the case study university. The TDGs are funded by national government and more than 40 projects have been implemented across the university. New and adapted institutional structures and policies have emerged in order to meet the educational goals of the projects and the accountability requirements of the state.

This study will contribute to the improvement of specific policy and practice at the case study university in the implementation of interventions to enhance the quality of teaching as it strives to improve student access and success. The contribution to the literature would be an in-depth case study on institutional change in a well-resourced South African university as it responds to external and internal demands for change in the provision of teaching and learning.

Methodology
I will draw on four research methods:
- Documentary analysis of national and university policies and structures, including the use of secondary data to situate the single-site case study within the context nationally
- In depth interviews with project leaders, institutional managers at the university and national government officials
- Participant observation of committee and project meetings
- Evaluation of TDG projects

Research Ethics

Besides confidentiality and anonymity, my position within the case study university would raise ethical considerations for the proposed study. The proposal for the study would have to be rigorous enough to be cleared by the faculty and university Research Ethics Committees.

Commentary on revised sample proposal 4

This is now much better: more cohesive and convincing. However:

1. There is a shifting focus at the beginning between the *quality* of teaching and learning generally and changes in teaching and learning in line with the transformation agenda (that is, redressing the inequalities set in place by the apartheid regime). This potentially makes the research too broad. A supervisor's advice would probably be to concentrate on issues around the transformation agenda.

2. The research questions do not offer something that is of broader applicability. What is the significance of this research for **other** institutions or for national policy etc?

3. The discussion of Badat's work offers a clue to the answer to this question - the research offers an empirically-based detailed analysis of the structure versus agency debate in institutional change. This could have been highlighted in a new, final, research question. Similarly, the Teaching Development Grants as a policy instrument could have been contrasted with other policy instruments which will undoubtedly be operating within the case study university, comparing relative effectiveness, the reactions to them and so on. This would also give the study broader significance.

4. The contribution to the literature section describes the study but does not really say what the contribution is. It says:
"*The contribution to the literature would be an in-depth case study on institutional change in a well-resourced South African university as it responds to external and internal demands for change in the provision of teaching and learning.*"
This descriptive but not explanatory sentence confirms the impression that there is a weakness in the proposal in terms of its answer to the "*so what?*" question.

5. There is an issue about whether the methods described fully align with the research questions. In particular, practice on the ground appears to be missing, unless this might happen in the evaluation of the TDG projects. How do lecturers and their students respond to the policies researched and how is practice actually changing in the classroom?

6. The final bullet point in the methodology section is not specific enough: how will that evaluation occur, what methods will be used?

7. The detail of samples, selection criteria and so on is missing from the methodology section. For bullet points are not enough to describe data collection methods, analysis approaches, sampling strategies etc. There is a gap in the proposal in terms of these details.

8. For a confirmation document (as opposed to an application for study, which this is) the literature would need to be more extensive.

Section 2: Making Theory Work

About this section

This section examines different ways of seeing 'theory', the different senses in which that word is used and what that all means for doctoral research into higher education.

2.1. The nature of theory

Tight's work (2004, 2011, 2012b) has shown that much work in higher education research is theory-poor. What this really means is that there is no *explicit* theory being used; that much of the work is 'purely' empirical in nature. Methodologically the field is limited too, studies into higher education very often use survey-based multivariate analyses, documentary analyses and interview-based studies (Dobson, 2009; Huisman, 2008; Ross, 1992; Tight 2007, 2011, 2012a, 2012b). So reports of research in journal articles are often simply reports of data analysis based on these methods.

To say that a study is 'atheoretical' is to say that it is largely devoid of 'theory' understood as explicit, bounded sets of ideas which string a series of concepts together to explain the world in some way. That kind of depiction of theory is the one often used in definitions of 'theory', focusing on explicit, thought-through sets of ideas. Examples explicit, coherent theories which link sets of concepts together to offer explanatory power would be: complexity theory; Marxist theory; or social practice theory (which is discussed below).

Merton (1949) helpfully identifies different 'levels' of theory which vary according to the level of analysis at which they apply, and vary too according to the scope of their ambitions. They are:

> grand theory,
> middle-range theory and
> micro-theory

Grand theory includes the 'isms' – postmodernism, radical feminism, functionalism, Marxism and the rest. It also includes ontological theory – theory about the nature of reality, for example critical realism. Theories at this level are reasonably unambiguous and explicit about how they view the nature of reality and what can be known about it. They make big statements about the nature of society and its direction of change, as well as the drivers of that change. In the study of higher education an example is Trow's (1970) theory of the shift in higher education systems from elite to mass and finally to universal higher education. Of course versions of Marxist theory can be applied in that domain, as for example by Rhoades (2007).

Micro-theory by contrast makes small propositions about the relationship between particular phenomena: it is often little more than a set of locally situated hypotheses. So in the study of higher education an example is a theory relating assessment outcomes to the use of a particular form of virtual learning environment (VLE).

Middle-range theory links the two. It builds and uses a form of theory which is empirically-grounded and can be disproved, but is of general validity. An example is communities of practice theory (Lave & Wenger, 1991) which is rooted in anthropological data and makes testable claims but which also makes general statements about the nature of learning. Another example which is sometimes deployed in the study of higher education specifically is neo-institutional theory (Johnson, 2012). So middle-range theory is testable and has an empirical basis (which is not always true of grand theory) but unlike micro theory it has some degree of generalisability beyond the local.

In differentiating these three sorts of theory Merton is discussing explicit theories. But in order to carry on effectively in our everyday lives we rely on theory and concepts of a different sort: *tacit* theory. Tacit theory is actually inescapable, and not to recognise its presence is dangerous:

> ...the absence of [explicit] theory leaves the researcher prey to the unexamined, unreflexive preoccupations and dangerously naïve ontological and epistemological *a prioris*.... Ball (1995, pp 265-6)

So research work that is free of explicit theory is in danger of serving to justify and sustain the status quo. For example Dimitriadis (2009) shows how, the so-called 'gold standard' of randomized control trials and experiments deployed in the name of usefulness and finding out what works can marginalize theory used to 'think otherwise'. It's not surprising, then, to read that during the Bush period in America this approach became the standard by which proposals for research were evaluated for government support (Anyon, 2009, p 1).

The most difficult tacit theories to escape (because normalisation lends them invisibility) are what Gouldner (1970) calls domain assumptions. These have a huge gravitational pull because they seem to be 'just normal'; simply stating the obvious. They might include, for example:

> dispositions to believe that [women and] men are rational or irrational; that society is precarious or fundamentally stable; that social problems will correct themselves without planned intervention...[Domain assumptions] are an aspect of the larger culture that is most intimately related to the postulations of theory....they are often resistant to 'evidence'....to understand the character of [a thesis] we have to understand the background assumptions with which it operates. (Gouldner, 1970, pp 31-33).

Assumptions about supposedly immutable gender or 'race' differences have of course influenced data collection, analysis and interpretation in negative ways over the years, and continue to do so. So do assumptions about the causes of behaviour. They continue to influence the selective reporting of research in the mass media too, which seem to give greater news value to results which claim to demonstrate imitative behaviour ('watching that video made him do the crime') based on a simplistic and unstated social learning theory . Such domain assumptions can become ingrained in dominant discourses which come to influence ways of seeing, and these can also be invisible to those using them - it takes 'work' to counter them (Trowler, 2001).

So different levels and types of theory inform decisions, processes and outcomes in research. Despite the etymology of the term, data are not 'given' but are 'contrived' with the inevitable help of concepts and theory, much of which remain tacit. To say this however is not to adopt automatically a relativist ontology or a dismissive attitude towards the need to establish the robustness of research:

> The influences, however deep, of theories upon [people's] perceptions or understanding is one thing; the claim that there are no theory-independent objects of perception and understanding is another. Similarly, the influence of theories upon what [people] may count as valid or consistent is one thing; the claim that validity and consistency are theory-dependent is another. (Lukes, 1973, p 236)

What theory can do

Under one reading of the nature of theory - and more particularly social theory, as discussed here – it has six key characteristics, each enabling a particular function. These functions are: classification; depiction; explanation; prediction; contextualisation and guidance.

First, it uses a set of interconnected concepts to *classify* the components of a system and how they are related. So in Marxist theory the capitalist system comprises components such as the proletariat, the capitalist class, the means of production.

Second, this set is deployed to develop a set of systematically and logically related propositions that *depict* some aspect of the operation of the world. So in Marxist theory the components are then used to how capitalism works through the exploitation of the surplus value of the labour of the proletariat.

Third, these claim to provide an *explanation* for a range of phenomena by illuminating causal connections. In Marxist theory, the depiction of capitalism explains the periodic crises it goes through and why there is a tendency towards monopolisation of industries.

Fourth, theory should provide *predictions* which reduce uncertainty about the outcome of a specific set of conditions. These may be rough probabilistic predictions, and they should be corrigible – it should be possible to disconfirm or jeopardize it through observations of the world. In the hypothetico-deductive tradition, from which this viewpoint comes, theory offers statements of the form 'in Z conditions, if X happens then Y will follow'. Again, to use the example of Marxist theory, it predicts an age of monopoly capitalism which will eventually crumble under the weight of the internal contradictions the theory describes.

Fifth, theory helps *locate local social processes* in wider structures and contexts, because it is these which lend predictability to the social world. So consumption of the mass media, in Marxist theory, is seen as one of the ways capitalism suppresses opposition.

Finally, theory *guides research* interventions, helping to define research problems and to indicate appropriate research designs to investigate them. A Marx-influenced study of higher education might look at its role in social reproduction, for example, and the ways in which the HE 'system' privileges and represses different groups.

To sum up this position, social theories offer ways of seeing which provide an interpretation of aspects of the world and make descriptive, explanatory and predictive statements about them. But in doctoral research into higher education, and in social scientific research generally, it is not necessary or even usual to deploy all these functions of theory, and it is certainly not usual to give each function equal weight. What the theory is actually *doing* in doctoral research depends, of course, on the research questions: categorisation, depiction and contextualisation may be its key tasks, for example. And some levels of theory are better at different tasks than others.

Social reconstructionist theory

To this point the paper has followed a fairly traditional Popperian line on the nature of theory. In this account good theory should have withstood attempts at refutation (Popper, 1963) so that there is some degree of confidence in its depiction of the world. So a good theory offers classification, contextualisation, depiction, explanation and (crucially) prediction that have withstood attempts at refutation. Where this is the case we can operate as if the theory is true, until proven otherwise.

However an alternative viewpoint is to see theory as creative and emancipatory. From this perspective theory does not just describe the world but seeks to change it (a point, incidentally, which echoes Marx, on whose work Popper directed a good deal of critical fire: Popper, 1945, 1957). Here explicit *values* underpin how and why theory is deployed. For feminists and others, theory can be a valuable ally in realising ambitions, illuminating structural inequalities and disadvantage, seeing the world differently, changing attitudes and practices and exploring the different dimensions of 'the enchantment of being human' (Archer, 2000). In this account the relationship between theory and the world is turned on its head: theory does not only *explain* the world: the world is constructed and reconstructed *through* theory.

Moreover the Popperian account above, which depicts theory use as rooted in rational cognitive processes, is too simplistic in this alternative, account:

> how often their own cherished analytical rationality is broken up by glimpses into the imagination of more provocative thinkers. I have come to the conclusion that it is not so much that we self-consciously assemble all the resources for the making of research imaginaries as those vivid ideas (and frequently their authors) come to haunt us. (Hey, 2006, p 439)

For Clegg (2007) as well as many others, there are multiple hauntings as the echoes of theorists and theories inhabit the walls of the studies and libraries where research is done and find resonance in the minds of the living:

> I have defended thinking about theoretical questions because they are an indispensable resource for critique. My work on critical realism is based on a commitment to understanding and explanation, but also involves a commitment to a view of human agency that means that critique is not just intellectual but is also grounded in our human capacities to act. It

is, therefore, hopeful in terms our capacities to change the world at both the micro political level of the institution, but also more broadly in terms of imagining different futures and outcomes. (p 11)

What theory is for

There is no real agreement about what theory is *for* or, in social science at least, how far we can take it. Is it part of the human capacity to imagine a better future, or is it a tool for the progress of science? Can social science use theory in the way that natural science does, or it is a completely different animal in the social world?
How theory stands in relation to data looks very different from standpoints whose location is fixed by these different compasses. From this alternative perspective theory can help us re-imagine, it can ignite and liberate the sociological (or other) imagination if we use it with skill and flexibility. It can help us perform 'epistemological reversals' which refract the gaze from what is accepted as self-evident and makes us think otherwise (Fine, in Anyon et al, 2009, p 183). Theory can counter dominant discourses and foster criticality. Ball makes this point well:

> Theory is a vehicle for 'thinking otherwise', it is a platform for 'outrageous hypotheses' and for 'unleashing criticism'. Theory is destructive, disruptive and violent. It offers a language for challenge, and modes of thought, other than those articulated for us by dominant others. It provides a language of rigour and irony rather than contingency. The purpose of such theory is to de-familiarise present practices and categories, to make them seem less self-evident and necessary, and to open up spaces for the invention of new forms of experience. (Ball, 1995, 265-6)

2.2 Making theory work

There is an argument that the use of theory in empirical research is like mist on spectacles: it obscures more than it illuminates (Shaw & Crompton, 2003). However I would argue that this is only sometimes true. As I argued above, it is better to deploy explicit, challengeable, theory to edge out the sort of tacit theory that inevitably exists anyway and which is invisibly embodied and encoded in our understanding and use of data if not surfaced. Foucault (1977) talks about 'blind empiricism', but empirical work is always underpinned by theory which conditions how we see and what we see; it's just not *explicit* theory and it tends to lead to undiagnosed myopia. Using explicit theory in empirical research, at its best, achieves a number of important goals. It illuminates 'reality' – simplifying and identifying what is important and what not, suggesting how things relate to each other, highlighting causality, providing explanations. Patton says that 'causal inferences flash as lightning bolts in stormy controversies' (1997, p 216). He argues that these inferences are rarely carefully considered and structured with any established degree of robustness, but they should be. Explicit theory, then, surfaces sets of propositions and so renders them amenable to critique. It generates hypotheses which can then guide questions, methodology and methods. (ie very much prior to the stage of using theory to illuminate data, or data to test theory). As Deming says:

> Without theory, experience has no meaning....one has no questions to ask. Hence, without theory, there is no learning. (Deming, 1993, p 105)

Theory can function to take research beyond what appear to be 'simply' descriptions - 'abstracted empiricism' (Mills, 1959) – though even the simplest description is infused with theory of a sort. Theory helps avoid a 'market research' approach which is rooted in one context only and describes correlations but offers no explanations. With theory, says one writer (perhaps too enthusiastically), data are lifted off the ground: 'data soar, data sing' (Dimitriadis, 2009). Theory therefore allows even single case study research to 'generalise to theory' (Yin, 2008), to engage in theory-building and the move from substantive to formal theory (Glaser & Strauss, 1967) - theory about the particular to larger scale theory. Theory can shift the level of analysis and bridge different levels of analysis, illuminating links between them and, as Mills in his classic work *The Sociological Imagination* (1959) did, linking the everyday life with the broader social structures which condition it.

Tooley & Darby (1998, p 67) criticise non-cumulation in educational research, and this is certainly true of HE research too – there are a lot of individual studies unconnected with each other. The use of appropriate theory would go some way to countering this. Tooley & Darby also criticise the tendency of educational researchers to defer to a small number of theorists (Bourdieu is mentioned) for no good reason other than the fact that others do likewise and these theorists are considered 'eminent'. There is, they argue, 'adulation of great thinkers, (pp 56-62). Ball (1995) refers to this as the 'mantric' use of theory, and Dale (1992) 'theory by numbers'. Eminence-based practice in educational research is certainly a problem, and it includes the use of sometimes poor theory and ill-defined concepts (like 'habitus', or 'culture') as well as the substantiation of argument simply by reference to the work of the Greats. This is social science as sorcery (Andreski, 1972)

Insider research presents particular problems in terms of the theory-data relationship (Trowler, 2012b). Insider researchers are themselves liable to be influenced by tacit theories held by respondents. In such cases it becomes particularly difficult to 'render the normal strange' (Delamont, 2002). Moreover human behaviour viewed through the microscope tends to bring to attention impalpable drivers of behaviour far more than when it is seen through a telescope: by their nature these are difficult to apprehend through data collection alone. In fine-grained, insider, qualitative research, knowledgeability and sense-making are foregrounded as explanation is sought more than correlation. Here the nature and status of data and conclusions becomes contested. As the data become contested, so does the relationship between theory and data: in particular the extent to which theoretical assumptions condition the interpretative process.

So how can theory best be made to do the great work it can do in doctoral research, and how can some of these problems be avoided?

First, there needs to be clarity and explicitness about the significance and purposes of theory, as against data, and a clear rationale explaining the fitness of the theory deployed for the purposes stated, clarity about what it offers. As Ashwin argues (2009, p 131-132), it is necessary ensure that the theoretical perspective adopted is appropriate in two ways: that there is internal consistency between the different positions adopted, conceptually, theoretically and methodologically; and that the theoretical approach is fit for the purpose for which it is intended.

Sibeon (2007) asks the question 'theory for what?', and exemplifies different purposes by distinguishing between 'sensitizing' theory and frameworks, on the one hand, and 'substantive' theories on the other. The former give new perspectives on habitual practices: better ways of conceptualising the world. The latter form the basis for rigorous testing and 'aim to generate new empirical information about the social world' (p 13).

Second, there is a further question: 'theory for whom?' Adopting a theoretical position involves a process of privileging: privileging some data over others, some insights over others, and sometimes some groups over others. It is important to be clear about whose perspectives and interests are foregrounded. The key question here is: 'in deploying this theoretical perspective to do some work in this research, what is being occluded and whose perspectives and interests are affected by this?' So, for example, a study examining sustainability in universities might adopt a Marxist lens, or a social practice theory one. The Marxist lens would situate the issues in the wider imperatives of a capitalist economy and society whereas a social practice lens would shift the focus to a lower level of analysis and occlude broader structural issues.

This example points to a third issue – the question of spanning the different levels of analysis. Generally there is a tendency towards lack of integration between meso and micro levels of analysis. For example the literature on higher education policy on the whole operates on the levels of whole organizations, professions and middle range theory, while fine grained insider research tends to operate at the micro level. The danger of the latter is that researchers miss structural conditioning of behavior (Webb, 1991). The danger of the former is that research misses the significant, nuanced, social processes operating on the ground in different contexts. A theoretical appreciation of the implications of level of analysis issues in research design can mitigate these issues.

The fourth point concerns the significance of getting the balance right between commitment to a position and being self-critical. This relates to the distinction made in chapter one between Popperian hypothetico-deductive understanding of theory and a social reconstructionist one. Burawoy tries to bridge the gap between them:

> In our fieldwork we do not look for confirmations but for theory's refutations. We need first the courage of our convictions, then the courage to challenge our convictions, and finally the imagination to sustain our courage with theoretical reconstruction.(Burawoy, 1998, p 20)

However some would disagree, arguing that convictions are paramount when they address centuries of structured disadvantage for some.

Fifthly, and finally, is the key issue of the relationship between theory and data. Data can be used to test/ refine/ develop theory, and theory can be employed to interrogate data, to organize/ explain/ order it. Both are equally valid purposes, but clarity about which is most significant in any research is important. 'Good social science uses facts to inspire theory and/or to check the empirical validity of a theory' say Abell & Reyniers (2000, p 749). And good social science is clear about what it is doing.

Theory provides a discourse to describe the world and to explain it. The repertoires of each theory help us to organize apparent chaos and to produce texts which communicate these understandings to our audiences in particular ways. But other writers employ different discourses, and audiences themselves approach our texts from their own theoretical standpoints, from their own frames of reference. It is important, then, to be mindful of the specifics of the discourses we deploy, of the work they are doing (and not doing) for our project.

An equally important though difficult task is to maintain awareness of alternatives and the different ways of seeing those alternatives provide.

Distilling these comments into a few questions for reflection, these are:

- What work is theory being asked to do in this doctoral research project?
- Whose perspectives and interests are privileged, who's occluded?
- What levels of analysis are foregrounded by this theoretical approach
- What other flaws exist in the lens being used?
- What are the most beneficial relationships between theory and data in this project?

Personal preferences, affinities, and disciplinary trends (or fashions) will influence decisions about theory: they key thing is to interrogate any decision made, and to be ready to make and remake the decisions.

Seven deadly (and not-so-deadly) sins in deploying theory

Doctoral students, and researchers in general, sometimes deploy theory in ways which are less than helpful, and sometimes damaging. In this section I want to summarise seven of them.

First is the sin of **circularity**. If theory informs research design, then there is the danger that the findings simply confirm the theory. This is a point Ashwin (2013) elaborates about the dangers of mutual confirmation in the relationship between theory and data. If the research design, including methods of data collection and the approach to data analysis is driven by theory, then the results simply exemplify that theory in a circular and usually unhelpful way. For Ashwin this mistake is best avoided by real clarity about the purposes of theory in a research project. Making use of work by Bernstein (2000) and Brown (2006), Ashwin argues that the internal (theoretical) and external (data-derived) *languages of description* need to be explicit and related to each other in a non-circular manner if empirical data are to do more than simply exemplify theory.

Second is the sin of **occluded origins**. The sin here is not being explicit about, or giving a rationale for, where theory comes from. Theory may emerge from the data, as in the grounded theory approach (Glaser & Strauss, 1967) or data may be viewed through a pre-selected theoretical lens. In the former case there is a danger of myopia, in the latter the dangers of circularity, just described.

Alternatively theory development and data analysis may occur together, but this risks premature cognitive closure. The possible reasons why researchers deploy one theory rather than another are multiple: because one is likely to be more illuminative; because one is more likely to help answer the research questions; because of a theory's capacity in the social reconstructionist project; because one is felt to be more robust than another, and so on. Whatever the reasoning, it is really important to make it explicit (and challengeable).

Third is the sin of **obscurity**. Where there is lack of clarity about the relationship between data and theory, about how each relates to the other in a given research project or where there is there is confusion about this, then there is the potential for *nothing* to be done well. The nature of the relationship can be one of several things: data may be testing, interrogating or refining theory; theory may be illuminating, explaining or interrogating data. Once again, it is important to be explicit about exactly what is going on.

Fourth is the sin of **binary thinking**. This sin involves forgetting that data are derived from the social world and that, because practices in the social world are infused with tacit theory, those data themselves are also infused with respondents' theories. So data and 'theory' (understood as the theory deployed by the researcher) are not binary types, but simply different expressions of theory. This probably needs a little more unpicking. In educational research much data (though not all) derives from information about social practices – accounts or observations of about educational practices of various sorts.

The danger is that the researcher imposes a theoretical framework on those practices without understanding that the practices themselves are permeated by theory. To further complicate this issue, different theories may infuse the actual practices of respondents compared to their *accounts* of practice.

Here we need to distinguish between practical consciousness (going about doing something, and the knowledge and skills used in that) and discursive consciousness (a different way of thinking used when talking about doing that thing, describing and explaining it) (Giddens, 1984). Different tacit theories will be deployed in these different forms of consciousness; and what researchers often access is discursive consciousness. So, theory infuses all dimensions of research, and researchers need to keep this in mind.

Directly stemming from the sin of binary thinking is the fifth sin; that of **ventriloquism**. This involves making respondents say things they did not say because the researcher's theoretical perspective indicates that that is what they should be saying, or what their words *really* meant or that their utterances betray an underlying, unrecognised (to them) truth. Fine (2009) points out this problem. He worries about....

> ...imposing theory onto the words of participants; ventriloquating or editing participants to speak the theory; or occluding the complicated, sometimes contradictory narrations of participants in order to fit with well-ironed theory. (Fine, 2009, pp 192-3)

What links the fourth and fifth sins, binary thinking and ventriloquism, is that respondents and researchers are existing in alternative theoretical worlds, with the two not touching. In this case one wonders about the real significance of that research. Jonathan Jansen illustrates the dangers of this disconnect, which he calls *the challenge of the ordinary*:

...show me a theoretical framework particularly in the critical tradition that begins to grapple with ...imperfect practice. There is none, for what critical theory does is to stand self-righteously at the other end of this struggle and declare the impossible ideals that real practising teachers and principals – the ordinary ones – must but simply cannot attain without working through the ruins of a troubled past, a testing present, and a future from which the lifeblood of hope is drained by the burden of the everyday. (Jansen, 2008, p 155)

The sixth sin is **eminence-based theorising**. Easy options are sometimes adopted to mitigate the challenges of writing theory against data in a way which makes them imbricate and instantiate each other. PhD theses, chapters, articles, often begin with a panoply of famous men (and sometimes women) rolled out, held up for admiration and then put back into the cupboard. Their role is simply to give their warrant to what follows. Often, too, theories are simply used, not engaged with. There is a tendency to simply take, not make, theory, to use it as a frame into which data is shoved. No matter how eminent the theorist nor how frequently cited the theory, there is always room for engagement, challenge and reconstruction. Abell & Reyniers (2000) make the significant point that theory has great value but is sometimes misused. They employ the example of Castells (2000) to argue that "social theory has failed intellectually" (p 739) yet it has the trappings of success. For them, Castells' writing conceals what are essentially obvious ideas behind florid idiom and that ill-defined concepts are made to fit the argument. Not only Castells is culpable in this respect, many of the 'Greats' use wooly concepts and high flown language that masks fairly simple and obvious ideas.

The final sin is **theoretical fundamentalism**: rigidly adhering to one theoretical perspective, deploying it no matter what. This can be as myopic as not having an explicit theory at all. For example Anyon et al. relentlessly apply *critical theory* to all of their research without challenging their own assumptions or perspective. So,

> An urban school may present as a collection of harried teachers and unmotivated students, until it is studied as an institutional repository of the effects of discriminatory macroeconomic, political and racial forces...This is a theoretical stance that informs our work. (Anyon, 2009, p 4)

Here the danger is that one's professional identity becomes bound up with a particular theoretical approach, indeed sometimes one's whole persona. This can be dangerous, as Ball recognised:

> [t]heory can, and often does, function to provide comforting and apparently stable identities for beleaguered academics in an increasingly slippery world. Theory can serve to conjure up its own anterior norms and lay its dead hand upon the creativity of the mind. Too often in educational studies, theory becomes no more than a mantric reaffirmation of belief rather than a tool for exploration and for thinking otherwise. (Ball, 2006, p 64)

When used in this way, theory informs, but it can also occlude. In this case Shaw & Crompton (2003) would be right: it offers spectacles, but misted ones. One way to avoid this is to challenge theory and one's own approach. But this takes difficult work, and much more difficult when the theory and the self become intertwined. And of course when theory is being deployed for social reconstructionist purposes, as discussed above, theory *should* become intimately connected with the self – without feminist theory (for example) women can be disempowered, with more feeble ways of seeing and possessing a more limited arsenal in the struggle against oppression

2.3 Social practice theory & studying change in HE

This section illustrates some of the comments above through one example – social practice theory (SPT) as applied to the study of change. SPT has been developed by authors such as Bourdieu, 1990; Giddens, 1984; Schatzki et al, 2001 and Warde, 2005. There is no accepted canon in this body of literature, though Reckwitz (2002) has provided a very useful summation, and subsequently Shove et al (2012) have written interestingly and entertainingly on the approach, applying it to practices in everyday life.

Rather than focusing on individuals, SPT looks at the social world as clusters of practices; regular sets of behaviours, ways of understanding and know-how and states of emotion that are enacted by groups configured to achieve specific outcomes. Examples of such outcomes in universities are: curriculum development; research; undergraduate provision. Individual people are conceptualised as 'carriers' of practices that are mobilised those individuals, with others, in specific contexts. People enact ways of behaving, understanding and responding that are commonly understood and accepted in that particular social field. Templates for practice might be a good metaphor. This involves acquiring and deploying a set of dispositions, perceptions and actions which give people who are immersed in them a 'feel for the game', an intuitive understanding of what is 'right': what Bourdieu calls 'habitus'. Individuals develop a 'practical sense' which they deploy through the 'practical skills' they acquire (Bourdieu, 1990).

There is then a shift from the 'ABC' theory of change; from a concentration on *individual* Attitudes, Behaviours and Choices, towards the social enactment of practices. However each enactment is unique. While people draw on and enact practice templates or *reservoirs* (learned and commonly understood and deployed practices), practice theory also recognises individual and group *repertoires* (Bernstein, 1999): specific ways of accomplishing different types of practice that are particular to the individuals involved. The background knowledge and motivating characteristics of each person in the social field are significant in determining specific outcomes and levels of success, as are the resources to hand, the affordances available (Barnes, 2001; Shove et al, 2012). These unique 'murmerings of the everyday' (De Certeau, 1984) are very significant, and are one reason why SPT stresses the significance of *context* for social science analysis.

Examining higher education contexts in detail suggests that there is both consensus and conflict over each of the characteristics of practice as identified by Reckwitz. Practice is, he says:

> a routinized type of behaviour which consists of several elements, interconnected to one other: forms of bodily activities, forms of mental activities, 'things' and their use, a background knowledge in the form of understanding, know-how, states of emotion and motivational knowledge." (Reckwitz, 2002, p 249)

Both consensus and dispute (or at least unspoken difference) characterise these different dimensions of motivation, emotion, understanding, knowledge and appropriate bodily practices in most university departments. Yet as Archer (2007) points out, there is a common set of contextual concerns which shapes agendas and priorities there and which form a common focal point for everyone there.

Because of this, the analytical distinction between 'practice-as-entity' (the template or reservoir of understood practices) and 'practice-as-performance' (their situated instantiation in the social world) is important: practice-as-performance always involves a unique configuration of know-how, resources, affordances and purposes. But practice-as-entity is the template within which this reconfiguration is accomplished, and it has much greater longevity than practice-as-performance. This distinction helps us to explain the difficulties experienced in scaling up change from small pilots to large populations, from enthusiasts to others: what's involved is a shift from practice-as-performance to practice-as-entity, a shift that is not easy.

So, to develop an effective theory of change it is necessary to move beyond *ethnographies* of situated practice, such as those produced in actor network theory, and to show how practice-as-entity changes, not only differences in, or the ability to re-shape particular instances of practice-as-performance. While Warde (2005: 140) rightly argues that 'the source of changed behaviour lies in the development of practices', the word 'practices' should be understood to mean practices-as-entities. Changing local, temporary performances represents an achievement, but one that is unlikely to last or to spread.

However some authors (for example Turner, 1994) have perceived a problem in this theoretical project: they have criticised SPT for not having a mechanism for explaining change. As the account above has indicated, there is an emphasis on the shared understandings of practice-as-entities, well-integrated arrays of practices to achieve ends and consensus about how to 'go on'. For example Schatzki (2001: 11) says that practices are 'embodied, materially mediated arrays of human activity centrally organized around *shared* practical understanding.'

Both Shove et al (2012) and Reckwitz (2002) argue in reply that change comes about because practice is an accomplishment involving the assemblage of different elements, summarised by Shove as: materials; competences; meanings. The configuration of these three elements, and long term changes to them, is the key to social change according to those authors. From an SPT perspective one important element of change involves the interaction between material artefacts and practices. 'There are no technical innovations without innovations in practice' (Shove et al, 2012: 12). Competence is distributed between artefacts and people, and it can be re-distributed. Artefacts can 'configure' activity, and the discursive repertoires they carry are often significant in this. Symbolic structures, particular orders of meaning in particular places evoked by specific things, are very significant in conditioning practices, and in changing them. Relations between people can be inscribed and hardwired into the design of material artefacts, and discursive and substantive agendas set by them too. It is misleading to think of *things* as infinitely flexible carriers of ascribed meaning, but at the same time the power of artefacts alone to inscribe practices should not be over-estimated. There is an on-going co-adaptation of artefacts and practices, a constant search for effective configurations of materials, competences and meanings: provisional equilibria are established and then remade. Multiple things have to be brought together in a spatially and temporally structured arrangement: software and hardware; architectural characteristics; policies and processes. Each has its effects in relation to each other and in conjunction, with people achieving the active integration of material artefacts and practice, and sometimes achieving new conjunctions.

So from an SPT perspective the accomplishment of university life for students, academics and others involves actively and effectively configuring and integrating complex assemblies of artefacts into sets of recurrent practices.

There are trajectories of innovation, but fossilization also occurs and often a 'snapping back' to old practices. There is 'recruitment to practices' as well as defection from them (Shove et al, 2012). The trajectories of practices-as-entities are inherently unstable, depending as they do on the recurrent integration of materials, images and forms of competence by more or less 'faithful' cohorts of practitioner-carriers.

Meanwhile there are sets of interests, emotions and subjectivities involved. Barnes (2001: 28) notes that: 'To engage in a practice is to exercise a power' and that often involves contestation over subjectivities as well as more concrete interests, and is an emotionally-charged business. What is rather awkwardly referred to as 'teleoaffectivity' (the influence of emotions in purposive activity) is significant, then, in conditioning practices. In universities what is mostly seen is contested conventions and understandings, the interplay of repertoires derived from different reservoirs, including educational ideologies which shape purposes.

Moreover academics come from a huge range of backgrounds and bring multiple sets of understandings and conventions into play: departments in particular are natural, open systems and this means that practices-as-performance tend to vary considerably between them. Finally, I indicated above that the interplay of practices and artefacts is a dynamic system. As Warde (2005, p 141) says:

> ...practices also contain the seeds of constant change. They are dynamic by virtue of their own internal logic of operation, as people in myriad situations adapt, improvise and experiment.... In addition, practices are not hermetically sealed off from other adjacent and parallel practices, from which lessons are learnt, innovations borrowed, procedures copied.

The trajectories of practices are inherently unstable because they depend upon the recurrent integration of artefacts, meanings and forms of competence by groups of practitioners who 'carry' but also adapt practices.

Social practice theory applied

In terms of the role of leaders and followers in universities, it follows from the above that the methodological individualism which permeates advice on how to lead change, envisaging individual leaders as being able to shift practices with relative ease, is misplaced:

> Patterns of stability and change are not controlled by any one actor alone, but policy makers often have a hand influencing the range of elements in circulation, the ways in which practices relate to each other and the careers and trajectories of practices and those who carry them. (Shove et al, 2012, p 19)

These key propositions from this theoretical and conceptual tradition as well as their corollaries in terms of leading change show that effective configurations of practice are composed of artefacts, meanings and forms of competence. Practices have sets of understandings, procedures and objectives. The change agent's challenge is to direct them in appropriate ways. Reconfiguring these brings about change, and providing circumstances in which lessons can be learned, innovations can be borrowed and procedures can be copied is one way in which change can be facilitated.

To conclude, SPT is an example of Merton's Grand Theory: it has large things to say about society and the relationship between what people do and their social location. It deals with ontological issues as well as offering a lens through which the social world can be viewed at whatever level is called for by the research project in question. Adopting it foregrounds some things but pushes others into the background. Individual choice and personal attitudes are de-emphasised while social process and the social construction of reality at the group level is highlighted. Individual agency and the effects of personality and (for example) learning styles are not entirely discounted, but they are given less emphasis than is common in most approaches to researching education. Artefacts, the things in use to achieve ends, are foregrounded as important influences on practices. Many other dimensions of social reality are cast into light and shadow by this theoretical perspective. There are then significant consequences for research design, for methods of data collection and for interpreting what the data mean and how far conclusions can be stretched. So it is really important to be wide-awake and wide-eyed when applying theoretical lenses in doctoral research.

For a full example of how social practice theory has been used in a successful doctorate, see Brian Boag's 2010 thesis *The Role of the Programme Team in the Implementation of Policy at Institutional Level - a Case Study in the UHI Millennium Institute.* This is freely available in full via the University of Stirling: http://tinyurl.com/hqer4xt. In conducting his study Boag deploys social practice theory and a number of the concepts and theoretical devices I have developed over the years.

2.4 Examples of theory use in doctorates

This short section examines ways in which theory has been made to work in completed doctoral theses, using Index to Theses and EThOS.

K. Hinnet's thesis (1997) developed theory from data: *Towards meaningful learning: a theory for improved assessment in higher education*. Her aim was to theorise how assessment can be improved, and so one of the aims of the thesis was educational enhancement, achieved through theoretical development. This was not situated as grounded theory however because theoretical resources were deployed from the beginning.

A similar purpose for theory development underpinned W. I. Warburton's thesis (2005): *Towards a theory of computer-assisted assessment uptake in UK higher education*. This one however did deploy grounded theory: "A grounded theory analysis of the interview and survey data was carried out and a theory of dual path CAA uptake in universities emerged from which three models of uptake were derived."

M. Ramrattan's thesis (2010) used theory in a different way, within an action research design: *Developing web-based information systems for emergent organisations through the theory of deferred action: insights from higher education action research*. Here an already-existing theoretical resource ("deferred action") was used to understand, interpret and create associations between the factors which constrained and facilitated the process of developing web-based information systems.

A further example of theoretical development is S. J. Aston (2001): *Student experiences of full-time education courses in higher education: an empirical and theoretical investigation*. Here however the purpose is less oriented to enhancement of practices on the ground and more to better understanding and the further refinement of theoretical debate. The abstract says that the ..."study developed a theoretical model that represented the decision-making processes of students both prior to and within higher education. The theoretical framework recognised the relationship between macro (society), meso (institutional), and micro (individual) factors, and attempted to develop the agency-structure debate."

One or two doctorates have deployed "living theory" (Whitehead, 1989). One example is M. Goldrick (2010): *Effective Learning Support in Higher Education: My Living Theory of student-centred learning support in National College of Ireland*. This involves the researcher centrally in developing theory through reflection on their own circumstances, approaches and reactions (somewhat in the style of auto-ethnography) but will also use other methods.

K. Glaston (2000) seeks to integrate various theoretical traditions: *A study of progression and retention in Higher Education: the search for an eclectic theoretical framework*. Glaston says in the abstract: "The main aim of this thesis is to create a new eclectic theoretical framework which will assist in the identification of students 'at risk' before underachievement, withdrawal or failure occurs. This universal model takes the form of a composite set of models which identifies the determinants and associated critical points of withdrawal or failure and processes behind student underachievement, withdrawal and failure."

L. A. Smith's thesis (2007) *Academic work practices in transnational education: a social practice theory approach to understanding the implementation of assessment-related policy in an offshore campus of an Australian university* uses theory as a lens through which to understand the implementation of policy at an offshore university campus. Here a particular approach, social practice theory, is adopted *ab initio* and the research design and data collection and analysis are informed by this.

X. Cheng's thesis (2006) *Investigating Chinese students' academic reading practices in a UK university: a new literacy studies/activity theory approach* took a similar approach using two theoretical traditions in a combined way. This used new literacy studies theory and activity theory to investigate Chinese students' academic literacy practices at a UK university.

There are of course plenty of other examples to be found among the abstracts: using the advanced search function specifying keywords and their location within EThOS (http://ethos.bl.uk/Home.do) will find them.

Section 3: Thesis structure, content and completion

About this section

This is designed to be helpful for anyone who wants to create a good structure for their doctoral thesis; one in which they can be confident that they have covered all the bases.

The section is not designed to create a template for thesis structure to be followed slavishly, rather it offers suggestions and advice as well as indications of where some options are low risk and others high risk when it comes to examination of the thesis.

It gives guidance on the contents of thesis chapters and subsections of those chapters, indicating what needs to be covered and how to prepare the content in the best way.

3.1 Starting at the End: Questions examiners ask (themselves)

Candidates for a doctorate are doing at least two things simultaneously: researching a topic that is of real interest to them (it has to be – they will be investigating it for at least 3 years) and undergoing an educative process. This book is about both but has success in the final assessment of the research uppermost among its objectives.

It is not yet another book about research methods, research design or the philosophy of research; there are already very many of those. Nor is it a book about how to *write* at doctoral level; there are an increasing number of those too. Its primary goal is to help the reader think about the best way to organise the content of their doctoral thesis, and what that content should be. That is very important: with a clear view of what the thesis will look like, what its shape will be, it becomes much easier to write it and to give it a coherent shape with a strong line of argument.

Mostly the way this book is structured follows the way in which a thesis in education is usually structured. But this chapter is an exception because it starts at the end: the point at which the thesis has been completed and is about to be examined. The examination process is different in different countries, but the dominant model is to have more than one examiner read and evaluate the thesis (sometimes with a viva voce with the candidate, as in the UK and some other European countries) and then come to an agreement about the outcome. So this chapter asks the question: what are these examiners looking for in a thesis?

Trafford and Leshem (2002) investigated this issue **empirically**. They reviewed the questions asked in 25 vivas, textually analysing the questions asked by examiners to identify clusters of themes. The topics of the doctoral theses examined included (in order of frequency) education (including education management) (14 vivas), applied sciences (4 vivas), business (2 vivas) and the following with 1 viva: psychology, bio-medicine, marketing, computing, history. From this they developed a template of questions "which prospective researchers can use to write...a doctoral thesis" (p. 31).

At the time of writing I have examined around 40 PhD candidates in 17 different universities, including several outside the UK. This experience tells me that Trafford and Leshem's template is useful, at least for doctorates on the topic of higher education, the focus of this book. It is a good starting point, but it needs qualification and elaboration, not least because their method of data collection was to record questions in viva examinations that they attended either as examiner or as independent chair. Clearly this design shapes the range and nature of questions asked. There are some odd omissions in their account, so what follows largely uses their headings but the content is mine.

Their template looks like this:

Cluster 1: Opening question or questions. This cluster only applies to viva voce examinations, live interrogations of the candidate by examiners. These questions are often used to allow the candidate to 'warm up' so usually involve an unchallenging question such as "why did you choose this topic?"

Cluster 2: Conceptualisation. This cluster concerns the candidate's understanding of the relevant literature and how it applies to their research, their theoretical lens and the work it does and doesn't do in the thesis, as well as the concepts they are deploying. Examiners want to know whether the different parts of the thesis hang together properly and whether the candidate has good reasons for making the theoretical and conceptual choices s/he did. No theoretical approach is perfect and very often the examiners will interrogate the one predominantly applied in the thesis, the candidate's use of it, their appreciation of its deficiencies and the particular slant it gives on the social world and the topic. So the thesis may deploy activity theory, communities of practice theory, actor network theory, a dimension of feminist theory or something else. All of these foreground and background particular things and have consequences methodologically and empirically which raise questions in examiners' minds.

The next four clusters I put together because they are normally treated by examiners in one group:

Cluster 3: Research design.
Cluster 4: Research methodology.
Cluster 5: Research methods.
Cluster 6: Sampling.

Together these are about the choices made **methodologically** and in terms of research **methods** as well as questions about the underpinning understanding of the nature of the social world and what can be known about it (**ontological** and **epistemological** issues). Here the examiners want to know that the approach taken (say a case study design) and the choices made within that (the sample chosen and the data collection methods used) are appropriate to the research questions and can lead to robust data.

Cluster 7: Conceptual and other conclusions. A doctoral thesis is not market research or just evaluative research, which each look at very particular issues, have findings which are empirical in nature and which are used to develop proposals for action. It can have these characteristics, but it needs something more: a conceptual and theoretical basis (see Section 2). This cluster explores the findings in the thesis on theory and concepts. Oddly Trafford and Leshem do not include a cluster on non-conceptual or empirical conclusions. Yet examiners also ask questions about these, and about how they are presented, in other words about empirical conclusions.

Cluster 8: Robustness. (Trafford and Leshem name this cluster "fundamentals", but that is unhelpful). Here the topic is the level of confidence that the conclusions can be defended. There are almost always questions about the role of the researcher in the research, issues of "objectivity", the way the data were analysed to derive outcomes and the ways in which "validity" and "reliability" were established. Ethical issues can arise here too.

Cluster 9: Contribution. The key issue here is the contribution to knowledge that is claimed by the candidate and how far this can be defended. This is one of the key criteria for judging a doctoral thesis and so is very important indeed. Here or within one of the other clusters is a compound question not addressed in Trafford and Leshem's list, but one that is almost always in the minds of examiners: "are these conclusions generalisable to other situations, and if so which and to what extent (and is the concept of "generalisability" used like this appropriate here?)"?

Cluster 10. Being critical. Here the examiners ask whether the candidate might have taken a different course; they consider the roads **not** travelled and why. They may well do this when they consider different issues within the thesis rather than asking such questions within a single, discrete, cluster.

The next two clusters I consider together. They only apply to examination by viva voce.

Cluster 11. Returning to the beginning.
Cluster 12: And finally...

Where the examination takes the form of a viva the candidate may be asked to make some general reflections on the whole research process, think about next steps in their career or research, and be given the opportunity to ask questions of the examiners.

So, understanding how the thesis will be approached by examiners, and the sorts of questions they are likely to ask the candidate or of the thesis helps in the process of planning and writing the thesis itself. This insight indicates content areas that must be addressed somewhere within the thesis and shows how and why the thesis must be shaped in a coherent way.

The following chapters give suggestions about how to do this.

3.2. Writing the Abstract

An abstract gives a brief overview of a thesis or article. This fulfils two purposes:
1. It gives readers an **advance organizer** which prepares them to navigate and properly understand what is a long and sometimes complex text.
2. It helps other researchers who are accessing a number of abstracts through a database to determine whether it is worth them gaining access to the full piece for their own research or writing.

For doctoral students the first purpose is paramount, and the readers they should have in mind are their examiners. The abstract is the first thing the examiners read, and it creates first impressions. Examiners may use it to navigate the thesis and to assess whether the broad purposes have been achieved. They may get the impression that this is a valuable piece of work with broader significance, or they may get a less favourable one. So it is important to make sure the abstract is absolutely right.

A large number of abstracts can be viewed at http://ethos.bl.uk/ (these must be accessed through a registered HE institution or by becoming a subscribed user).

An abstract needs to be short – around half a page is the norm. Most abstracts do the following: describe the purpose of the research; describe the research design, in brief; summarise the findings; explain the relevance for other contexts and the truth claims being made.

Here is an example, adapted for better readability from my own doctoral thesis abstract:

This is a single-site case study in an English new university using a mixed-method quasi-ethnographic approach to examine the implementation of a group of features collectively referred to here as the "credit framework". By this is meant those aspects of the higher education curriculum facilitated by the assignment of credit to assessed learning including: modularity; the semester system; franchising; accreditation of work-based learning and of prior learning.

At the time of the research the framework was being implemented in the context of expanding student numbers and a declining unit of resource. The study describes and tracks the sources of the attitudes and values of academic staff concerning the framework's features. The implications these attitudes and values have for the implementation of institutional policy in this area are described and analysed.

In addressing this task the thesis critically interrogates a number of conventional approaches to the study of higher education, including approaches to understanding the dynamics of change as well as organisational and professional cultures and the role and importance of the epistemological characteristics of disciplines in higher education.

It is argued that there has to date often been an inappropriate generalisation to the whole higher education sector of findings in these fields that are derived from studies of elite institutions, disciplines and individuals. No such general truth claims are made for the specific findings from this research concerning academics' attitudes to change or their related policy implementation strategies.

However the conditioning factors affecting these are likely to be found in many contemporary higher education institutions, albeit in different configurations. Additionally, the study's theorisation of the nature, construction and impact of cultures within higher education institutions and the research strategies deriving from this are commended as appropriate for the study of academics' adaptive responses in university contexts.

Looking back on this now, many years later, I think the original version was rather obscurely written (this version remains quite dense). There is not enough detail about the methods used and the findings are referred to only obliquely. The last two sentences in particular are quite obscure. However writing an abstract is quite tough – the author needs to convey a lot of information in a very restricted space.

3.3 Structuring the Introductory Chapter

This first chapter should prepare the reader for what is to follow, ignoring the fact that some information is already in the abstract. Typically this chapter will:

- Set out the aims and rationale for the study

- Set out the research questions for the first time, and explain them

- If appropriate, give brief details of the context of the research: the research site; history; policy context and so on. Chapter 4 of this book gives more detail on the larger chapter which does this, and it is usually best to write that before this summary.

- Give a brief summary of the methodology and methods used, and the rationale for choices made in this respect. This is a precursor to the methodology/methods chapter of the thesis. Again, a section of this book covers that chapter later, and it is best to write that before this summary.

- Offer initial insights into the theoretical tools deployed and their purposes, and/or significant debates being addressed. This will usually be drawn from the literature review chapter.

- Set out an initial statement of what the claims to originality and significance will be, and where the boundaries of the truth claims lie. This will form a part of the final chapter and again this précis should be written after that section has been completed.

- Give an overview of the thesis structure to follow, and introduce the next chapter.

Writing the aims and rationale for the study should be reasonably straightforward. Sometimes candidates ask about the extent they should talk about themselves and their own motivations for doing the research, as well as other reasons behind doing it. If these are relevant to the research, and they usually are, then it is important to talk about personal motivations, but not to allow those to form too-large a part of this section. Nowadays it is really important to acknowledge the role of the researcher in the research and the write-up of it, so saying some things about the person writing the thesis has become the norm. This account should lead on to the next, very important, section:

Writing research questions.

Research questions should:
Be answerable: it must be possible to know when a question has been answered
Be specific, that is set clear boundaries in terms of what is being studied, and what is not
Include at least one analytical question which goes beyond the descriptive
Be capable of **operationalisation**; that is, use concepts that can be turned into measureable, observable, describable phenomena
Be bounded in what they require, that is they can be realistically answered given the resources available
Be significant; that is, they should provide an answer to the '**so what?**' question - the issue of offering wider interest to a larger audience

One role of research questions is to guide research design, and there needs to be congruence between that design and the questions. This means that the research design chosen must be capable of answering the research questions.

A thesis should unambiguously answer the research questions. The answers may be subtle, conditional, nuanced and give rise to new questions, but there should be clear answers of whatever sort.

Here is a problematic attempt at constructing research questions:

This thesis aims to explore academic staff's reception of the teaching and learning policy of a university. The analysis focuses on the discourse that arose from staff's reaction to the policy as well as factors that could undermine or facilitate the achievement of the policy.

This is more like part of an abstract than research questions: while these statements give a feel for the research, there is no specificity, only broad aims. While they give licence to the writer to cover ground that seems interesting, they fail to set boundaries. It will be unclear to the writer when their work has stepped outside the limits of the study. The word 'explore' is particularly dangerous in this respect - it does not set boundaries or specific goals. 'Reception' is capable of multiple interpretations and needs to be operationalised. There are too many questions wrapped up in these two sentences: they need to be unpicked.

Those two sentences could be reconfigured as follows:

1. To what extent do academic staff in one Faculty in a new university in the UK display knowledge about and understanding of the formal teaching and learning policy there?

2. In what different ways do academic staff there interpret and respond to that policy?

3. What reasons can be given for the differences identified in answering questions 1 and 2?

4. What different **discursive repertoires** do they draw on when they discuss the policy?
5. What are the implications of the answers to questions 1-4 for policy implementation in the area of teaching and learning in the case study university?
6. To what extent do these findings confirm what is known about policy implementation in that context?
7. What are the implications of the findings for university managers at senior and middle levels in that context?

These research questions, unpicked in this way, themselves raise issues about the **truth claims** that can be made from a study of one Faculty in one university, but the writer should address this issue in writing the thesis, and the limits of generalisability made clear both there and in the abstract.

Analysing these questions further:

Question 1 requires a fairly descriptive answer but there are more analytical ones to follow.

Question 2 is possibly still too open, but it is an improvement on the original version.

Question 3 allows the writer to do some analysis which might get him or her into disciplinary differences, institutional location etc. The data collection needs to be thoughtfully constructed to be able to answer it, and a pilot study undertaken to ensure this.

Question 4 (based on the original version) stands out as possibly belonging to a different thesis, and being potentially too big, especially when Question 5 is attempted.

Question 6 allows a discussion of the literature and gives the thesis a theoretical edge.

Question 7 might be further refined, or possibly dropped if the thesis becomes too big - question 6 covers some of this already. It also begs the '**so what**' question – why should anyone other than senior and middle managers in that institution be interested?

The issue of **truth claims** is not obviously addressed in the questions: how far are the results from this study significant or applicable to other contexts, for example? Because of question 6 the main answer to the 'so what' question appears to be a theoretical one in relation to the literature on policy implementation. That would be fine, and the candidate needs to make it clear that this is the main priority of the thesis, with other findings being significant but perhaps not central.

Often it is useful to distinguish between the locus and the focus of a doctoral dissertation – a topic of study can be merely the location through which deeper questions are explored. In this case the locus is the teaching and learning policy in one Faculty in one university, but the focus is actually achieving a better understanding of the implementation of change. Research question 6 is the key one, if this approach were to be taken in this example.

Research Questions: The seven deadly sins

1. Too descriptive – *"What are the management styles in place in Saudi Arabian universities?"* (This is OK if there are more analytical questions after it).
2. Too narrow – *"How can the use of e-portfolios at the University of Bentham be improved?"* (Who cares – apart from people at Bentham?).
3. Too ambitious – *"What teaching and learning approaches are in place in UK higher education and how can they be improved?"* (Impossible to answer).
4. Only focused on perceptions – *"In what different ways do Accountancy lecturers at the University of Bentham view the merger of their Department with the Department of Statistics there?"* (So what?).
5. Too vague – *"How does the higher education system in Chile differ from that in Argentina"?* (How long have you got?).

6. **Normative** – *"What are the benefits of linking research and teaching in universities?"* (What about the dysfunctions?).

7. Too **prescriptive** – *"Why does the modular system in UK higher education need to be changed?"* (Predicts the outcome without actually doing the research).

Note how the deadly sins are rarely found alone – problematic questions often combine two or more.

3.4 Contextualising the Study

On the face of it a chapter describing the context of the research, the institutions, national scene, professional environment or whatever, is a straightforward task, an exercise in description.

However for a doctorate and serious research in general, the task of planning the structure and content of the contextualising chapter involves thinking through the nature and significance of 'context' for the specific research project. It also means finding a balance between competing tensions, a balance that is right for the thesis.

The nature and significance of 'context'

Addressing what 'context' means for a research project requires thinking through questions of **ontology** and being explicit about the theoretical position adopted.

The ontological issue is about the nature of 'reality' and its significant aspects. For social realists like Margaret Archer (2007) the 'real world' sets limits on possibilities and shapes the situation, including on how people think about it. There is no escaping the limits imposed by resources, by power relations and by the physical environment and level of technological development, for example. However within these constraints people in groups do develop particular constellations of concerns according to Archer, and these are socially constructed, as are sets of meanings ascribed to circumstances. At another level, individuals reflexively deliberate and determine their own practical projects.

So, 'context' is a mix of pre-defined structures and enacted constructions from the social realist point of view. Other ontological positions are possible of course – for example a hard social constructionist position which holds that everything of significance is the product of meaning-making, and so accounts of context need to concentrate on that.

In short then, it is usually best to think in terms of 'contextualisation' rather than 'context', to take account of the active *creation* of context within the constraints set by structural realities. The concept of 'context' has a feel of solidity and inevitability about it, while the notion of 'contextualisation' places some emphasis on the active creation and recreation of context, as well as recognising that 'describing' a context is partly a creative process..

The Significance of Theory and Topic

Clearly both the topic and the theoretical approach adopted in addressing it will, in their different ways, impact upon how one should approach this chapter. A thesis based on a case study of a single university needs to situate that institution and give the reader a feel for it, whereas one which looks at a profession (for example academic developers) needs to adopt a different level of analysis and type of account. A thesis about environmental issues and sustainability which adopts a Marxist approach will take a perspective on 'context' which is different from one which takes a social practice approach. The level of analysis will be different, as will the focus of the account itself. Arguably a thesis which adopts an actor network theory (ANT) perspective on anything will not actually need a contextualising chapter at all because ANT is all about elaborating situations and describing links between actants, both human and non-human.

Doctoral candidates therefore need to be clear about what their use of theory is intended to do, and what its implications are for situating the context of the research. In Trowler (2012b) I discuss the different purposes of theory and show how they have very different implications, including for the understanding of the social world and how one describes it. It is really important that, once having established the theoretical approach taken and the basis upon which it is used, that this remains consistent throughout the thesis. Theoretical **incommensurability** is one of this area's seven deadly sins (see below).

Balancing tensions

The purposes of a contextualising chapter are multiple and sometimes contrasting. Issues around ethics and establishing the robustness of the study come into play too. For the doctoral candidate the task is to be explicit about how these tensions play out in their particular thesis and to find an appropriate balance between sometimes-competing requirements. The following table sums up some of these tensions.

Offering a transparent account which will enable readers to judge the robustness of the study.	V	Maintaining the anonymity of institutions and people.
Providing sufficient detail so that readers will be able to judge the extent of similarities to and differences from their own contexts, and so evaluate the salience of the findings and recommendations in their own contexts.	V	Giving a succinct account which focuses on the aspects of the context relevant to the research questions and design.
Offering a neutral, often	V	Painting a picture in interesting

quantitatively-based account, which attempts to be objective (but which may quickly date).	colours with narrative detail which could engage readers but may be difficult to substantiate.
Writing for a wide variety of readers, as if for publication, and so making few assumptions about background knowledge.	Writing with examiners in mind, and so making assumptions about reasonably extensive background knowledge.

Contextualisation: the seven deadly sins

1. Taking descriptive content from a website. (Web pages are written for different purposes and different audiences).

2. Theoretically **incommensurable** positions adopted. (Contextualising chapter takes one ontological position, the rest of the thesis takes another).

3. In insider research, statements are made about the context without substantiation. *("Well, everyone knows that's true, don't they?")*

4. Assumptions remain unchallenged. (For example, in talking about the 'higher education system', the assumption that there is such a system, in the singular, is simply accepted).

5. Contextualisation is done in such a way as to support the approach and findings of the thesis. (Only those parts are described which tend to support the argument made, other aspects are occluded).

6. Contextualisation stops too early. (For example the European context, including the Bologna process, might be relevant but is not described).

7. Contextualisation is unfocused. (There is no clear rationale for what appears in this chapter compared to the substance of the rest of the thesis, and the criteria for inclusion and exclusion from the chapter are obscure).

3.5. Structuring the Literature Review Chapter

Literature reviews are written, firstly, to scan the research that has already been done on the topic at hand. The aim of this is to find out what is already known in that field of study, what approaches have been used, where the gaps are, and how the current study will relate to what has been done already. The latter might include, for example: testing conclusions by replication of the research design; testing claims of applicability in other contexts; elaborating or critiquing theoretical positions deployed.

So, for example, in reviewing the literature on the 'teaching-research nexus' in higher education (the linkages between teaching and research) I concluded that, with only a few exceptions, the studies that had been done to date were characterised as **normative**, **foundationalist**, **empiricist** and **instrumental** (Trowler and Wareham, 2008). Thus they took a committed position on the subject, understood reality as something that could be 'captured' in a scientific way, adopted an apparently a-theoretical position and had undertaken the research in order to bring about change in a pre-determined direction (or defend the status quo) rather than being dispassionate in their approach. On the basis of this, the study I conducted took a different approach, I hoped one that had something to add to what had already been done.

One's own work should be thoroughly grounded in research that has already been done and should take account of its findings; the doctoral candidate should be a very knowledgeable specialist in the field, with a detailed grasp of related work at their fingertips.

A second purpose of the literature review chapter is to assemble the theoretical resources needed to conduct the study. So, this part of the review will explore previous elaborations of whatever theory and concepts are being used. Importantly it is also a place for the thesis author to determine his/her own definitions and accounts, conceptually and theoretically. Rather than simply recounting how other authors have understood particular concepts or employed theory, and stopping there, a brief account of that type acts as the basis for putting forward one's own position.

Literature Review: The seven deadly sins

I have elaborated on the following 'sins' in more detail than on those in other areas of the thesis because they tend to be very prevalent in candidates' writing.

1. There is there is little or no attempt to organize the literature – a 'listing' approach is taken. It is important to impose a relevant organizing schema on bodies of literature - they are usually very chaotic in their content and approaches. In order to do this a good feel for the relevant literature is necessary as it enables the categorisation of different types of work in a way which makes sense for the argument of the thesis. It is often best to start with work that itself tries to offer an overview of the literature, even with a textbook, and then work back to the specific articles and books.

2. There is little or no attempt to relate the discussion to the research questions/argument or the thesis generally. It is important to regularly show how the discussion of the literature is significant to the argument of the thesis, to tell the reader why this or that book or chapter is worth discussing, what light it sheds on the research questions being addressed by the doctoral thesis, or how it relates to them.

3. The discussion of the literature is descriptive rather than critically engaged. Make sure that the review doesn't just offer a description of the literature - this is, after all, the job of a textbook, not a postgraduate thesis. Rather it should engage in a dialogue with authors, and contrast one approach against another. The review is searching for deficiencies and strengths in the argument, areas that have not been covered, consistent bias in the approach taken as well as comparing and contrasting sets of approaches and findings. Dunleavy (2003: 30) argues that one should beware of being too critical of existing literature for fear of raising unrealistic expectations in readers' minds about one's own contribution, and particularly in the minds of the examiners. While this is a fair warning, my own experience is that doctoral candidates generally are not critical enough. Certainly one should resist the urge to make claims about going far beyond the state reached by the current literature if such claims are not realisable. A doctorate need only make small steps into previously unknown territory, not undertake an armed invasion.

4. There is too much or too little material included. It is sometimes difficult to know what to include and exclude in the literature discussed. The key thing is to make clear decisions about this, to plan the different sections of the chapter (with word limits) and to make the rationale for those decisions explicit in the thesis. The guiding principle is alignment with the argument of the thesis. There will be areas of literature that are peripheral to that argument but still significant, and so judgement is required about how much attention to give them. One way to think about this is to remember that it is acceptable not to have a literature review chapter but instead to engage in a dialogue with the literature in other chapters (usually most significantly in the data analysis chapter and subsequently). When this route is taken it is necessary to engage with different literatures in different chapters, and thinking this through can be helpful in deciding what literature to include. In practice it is usually easier to have a separate literature review chapter, even if this gives a slightly disconnected feel to the argument as a whole.

5. Literature is selected according to criteria which are too restricted or oriented in a particular direction. Unfortunately journal articles and books are not written into neat categories and where keywords are selected, this is not always done in a consistent way. Thus, for the researcher seeking to review the literature in a field it can be quite tricky ensuring that all of the relevant literature has been identified. So, for example, in a review of the literature on 'student engagement' in higher education (Trowler, V. 2010) it was necessary to limit the work discussed to that which was defined *by its authors* as concerning that topic. This was because the term 'student engagement' covers a multitude of issues and practices and not setting this criterion for inclusion would have resulted in a huge review. But because authors do not necessarily tag their piece with the 'right' terms, arguably quite a bit of relevant literature was missed. The worst form of this fifth sin is to deliberately **cherry-pick** literature which suits the argument of the thesis, ignoring more difficult areas entirely.

6. Consistently taking an overly-critical or too-forgiving approach. Finding the right balance between recognising the strengths of previous work and being critical of deficiencies is difficult. And it can be made harder when one's own position interferes, so that some authors receive more critical fire than others simply because their position is some distance from or opposed to that of the review author. One solution to this is to ask another person who knows something about the field to assess whether this sin has been committed; and of course the doctoral supervisor is a suitable person for that task.

7. There is a disconnect between the review of the theoretical resources to be deployed, as set out in this chapter, and what actually happens in the rest of thesis. Sometimes big claims are made in the literature review chapter which are not fulfilled later, either because the theoretical resource is not really applied, or is not taken as far as it could go. Another variation of this sin is to attempt to take theoretical perspectives to places they were not designed to go (for example using actor network theory in an explanatory way). Again, my article on the relationship between theory and data (Trowler, 2012a) covers this in more detail.

To conclude: a literature review should:

- Cover the main perspectives, traditions or schools in the area (and explain why some are excluded, if they are)

- Identify commonalities, differences and debates present in the literature

- Identify any gaps in the literature, including alternative perspectives or methodologies that have not been employed

- Explore any differences in methodological approaches found in the literature and their implications

- Relate the significance of the review for the topic of the thesis, and offer a position on the account of the literature, a perspective on it.

3.6. Structuring the Method/ology Chapter.

The rather awkward term method/ology is here used to refer both to data collection methods and to broader research approaches and designs based on **ontological** and **epistemological** positions. This chapter in a doctoral thesis needs to cover both areas, as methodology and methods are linked but different.

A traditional chapter on method/ology should contain the following sections:

Firstly there should be a brief overview of the research design to give the reader an **advance organizer**, even if the design has been described briefly earlier in the thesis. Secondly there should be an explanation of how this design relates to the research questions; how the two fit together.

Following that introductory section the usual approach is to follow a step-by-step walkthrough of the detail of the method/ology and related issues. A sensible order is to begin by describing the type of study it is: 'single site case study'; 'quasi-**ethnographic** study'; **'elite policy study'**; 'policy trajectory study'; **'insider research'**; 'action research', or whatever. Next comes the detailed account of the research design: the sites or samples chosen, and why. Detail here is really important, and examiners appreciate summaries in graphical or tabular form.

Then follows a description and discussion of data collection methods, including choices made, the rationale for them, and the possible disadvantages of options chosen. After that comes a description of data analysis methods, including options not chosen, again with a rationale and a realistic appraisal of the strengths and weaknesses of the path taken.

After those main sections there should be a discussion of the broader issues which are related to method/ological issues. First is the approach taken to ontological and epistemological issues and how the chosen design relates to this approach. This section should discuss the view of social reality and what is knowable about it follows from the theoretical and method/ological options that have been used. This can then lead in to a section on the approach taken to issues of 'reliability' and 'validity', and whether those terms are accepted. The point is that such concepts are founded on a particular ontological position, a **foundationalist** one, which sees the social world as unproblematically describable, with research being closer or further from the 'truth'. The literature on research is replete with alternatives to these terms, but for now it is enough to talk about the 'robustness' of the research: how well-designed it is to achieve its goals and how securely it was carried out. So this section needs to describe the measures taken to ensure robustness and to avoid dangers such as premature **conceptual closure**, **cherry-picking** of data etc. It should explain to the reader what warrants are being offered that this is a worthy enquiry.

Two further sections remain. One should deal with the ethical issues raised by the study and how they were addressed. The final section should discuss the status of the findings, given the method/ology described in earlier sections, and in particular how generalisable the findings are are to other contexts (or why this does not matter). The claims being made for the findings should be discussed in detail, and this may well relate back to the ontological and epistemological position taken.

Method/ology: The seven deadly sins

1. Adopting a research design which is not appropriate to answering the research questions.
2. Not being specific enough about the details of the sample selected for study and the rationale for that selection.
3. Taking contradictory ontological positions in different places – falling into the trap of **incommensurable** positions while discussing different aspects of methodology, method and theory.
4. Adopting a 'convenience' sampling approach without recognising and taking account of the consequences of this for the robustness of the study.
5. Not showing how the different components of the research design can be integrated during analysis – especially in a mixed-methods design.
6. Dismissing potential ethical concerns without fully addressing them.
7. Tackling the question of generalisability of findings and **truth claims** in an ill-considered way, or contradicting statements elsewhere in the thesis about this.

3.7. Writing the Data Presentation and Data Analysis Chapters

Data *presentation* is about offering the data in a relatively unmediated form. Data analysis involves a process of reducing the data down to a form which brings out key issues. Data analysis involves processing data so that it becomes *information*. Presenting the data before analysis can assist in offering further guarantees of the robustness of the research. It gives greater transparency concerning the nature of the data before analysis, though of course it is never possible to offer the data in totally unmediated form. Clearly some reduction of the data will be necessary even in presenting the data initially, it being impossible to offer raw data in a chapter of a few thousand words (as well as having potential ethical implications).

The process of data *analysis* brings out the significance of the data, rendering information more useable. Data analysis always involves the reduction of data in a way heavily mediated by the author. So, in analysing the data, reducing them and shaping them into useable form, it is necessary to be clear about criteria used in the reduction process; what is included, what excluded and how the data have been reduced.

In conducting data analysis the author is reducing the data to a form appropriate to the purposes of the thesis. These purposes are multiple and include:

- Answering the research questions

- Developing and substantiating an argument

- Offering further guarantees of robustness by searching for and addressing counter-instances which challenge the developing answers and argument.

It is important to remember that the Conclusions chapter of the thesis will offer the final summation of the argument and answers to the research questions, and so it is necessary to refrain from succinct summaries of answers and argument at this stage. The Analysis chapter is more discursive, using both evidence from the data and argument to play out possible alternative interpretations and discuss absences in the data.

The final section of the Analysis chapter should reflect on the analysis method chosen and the ways in which that might have structured the findings. Qualitative data analysis software, for example, may inadvertently lead the researcher to think in certain ways, to rule out other ways of seeing the data (see my paper on "technological somnambulism" for more on this: Trowler, 1997)

Data Chapters: The seven deadly sins

1. There is lack of transparency generally about the data collected and how it was analysed.
2. Analysis methods appear to be inadequately rigorous so that the findings are not robust.
3. Data are presented with inadequate information – for example about where in the sample they derive from.
4. Too much space is devoted to presenting data (it can sometimes be hard to edit data down because so much effort was expended in acquiring them, and to the author they appear very valuable).
5. Data are presented without adequate reference to the argument of the thesis or to the research questions, even after analysis.
6. Data are not rich enough to adequately answer research questions.
7. There is an unclear relationship between the data as presented and the outcomes of the analysis.

3.8. Structuring the Conclusions Chapter

The key purpose of the Conclusions chapter is to answer the research questions in full, based on the foregoing analysis and argument. Having done that it is extremely advisable to state very clearly what the claim is in terms of offering an original contribution to knowledge. It is also important to state what the **truth claims** are: how far and to what contexts the findings of the research can be applied elsewhere.

Usually the thesis will have uncovered the complexity of the situation being analysed and so it is appropriate to offer some final comments about how the situation and the 'problem' as originally conceived can now be better understood.

Where the research questions involve considering the implications for practice or policy, there is usually plenty to say. Such implications raise the question, again, of truth claims, and in particular the circumstances in which the findings can be appropriately applied. Rather than offering axioms for practitioners, or 'tips and tricks', a more nuanced approach is necessary, one that recognises the importance of context in conditioning what might work and what might not, what is appropriate and what is not. Elsewhere (Bamber, Trowler, Saunders and Knight, 2009; Trowler and Trowler, 2010) I have suggested the notion of 'Frameworks for Action' to help with this: conceptually and theoretically-informed guidance which highlights significant issues for readers to consider in their own situation. These frameworks will usually draw in findings from research to assist readers in making evidence-informed decisions about their own university or policy-making arena.

Often there is a section about the scope for further research: it is probably best to keep this to a minimum It emphasises what was **not** done, and so is not a good way to finish, and experienced examiners can be somewhat jaundiced about such discussions.

A Reflections Section?
Some people add a section reflecting on the research process, considering what they would have done differently, what they have learned during the process of the research and so on. While I have said that doctoral study has both a research and an educative function, generally I would not recommend this. Critical appraisal of choices made, and the rationale for them, normally belong in the relevant section of the thesis – for example strands of literature not reviewed, methods of research not adopted, research design options not taken. As to reflections on what was learned, or the personal journey of the researcher, these do not belong in a doctoral thesis in my view: it should confine itself to research. Although doing a doctorate does involve a huge amount of learning, this is not the point of the thesis – that point is to make an original, and publishable, contribution to knowledge.

Research Evidence on Conclusions Chapters
Trafford et al (2014) conducted some interesting empirical research into the contents of the concluding chapter of 100 PhD theses from four higher education institutions in three different countries (England, South Africa and Israel). These theses were mainly in the field of education, but included other disciplines too for comparative purposes. They also conducted a valuable review of the literature around the topic, which is worth reading in itself.

Perhaps the most interesting finding is that in nearly half of the cases analysed the candidates made no explicit claim for making an original contribution to knowledge, and in almost of the cases where there was such a claim the explanation was judged inadequate.

Concluding: The seven deadly sins

1. Forgetting to return to the research questions in order to answer them.

2. Continuing the discussion so that the chapter becomes a continuation of the previous ones, introducing new evidence, literature and concepts.

3. Answering the research questions in an over-mechanical, un-nuanced way (taking each one in turn and giving it a few paragraphs).

4. Repeating earlier information in a mechanical way.

5. Spending too much time on discussing the need for further research and what it might look like.

6. Omitting to press key buttons for the examiners: pointing out the significance and originality of the research (the answer to the '**so what?**' question), its key findings and its **truth claims**.

7. Being either unrealistically positive about the achievements of the research, or overly critical about its deficiencies.

3.9. Sequencing the Writing

A doctoral thesis is not usually written in linear fashion. Parts can be drafted quite early, at least in outline. These include: a few parts of the introductory chapter; the contextual chapter; the literature review chapter; parts of the method/ology chapter, especially the description of the research design, data collection and analysis methods.

It is usually helpful to have at least bare-bones drafts of these or, minimally, outlines of their structures with indications of content. This helps the author to think about how the various parts of the thesis fit together. Perhaps more importantly it acts as a good foundation for the iterative processes that almost always go on throughout the course of the research – bouncing data off research questions and perhaps amending the latter; considering whether the research design needs to be amended; amending design details in the light of ethical considerations and so on.

Usually there is an intensive writing up phase at the end of the period of registration at a university when chapters are finalised and early draft chapters are brought up to the necessary standard. This can be extremely hard work and quite stressful, so having a clear idea of the overall structure of thesis and some parts written in reasonably good draft is very helpful in both reducing workload and diminishing stress levels. A clear timetable for the writing is also helpful, with feedback from the supervisor at regular points.

3.10. Non-Conventional Thesis Structures

I stated at the beginning of the book that its structure follows a conventional doctoral thesis structure, but that sometimes a non-conventional structure is appropriate. This can take the form of a minor deviation from the usual shape, or be completely different. In the latter case, many universities have regulations in place for the submission of 'alternative format' doctorates. These are normally used in disciplinary areas such as Art and Design, Computing, Music or Performance in which the doctorate may contain some creative element.

There is no reason (regulations permitting) why a doctorate in the field of higher education should not be submitted under alternative format regulations. However this may be a high risk strategy, and in such a case special thought would need to be given to the skills and experience of the thesis examiners. So, for example, an **action research** project around the implementation of change within a university may contain media-rich forms of evidence about processes and outcomes during the course of the research. Instruments developed for such initiatives might also be included as part of the doctoral submission – while not being strictly part of the research, they may be significant as an outcome of it.

Less radically, there can be good reasons to use structures which, while based on the one this book adopts, deviate from it. I have already mentioned the probable lack of a Contextualisation chapter in a thesis which heavily deploys actor network theory (ANT), because ANT-based studies focus very strongly on situations. In a sense a very large part of such a thesis would be 'about' context.

My own PhD thesis lacked a literature review chapter for several reasons (its abstract appears in Chapter 2). A key one was that I considered it helped the flow of the argument if I addressed the relevant strand of theory at points in the argument when it became relevant, rather than in a separate chapter. So, for example, aspects of feminist theory were discussed and engaged with during the presentation of data around pastoral roles assigned to and taken by women, and the attitudes of male academics and students around this.

Different dimensions of organisational theory became salient at other points in the thesis, while 'grand theory' (in the form of Giddensian structuration theory) acted as an overlay to the argument as a whole. To discuss these different areas of theory, and others, together in one chapter would have made little sense. My choice allowed me to integrate the description and discussion of the theory with the depiction of the relevant data at appropriate parts of the thesis. I was able to deal with the non-theoretical aspects of the thesis that might normally appear in a literature review within the contextualisation chapter.

So the key point is to consider the nature of the specific research being undertaken and how it can best be written up. The structure used here is as close to a 'template' as there is in doctoral theses, but it is not fit for every type of thesis by any means. And of course it is only partly relevant for non-**empirical** doctorates, ones that are based on secondary data or are entirely theoretical in nature.

3.11. Successful Completion: Some pointers

There are many guides available for doctoral and other students about study skills, time management and so on. Unfortunately they tend not to take account of the conservative power of the habitual routines that individuals develop during their lives, nor of the power of social practices that are created and enacted in the social settings which those individuals inhabit. Good intentions often result in short-term changes, but practices have a tendency to 'snap back' to the status quo ante.

Individuals develop sets of habitual routines in their lives, both personal and professional, which they deploy to get things done. These are usually unacknowledged and can be most entrenched when they become associated with the identity of the person, when they become part of who the person sees themselves as or 'the kind of person they are'. Teachers of maths, music and art are well-used to having to confront this kind of issue; the student who says "I'm just not mathematically/musically/artistically inclined".

The problem is compounded by the fact that recurrent practices are also developed in social situations, and these become associated with sets of identities (or subjectivities), with sets of conventions and assumptions about the way to do things, and what's best. Emotional and other responses are evoked too when this happens.

In short, as individuals our capacity to radically alter the way we do things is somewhat confined. In this case the challenge is to suddenly begin devoting a large amount of time, intellectual energy and writing effort to something as complex as a doctorate, and over a very long period of time.

Changing routines, altering patterns of behaviour developed over years, and challenging self-ascribed characteristics of identity are not just a matter of reading a book on time management or study skills. That involves a gradual change over time, moving from where the individual is at the moment to gradually behaving in different ways. In this case the journey is towards becoming 'a researcher'.

This involves acquiring sets of recurrent practices (including those associated with discourse), ways of seeing, skills and sets of values and attitudes (often associated with emotions) that are particular to the researcher identity. But there is nothing unique about this as a process - analogous processes and personal change applies, say, to becoming 'a musician'. Arguably, doing a doctorate is quite different from earlier levels of education: if successful it involves quite fundamental personal change.

This journey often happens naturally, but it can be assisted by taking a number of steps involving interventions in routines that bring about step-by-step changes. The UK government in 2012 had what it called a 'Nudge Unit': the Behavioural Insights Team (Glover, 2011). Its task was to devise and implement such steps to change the population's practices in various areas, if only a little. A YouTube video demonstrates the idea:
http://www.youtube.com/watch?v=2lXh2n0aPyw&feature=player_embedded .

One important thing a new researcher can do to help this is to join or develop social groupings where recurrent practices, values, attitudes and conventions of appropriateness are such as to give assistance in completing the doctorate. For example in one university in South Africa a group of PhD students formed a support group called PaperHeaDs. They shared their writing and their problems at different stages of the research and gave each other moral as well as practical and intellectual support.

Writing groups and reading groups are helpful too, as is attending conferences and attending research seminars. Getting involved with more experienced researchers, perhaps on a funded project, is also helpful.

All of this can be done online as well as face-to-face for those candidates who are studying away from their university of registration.

Reflecting on one's own habitual routines and upon the conventions and recurrent practices in the different social situations one is part of is important too, and then making plans to change them where necessary. For example if those social situations do not value the use of an **academic register** and there are no conventions in place about the use of abstract thought, then the opportunities to practise the forms of language and thinking used in the doctorate are limited.

University departments can of course help in this by consciously working to develop an inclusive research culture in which postgraduate research students are both very involved and feel part of the research community, including those studying online. Departments can also take practical measures, such as making clear their expectations of progress at different stages of the doctorate.

The Department of Educational Research at Lancaster University offers its doctoral students a 'stages of completion' outline and evaluates them annually (more frequently in some cases) against this as well as against other criteria. For empirical projects it looks like this:

For Students in Year 1 (or Part-Time Equivalent):
- Research questions and research design finalised and agreed with supervisor.

- Good progress made with review of relevant literature.

- Scoping and pilot enquiries have validated research design in terms of potential of richness of data to answer questions.

- Key concepts and theoretical lens clear by end of year 1.

For Students in Year 2 (or Part-Time Equivalent):
- Data collection complete, or nearly so. Good progress on analysis.

- Some thesis chapters written in draft, including contextual-introductory chapters, methodology chapter, literature review.

- Good conceptualisation of probable findings and argument, including its engagement with the literature.

- Writing 'voice' for thesis now found.

For Students in Year 3 (or Part-Time Equivalent):
- Data analysis complete. Argument fully formed.

- Writing up full thesis.

- Presentations at conferences and departmental seminar to prepare for viva and improve structure of argument.

- Potential areas of discussion in viva identified and prepared for.

Social practice theory tells us that the use of tools such as this can help shape social practices in desired directions. This has certainly been the experience in the Department of Educational Research at Lancaster University with both its blended learning and residential-based doctoral programmes.

3.12. Seven Valuable Virtues for Doctoral Success

I would suggest that the following characteristics are usually present, for good reason, in successful doctoral theses:

1. Has clear sequencing of the argument, fore-grounded at the beginning and well-signposted throughout the chapters.
2. Offers clarity about the focus and limits of the research, about what it has to offer the academic community, and about what its design means it cannot offer.
3. Uses an appropriate **academic register** to manipulate authoritatively the relevant concepts and theory. The thesis avoids 'folksy' or idiomatic phrasing.
4. Demonstrates thorough knowledge of the previous literature and findings in the area.
5. Is well-balanced in presenting the relevant field, including those areas critiqued or not explored in depth.
6. Has findings which are original and valuable.
7. Displays attention to detail in presentation, with thorough final copy-editing as well as a succinct writing style.

Changes in the higher education policy environment mean that over time and in different places that there are differing emphases among these 7 virtues, and that different interpretations are placed on some of the words in them. So, for example, in the UK there is an increasing emphasis on the importance of the 'impact' of research on the wider community, the economy and culture. In developing countries there is often a stress on the significance of research for national economic and social development. In such areas, and especially for funded research, it is no longer enough for the doctorate to offer benefit to the discipline; its reach must go beyond this. So the definition of 'valuable' in the sixth virtue is becoming re-shaped to incorporate these concerns.

3.13. Useful Resources for Thesis Writing

While there are many books on research methods, on aspects of writing a PhD and on doctoral study generally there are few helpful ones on structuring the content of the thesis for success. One good example is Patrick Dunleavy's book *Authoring a PhD* (2003). Though the author does not state it to be the case, this is best used for social science theses (Dunleavy is a political scientist).

Murray's book *How to Write a Thesis* (originally published in 2002) also offers useful advice, but has a wider focus than content and structure. Its second edition in 2006 gets some poor reviews on Amazon for not itself being well structured. Murray must be doing something right though – it is now on its third edition (2011).

Generally, to get the most recent examples of helpful texts it is best to search the current catalogues of those publishers who specialise in texts for doctoral students. In the UK and USA these are: Sage; Open University Press and Routledge.

The British Education Index and EducationLine are databases for students of and researchers into education, including higher education. There are Australian and North American equivalents: the Australian Education Index and ERIC. These include articles on the experience of being a doctoral student, including in relation to writing the thesis. The Society for Research into Higher Education publishes its Research into Higher Education Abstracts through Routledge, which is also a helpful resource.

My own site offers further resources for doctoral research students: http://paul-trowler.weebly.com/

One of the best ways to get a feel for good (and bad) structures for a doctoral thesis is to look at a few examples of theses. An important website which offers access to PhD theses is the British Library's *ETHOS* service: http://ethos.bl.uk/.

It is often a good idea to publish from the research before the thesis is examined, because one of the criteria for a successful thesis is that it is publishable, at least in part. Meeting this criterion in advance of the examination can only be a good thing. The process of research will have identified the relevant journals for the topic being investigated, and these are the obvious places to submit to for publication. The convention is to only ever submit a piece of work to one journal, never a number at the same time. Of course it the article is rejected then another journal can be approached.

Nowadays, however, the maxim 'publish or perish' needs to be refined to read: 'publish articles in the right journals or perish'. Increasingly the word "right" has come to be defined in relation to the citation indeces of journals, which have taken to publicising them when the editors feel they are high enough. The freely available software *Publish or Perish* is elegantly written and offers citation indeces for journals, using Google Scholar as its search engine A more complex route, and one which is actually more limited, is to use the 5 year citation index of the *ISI Thompson Reuters* database or the Elsevier *Scopus* one. The latter two both exclude some journals and other publishing outlets, as well as requiring either institutional or personal subscription. The London School of Economics' *Maximizing the Impacts of Your Research: a handbook for social scientists* (nd, draft 3) offers a useful comparison of these three sources, coming out in favour of *Publish or Perish*.

For the doctoral student it is probable that the citation index of the journal is not of paramount importance, at least for their first article. But it is worth bearing that criterion in mind for the future. And it is important to avoid those 'journals' which have the sole purpose of making money: they often have names that are very similar to *bona fide* ones (Altbach and Rapple, 2012).

3.14. Appendix: Writing a doctoral project proposal

This section started at the end, the examination of the thesis. This appendix ends the book at the beginning: applying to study for a PhD.

Applicants for a PhD normally have to supply a project proposal as part of their application. This is one of the three ways in which universities normally make selection decisions. These are:

4. Is the applicant sufficiently qualified and capable to do a PhD (as judged by their CV and track record)?

5. Is the doctoral proposal of high enough quality, practicable and important enough to be acceptable (as judged by the written proposal and perhaps a defence of it in interview)?

6. Is there a supervisor who is able and willing to supervise the proposal?

Each university's requirements are different, but in the Department of Educational Research at Lancaster the requirement is for doctoral project proposals of up to 1,000 words to cover the following areas:

Title: A meaningful, provisional title that summarises the area of interest and planned programme of research. There should be a central problematic in the title, not simply a description of the field to be studied.

Research questions: Identification of the main research question(s) being asked. These should be succinct, researchable and significant. Bullet points are usually best.

Background: Explanation of how the questions are different from those asked by others, drawing on a brief review of the relevant research literature. This should show familiarity with the main literature in the field of interest.

Research Design & Methods: The 'who', 'what', 'where' and 'why' of the research plan. There should be an explanation of how the method(s) used will answer the research questions.

Significance of the Research: The contribution that this research will make. Identify the implications of the research for existing educational theories, policy or practice in higher education.

Timetable: A detailed timetable that shows how the research design can be managed within a three year time period (or a 5 year period for part time students).

Bibliography: The main written sources on which the research will be based.

Previous chapters of this book offer guidance to potential applicants to enable them to write a high quality project proposal which admissions tutors can assess. On writing good research questions, see Chapter 3. On the *Background* section, see Chapter 5. On *Research Design and Methods*, see Chapter 6. On the *Significance of the Research*, see Chapter 8, but also Chapter 3 on the 'so what?' question. A Gant chart is normally best for setting out the timetable, and the structure of the chapters of this book (which cover the main tasks to be done) should be helpful in constructing that, but see also Chapter 11 on the stages of completion in doing a doctorate.

Section 4: Ten Key Components of Doctoral Research: Maximizing Alignment and Significance

About this section

This section aims to help doctoral researchers ensure that both the research design and the thesis are well-structured, that they 'hang together' internally. Ten key components are identified, and common errors are highlighted in the way that the interlock. With a good understanding of how to make these components hang together, the candidate stands a good chance of writing a thesis which satisfies examiners in terms of structural issues.

4.1 Introduction

In the social sciences, at least, doctoral research design has 10 key components which work together dynamically as the research is being done to create a whole finished thesis.

The 10 *components* are:

1. The research questions addressed
2. The ontological position adopted
3. The epistemological position adopted
4. The domains of literature chosen for review
5. The context/s of study selected
6. The 'sample' selected from within the context or contexts
7. The types and extent of data 'collected' and analysed
8. The theoretical lens through which the data are viewed
9. How the outcomes of data analysis are presented
10. The conclusions drawn and claims made

These can be subdivided into 3 *categories*:

1. **Details of design:** Research questions; domains of literature, context/s of study; 'sample'; types and extent of data. (1, 4, 5, 6, 7, above).
2. **Social theory:** Ontological position; epistemological position; theoretical lens. (2, 3, 8, above).
3. **Results:** Outcomes of data analysis; conclusions. (9, 10, above).

The components and categories form part of an empirically-based thesis and are carefully scrutinized by examiners. A thesis which is non-empirical (for example is philosophical, theoretical or historical in character, using only secondary data or none) will of course be lacking those components related to primary data.

So, making your thesis "hang together" properly involves planning and implementing a research project which has internal coherence and congruence between the different components. They operate together to achieve the goal of a strong, low-risk thesis. There is a clear chain of evidence and argument which is assembled and deployed to answer the research questions, making claims which are robust and sustainable.

A design which doesn't hang together has internal disconnections; there are components which don't mesh properly. This means that conclusions and claims are shaky, the research questions are not fully or convincingly answered and that that there is a failure in the logic connecting two or more of the components.

That situation can be a disaster because when the thesis is examined and these flaws are identified there will be major changes needed to the very structure of the work: perhaps more and different data will be required; different research questions may need to be formulated and a fundamental reshaping of the claims made may be needed. There may be even worse consequences……

In writing a research proposal and in planning research design generally, many doctoral candidates zoom in too quickly on the detail. They start writing parts of the literature review, or they get tied up in details of 'sample' selection. This rush to the ground level of detail is dangerous because it can blind candidates (and their supervisors/advisors) to internal dislocations in the logic of the overall design, approach and claims.

Impediments to Good Design Alignment

Achieving design alignment across the 10 components is quite a brain-stretching exercise partly because a doctorate stretches over a number of years – though hopefully that number remains countable on the fingers of just one hand. In addition the task is made more complex because the components of a doctoral research project belong to several different orders of things. The components frame issues of salience, theoretical resources, truth claims, issues of 'sample' selection and context choices.

Practicalities such as access to research sites and the resources available can mean that the ideal design is not fully achievable. Ethical issues set limits around what can be done. The researcher's preferences, background knowledge and abilities also shape the project in particular ways which may, in some cases, be operating against a well-aligned thesis structure.

In short, the design and enactment of a doctoral research project takes place in the world as it is, not the pristine and hermitically-sealed world of the research methods textbook. Achieving 'perfect' alignment is next to impossible. It is the researcher's task instead to find as close a fit as possible between the 10 components, and to develop and be able to defend a good rationale for how they fit together. The aim is to present a bullet-proof thesis, but it is more realistic to produce one which is very low risk when it comes to its examination.

For the experienced examiner, however, the task is a simple one. He or she will read the abstract, then the introductory chapter and probably move to the last couple of chapters before s/he looks in detail at the middle chapters. The main question they ask themselves at this early stage of consideration is: "does it hang together?" - does the thing make sense as a whole or are there discontinuities in it?

What Does Misalignment Look Like?

Misalignment may be inadvertently designed into the project, or it may simply result from thinking and writing in different ways at different stages of the project – taking your eye off the original design.

An example of a misaligned design would be, for example, a project which takes an ontological position which stresses the social construction of reality in local contexts, but an epistemological position which claims it is possible to generalize from the study findings to other contexts. Another example would be a study which has research questions about academic staff attitudes to the introduction of online learning and the use of a virtual learning environment, but collects data about this only from learning technologists, not academics. A third example would be a design based on a single in-depth case of one department in a university to investigate the enhancement of learning and teaching, but makes claims about the implementation of change generally.

These are quite gross examples (though based on real ones), and relatively easy to spot, but there are more fine-grained, less visible, and more insidious ways in which research design can go awry in terms of alignment. Misalignment can creep in when writing up the study or focusing on detail and failing to see the development of a position which is incommensurable with that taken elsewhere.

Here is an edited example of potential misalignment creeping in as different parts of the thesis get written. This is a lightly fictionalised version of a real thesis. Potentially troublesome passages are in bold.

The first quote comes from chapter 1, the introduction:

> ...I did not wish to limit the data to one single case study as this would offer **a poor representation of the population**. I believed that eight departments in total would be both sufficient and adequate coverage to meet the initial research objectives. **I believed that the four case study universities, with two departments in each would enable me to make some naturalistic generalisations** about the topic under exploration.

In the methodology chapter, chapter 4, the author talks about two contrasting ontological and epistemological positions, and concludes that an interpretive, qualitative approach is appropriate for the topic of the PhD research being done:

> Philosophical assumptions are frequently overlooked in the initial research phase...I was initially naïve about how my values and experiences would shape my research philosophy. Axiological assumptions shape qualitative research and as themes emerge through inductive methods the research questions change to match them. In qualitative research, data emerges from the ground up in contrast to quantitative research where data often emerges from pre-existing theories. Merriam (2009:13) points out how '**Qualitative researchers are interested in understanding the meaning people have constructed, that is, how people make sense of their world and the experiences they have in the world.**'

...Denscombe (2010:118) points out that realists regard the social world as existing 'out there' and having properties which can be objectively measured just like in the natural world. This ontological position fits with the quantitative research paradigm where there is great emphasis on the processes of observation and measurement in the process of building knowledge. This contrasts with the ontological position of many qualitative researchers who consider the social world to be socially constructed, in part at least, and that contextual factors locally are intimately involved in this constructive process. **Knowledge about people's behaviours and understandings that is true for every context is very hard to come by, from this perspective.**

However in the concluding chapter we read, in self-criticism:

[A] limitation [of this study] is the case study approach where there **may be criticism that the four case study universities are not representative of the sector**. I have stated elsewhere in this thesis that universities will differ depending on a number of variables such as their local community, leadership as well as their financial situation. This exploration explicitly recognises that the findings and interpretations are within the four organizational contexts and I do not attempt to make claims for other organizations. However, **with this limitation in mind,** I have attempted to reference the wider literature pertaining to the HE sector to highlight either linkages or variances.

There is an issue, then, about a slightly varying ontological and epistemological position being elucidated in different places and, in the concluding chapter, a somewhat defensive posture on the issue of 'generalisation' of the findings to other sites, and lack of generalization being a 'limitation'. Stability of position and a robust statement of it are better than prevarication, cases of 'epistemological wobbles' and apologetic statements about lack of generalisability. The value of qualitative research usually lies elsewhere, and acknowledging this rather than defending qualitative research according to a positivist worldview is the best approach.

The Seven Deadly Sins of Misalignment

Unrecognised misalignment is always problematic in a thesis. But some types of misalignment are more serious than others, and can be fatal for the examination of the thesis. These are:

1. Drawing conclusions and making claims about significance which are not related to the research questions. (Components 10 and 1).
2. Selecting a context, 'sample' and type of data which are not appropriate to fully address the research questions. For example by omitting contexts, respondents or types of data which would be significant for a comprehensive response to the questions. (Components 5, 6, 7 and 1).
3. Drawing conclusions based on data which, taken together, cannot sustain them. For example making claims which have no basis in the data presented, but are, rather, based on the researcher's preconceptions or preferences. (Components 10, 7 and 8).
4. Presenting a literature review which fails to critically address the deficiencies as well as the strengths of the theoretical lens deployed, thus failing to acknowledge

those things the theory casts in shadow as well as those which it illuminates. For example by adopting a social constructionist perspective but failing to acknowledge the possible occlusion of structural conditioning factors this may entail. (Component 4 and 8, with misalignment in this example related to component 2).
5. Making claims about the nature of reality (ontological standpoint) and what can be known about it (epistemological standpoint) which are not reflected in claims about what can be known from the data. (Components 2, 3, 9 and 10).
6. Selecting contexts on samples in ways which have no clear linkage to the requirements of the research questions. (Components 5, 6 and 1).
7. Adopting a theoretical lens or lenses which do no work for the research in terms of analysis and conclusions. (Components 8, 9 and 10)

I'll go on next to give an example of a study in which alignment between the 10 components has not been achieved. After that I look at a more successful example.

4.2 Misalignment: An Example

Although not a doctoral thesis, I want to use just one article in this chapter to 'ground' the somewhat abstract comments made so far. I have chosen Tan and Prosser (2004) to do this as it offers in a single brief, accessible, article some examples of both poor and stronger component alignment.

I recommend that you download and read this article now before going any further in this book. You can download it here: http://tinyurl.com/p6rmpju.

In summary the research concerns 'grade descriptors': descriptions of the characteristics of assessed student work at different grade levels. It is a phenomenographic study, that is one which researches and describes different 'orientations' towards a particular object of research, in this case the alternative ways of understanding (orientations towards) grade descriptors found among academic staff. A policy encouraging the use of such descriptors had been introduced in the institution of higher education in which Tan and Prosser conducted the research. 7 academic staff (of the 15 identified as actually using grade descriptors) in this HEI were interviewed "in depth" and their responses analysed.

Four different orientations or conceptions of grade descriptors were identified from the data:

(1) as 'generic descriptors', ie depictions of achievement levels used as a description of standards for generic purposes.
(2) as 'grade distributors', to show the distribution of students' work amongst different levels of achievement.
(3) as 'grade indicators', ie indications for staff and students what a piece of student's work could mean in terms of specific criteria.

(4) as 'grade interpreters', ie authentic bodies of intrinsic meaning as to what actual achievement levels are.

For phenomenography, the significant outcome of research is not the description of different orientations, such as these, but the relations between them. This gives the research broader applicability and significance, according to exponents of the method.

This is just a bare-bones description: to be able to reflect properly on the sections that follow it is best to read the whole article for yourself.

The Ten Components in Tan and Prosser

Component 1: The research questions addressed

There is no explicit set of research questions as normally understood in a doctoral thesis. However there are a number of statements and questions throughout the article that describe the research objectives:

> a) [What are] the different ways academics [in a particular university] understood and practised descriptors? (p. 267 with insert from p. 268).

This is re-expressed in different ways in the paper, saying that it aims to:

> investigate and describe the variation in academics' experiences of using and understanding grade descriptors. (p.268).

> investigate…the different practices and understandings of grade descriptors. (p. 269).

> gain a sense of the variation of the ways in which grade descriptors were practised. (p. 269).

While not identical (the last is somewhat weaker than the others, for example), the different phrasing is close enough for consistency.

Component 2: The ontological position adopted

The view of reality adopted is not set out explicitly by these authors, but the phenomenographic position on this has been set out elsewhere, especially by Keith Trigwell who has collaborated extensively with one of the article's authors: Michael Prosser. For phenomenography the world has a concrete existence, but can be and is viewed in multiple ways, and these differences have 'real' implications. They are significant for meaning-making and subsequent actions and so have effects in the world. In effect then there is little point in distinguishing between 'reality' and perceptions of it. This is a so-called 'monist' (as against dualist) position:

> There is not a real world 'out there' and a subjective world 'in here'. The world [as experienced] is not constructed by the learner, nor is it imposed upon her; it is constituted as an internal relation between them. (Marton & Booth, 1997, p. 13).

> [P]henomenography takes the position that experience is relational, not purely objective, independent of people, nor purely subjective, independent of the world. Knowledge is then created from the relations between persons and in relation to the world. (Mann, 2009, p. 1).

Component 3: The epistemological position adopted

Because meaning-making is so significant from that ontological point of view, the focus of phenomenographic research is the perceptions of an aspect of reality in a specific context. The purpose of this kind of research is to explore perceptions of experience and to categorise those depictions into different orientations which together comprise an 'outcome space'. This is significant knowledge to acquire from research, and from a phenomenographic position there is no point in trying to acquire 'objective' knowledge about reality because, firstly, any significance it has stems from orientations towards it, and secondly because the researcher will him or herself approach it from a subjectivist position.

Component 4: The domains of literature chosen for review

Not being a doctorate, there is not a formal literature review in this paper. However analysis of the content reveals the following categories of literature referred to:

a) assessment in higher education
b) phenomenography as a method and perspective
c) teaching in higher education
d) student learning in higher education
e) policy implementation
f) professional development for academic teachers

Component 5: The context/s of study selected

The context is a large research-intensive metropolitan university. A policy of using grade descriptors had recently been introduced there, attempting to increase the use of standards-based assessment. The study was conducted in the first year of the policy's formal introduction. As a result the familiarity of the academic staff with the policy and with grade descriptors was limited.

Component 6: The 'sample' selected from within that context or contexts

Seven academic staff were selected for data 'collection'.

Component 7: The types and extent of data collected and analysed

In-depth interviews were conducted and the transcripts were analysed to identify distinct orientations towards grade descriptors. Though not specified in the article, phenomenographic analysis usually involves an iterative process of reading through transcripts, identifying, checking and testing the outcome space identified.

Component 8: The theoretical lens through which the data are viewed

Phenomenography is usually seen as a method. However it is also a perspective, a theoretical lens, which is part epistemological position (as outlined above) and part social theory. It holds that the world is effectively indistinguishable from the different perspectives that are held on it, and that the significant things about these perspectives is that they are relational – the 'patterns' that exist between them is their most important feature, together with the way they stand in relation to each other. The researcher is able to establish the nature of the variation in perceptions. The research participant is also able to do so if they are shown their own perception in relation to others (Pang, 2003). So the theory is a subjectivist one, close to phenomenology but not identical with it.

In addition to that account it is also possible to infer some theoretical aspects underlying this article from the stated claims about its contribution to knowledge. If a theory links concepts together to provide an explanatory framework which illuminates reality and, sometimes, helps us to shape it, then we can say the following, by looking at the claims made (component 10, below):

> a) Meaningful descriptions of standards bring about better learning and assessment.
> b) Different expectations about a phenomenon can be resolved by the individuals concerned coming to an understanding alternative orientations towards it, beyond their own.
> c) Such an understanding will change their own orientation towards the phenomenon and their associated practices

d) The nature of the different orientations towards a phenomenon such as grade descriptors can significantly affect the implementation of policy in a university.

e) But where there is a widened awareness of different orientations, implementation can go more smoothly.

These are not explicitly stated, but each is challengeable. Together they show that the authors are aligned with the case study university's approach to policy on this issue, rather than engaging with it critically. They also indicate a rational-purposive approach to policy and policy enactment – one which holds that clear, well-understood goals, good communication and a degree of mutual understanding will lead to the achievement of clear goals, carefully set.

For a doctoral thesis, the presence of such tacit theoretical propositions and assumptions is potentially dangerous: they should be made explicit and defended. The examiners may well challenge them if this does not happen.

Component 9: How the outcomes of data analysis are presented

Phenomenography focuses not on individuals but on variations of experience, on the outcome space which incorporates different orientations towards a phenomenon. Consequently the data are presented in terms of four different orientations identified by the researchers, with illustrative quotes from the respondents to exemplify and elaborate. The focus is not directly on the respondents, with their utterances analysed as a whole (as might happen in other types of research): they are not the significant unit of analysis here.

Additionally the different 'themes' which run through the four orientations are made explicit, as are (to a lesser extent) the attributed meanings of the grade descriptors – their referential aspect.

Component 10: Conclusions drawn and claims made

The conclusions are that there are four distinctly identifiable conceptions of grade descriptors which exist in an expanding hierarchy such that later ones are more complex than earlier ones, including all their elements and going beyond them. "The assumption is that the more complete the conception, the more sophisticated the understanding of the grade descriptors" (p. 271).

The claims made about (or aspirations for) the contribution of this research are described as being to:

> a) provide a basis for identifying and resolving different expectations for understanding and practising grade descriptors. (p. 267 and 280).
> b) clarify… the place of standards and criteria in assessment. (p. 267).
> c) contribute to the ongoing efforts in the university to achieve meaningful descriptions of standards that can assist students and teachers in their learning and assessment. (p. 268).
> d) identify the range of issues that the policy [on grade descriptors in the case study university] is raising. (p. 269).
> e) [be] the basis for further research and the development of the policy of grade descriptors in the [case study] university. (p. 269).

f) facilitate academic staff development. (p. 269).

g) [address] issues for...enhancing the use of grade descriptors as a form of standards-based assessment. (p. 279).

How Far Does the Tan and Prosser Study Hang Together?

Now that I have divided up the argument and evidence in Tan and Prosser's article into the 10 components you can probably write the next section, analysing its alignment, yourself. Doing that initial deconstructive work makes it much easier to see the strengths and weaknesses of an article or a doctoral thesis.

I can see five areas which would be interrogated carefully if this were a thesis coming to be examined:

1. First of all there is confusion about the scope of the research questions and conclusions/ of the study. This relates to misalignment between these components:

Research Questions – Conclusions/Claims

In one part of their paper Tan and Prosser describe the study as related only to this policy and this institution:

> The findings of this study serve to identify the range of issues that the policy [of using grade descriptors] is raising. These results are utilized as the basis for further research and development of the policy of grade descriptors **in the university**. (p 269, emphasis mine).

However elsewhere the aims are much more broadly described:

> [To] provide a basis for identifying and resolving different expectations for understanding and practising grade descriptors as well as clarifying the place of standards and criteria in assessment. [Also to] obtain a sense of the variation of the ways in which grade descriptors were practised and used in order to facilitate academic staff development. (p. 267 and 269).

> The study sought to contribute to the ongoing efforts in the university to achieve meaningful descriptions of standards that can assist students and teachers in their learning and assessment by articulating the variation in the purposes and practices of grade descriptors in the form of conceptions. (p. 268).

> By articulating the variations in the purposes and practices of grade descriptors in the form of conceptions, this study seeks to contribute to the ongoing efforts to achieve meaningful descriptions of standards that can assist students and teachers in their learning and assessment. (p. 280).

Later the authors ask:

> What can be done to enhance the use of grade descriptors as a form of standards based assessment? It is suggested that three issues must be addressed in order to achieve descriptions of requisite performance standards that are useful to both students and teachers. (p. 279).

Clearly, then, the truth claims being made are very elastic and, in some cases, stretch very far indeed. But then the research questions themselves are not well-specified, so are also inherently elastic. In a doctoral thesis this elasticity at both ends is a high risk strategy. Examiners would ask – 'What exactly are your questions, and what exactly are your answers, and claims about them?' If a viva is involved, it is not a good place to have to think on your feet about your answers to those questions.

2. Second, there is an issue about how far the research design, particularly the study context, is appropriate to answer the research questions. So here the alignment issue is between:

Research Questions – Study Context – Sample Selected - Conclusions/Claims

The study context and the sample of 7 academics are being asked to carry too much weight in terms of answering the research questions and in relation to the conclusions and claims made. The context of the study needs to be suitable for the research questions being asked, naturally. This means that any data obtained in that context must be appropriate and sufficient to answer them and that no issues are left unaddressed because the context was not sufficiently encompassing or was in some way not adequate for a full response to the questions. Moreover the claims made for the thesis must also not go beyond what can be said from the context chosen. Similarly the size and nature of the sample must be adequate to bear the weight of answering the research questions.

In the case of Tan and Prosser, while the study context is made to carry a lot of weight, it is a shifting weight because neither the research questions nor the conclusions/claims are stable.

Examining the research questions, as far as they are expressed (see above), it is unclear whether the word 'academics' in the research questions means a) all academics in every university b) academics in the case study institution or c) the 7 academics from whom data were gathered.

Similarly when examining the conclusions and claims, there are sometimes explicit statements relating claims to "the university", as in "contribute to the ongoing efforts in the university". However at other times the claims made are more generalized, as in "clarifying the place of standards and criteria in assessment".

As a result the single university as the context of the research is either being asked to bear a very considerable weight in terms of the questions asked and the conclusions drawn, at others a very much lighter load, with highly specific questions and responses relevant only to it.

The ambivalence is tempting for a doctoral student because it appears to offer one way of both having restricted and defensible truth claims (in terms of conclusions and claims to originality and significance) while at the same time appearing to have a very strong answer to the 'so what?' question: the significance of the research. However relying on ambiguity to help you to square this circle is never a good idea: the examiners will be watching for this tactic.

There is, however, a way out of this dilemma. This is to be explicit about the different categories of research questions and claims made. In the case of Tan and Prosser's study one could identify the following two broad categories:

1. Substantive questions and claims limited to the sample and to the case study institution.

2. Questions and claims of a more illuminative nature which have broader applicability.

Under the first could be included, for example:
- Detailed information about the outcome space relating to grade descriptors, including the relationship of the 4 orientations the research revealed.
- The development of the policy of grade descriptors in the case study university.
- Contribution to the efforts in the university to achieve meaningful descriptions of standards that can assist students and teachers in their learning and assessment there.

Under the second could be included, for example:
- Providing a model by which different orientations in particular locales can be identified and their significance there explored.
- Illuminating issues for the successful implementation of policy in this area in universities.
- Setting out ways in which staff development might address the nature and significance of the different orientations for the operation of teaching, learning and assessment in different locales.

This approach would require a greater degree of explicitness about the theory of change underpinning the research. I noted above that this appeared to be a species of 'rational-purposive' approach. Claims to broader significance of the type just set out would need an explicit elaboration of and defense of this theory.

3. Thirdly, the study extrapolates from *statements by respondents* about their practices to draw conclusions and make claims about practices themselves. This misalignment relates to these components:

Data – Outcomes of Data Analysis - Conclusions/Claims

This is illustrated in the following two quotes, though there are several instances in the article:

> The results of this study illustrate that academics understand **and practise** grade descriptors in markedly different ways. (p. 280, emphasis mine).

> This paper reports the results of a phenomenographic study on the different ways that academic staff in a particular university understood **and practised** grade descriptors. (p. 268, emphasis mine).

Kane et al (2002) are very critical of studies (and they discovered many examples) which interpret respondents' statements about their own practices to be the truth about those practices:

> [R]esearch that examines only what university teachers say about their practice and does not directly observe what they do is at risk of telling half the story. Our [literature] review revealed several unsupported claims about university academics' teaching practice, [and] raised concerns about data gathering and analysis methods…(Kane et al 2002, p. 177).

Tan and Prosser do not collect observation data and have no basis in this study to make statements about practices, yet they do so. They are assuming that "espoused theories" (as articulated in interviews) about grade descriptors and "theories-in-use" (as applied during episodes of professional practice) are the same. But as Kane et al and many other authors show, this assumption is usually fallacious. Attitudes and assumptions do not play out in practice in a direct way but are mediated by other factors, including those beyond the immediate control of the actor.

4. Fourthly Tan and Prosser make claims about the implications of their study that do not rest on the outcomes of the data analysis. This misalignment problem relates to these two components:

Data analysis outcomes – Conclusions/Claims

A sub-heading used in the article is *"Issues for enhancing standards-based assessment"* (p. 279). Under that some very generalised implications are drawn:

> Academics who decide to utilize grade descriptors should reflect on their underlying agendas and purposes….The question of whose purpose is ultimately being served must be addressed when using grade descriptors….Finally, it is suggested that students be involved in the formulation of grade descriptors. (p. 279).

However there isn't an adequate basis in the data and their analysis to support such propositions. They rely on a set of unexamined assumptions about the nature of change processes and the adequacy of reflection and of 'ownership' in facilitating effective change. These assumptions are neither stated nor tested in the research.

5. Fifthly Tan and Prosser's study identifies 4 orientations to grade descriptors which they treat as universal. This raises the question of how comprehensive and generalisable their findings are.

Data Presentation – Conclusions/Claims

As outlined above, Tan and Prosser identify four hierarchically-based orientations towards grade descriptors and their purposes. This comes from 7 academic staff who have recently started using them in an institution which itself has only just introduced a policy concerning their use. There is no way of knowing whether these four are comprehensive or fairly typical of other situations. They may be interesting in themselves, and perhaps illuminative and indicative of what might be found elsewhere. So might the relationship between them, which is considered very significant in phenomenography. But their status in terms of comprehensiveness and prevalence is unknown.

To be fair to phenomenographic studies, they tend to make no claim for the generalisability of sets of orientations discovered in research. Rather they stress the nature of the outcome space they inhabit, in other words the relations between the orientations. Tan and Prosser say that their four "meet the phenomenographic criteria for a well-structured outcome space" (p. 269).

Phenomenographically, the significant finding is that there are "evolving subsets [of orientations], each consuming and building on the previous conception" (p. 271). Tan and Prosser assume that the more complete the conception, the more sophisticated the understanding is. They say "conception 4 may be seen as the complete and sophisticated way of understanding grade descriptors" (p. 271). But on what basis, from this study, could we know that this is the most complete and sophisticated conception that there might be? And if one is clearly more sophisticated than the others, why do we later learn that each is appropriate for a particular purpose (p. 279)? Like the research questions and the claims, the basic argument about the significance of the data as presented shifts around.

I am not being original in pointing out the ways in which phenomenographic work can sometimes involve misaligned questions, claims and conclusions. A forensic examination by Meyer and Eley (2006) of Prosser and Trigwell's work (1999, as well as other work) is illuminative. It shows how that work was used to develop the 'Approaches to Teaching Inventory', yet was not fit for that purpose in numerous ways. While not using the 10 components framework set out here, Meyer and Eley's critique could easily be framed in its terms.

4.3 A More Successful Example

Rhonda Lobb (2015): *Organisational Citizenship Behaviour in the Further Education Sector – Deconstructing a managerialist positivist paradigm.* Lancaster University.

This PhD began with a question about when and why further education (FE) lecturers go beyond their contractual obligations, engaging in discretionary behaviour. It soon became clear that the research on discretionary behavior in organizations – the Organizational Citizenship Behaviour (OCB) literature – was largely rooted in a realist ontological position and a positivist methodological paradigm. It was almost always motivated by a search for the variables which would increase OCB in organizations, so the literature was also normatively focused.

What was needed was a study which would use a lens which focused on the significance of context, of individual meaning and of the complexities of lived realities. This would explore the nuanced motivations and drivers underpinning discretionary behaviours in the FE context, including values and attitudes, sets of meanings and emotions. This new lens would offer an important contribution to knowledge in the area and would plug what nearly every PhD candidate hopes to find: a gap in the literature.

I will analyse Lobb's thesis using the 10 key components, in the same way I did in the last chapter. However this time I will combine the description and discussion of how far the components hang together rather than having two separate sections as the last chapter did.

The Ten Components in Lobb's Doctoral Research and Thesis.

Component 1: The research questions addressed

The research questions are set out in chapter one and repeated at appropriate points in the thesis. They are consistently expressed as:

1. To what extent is the traditional conceptualisation of OCB deployed and applicable in a Further Education setting?
2. How can OCB be re-configured for a Further Educational context?
3. How does a social practice lens illuminate the working practices of lecturers in a Further Education setting?

Component 2: The ontological position adopted

Lobb is very clear that the thesis is, in part, a response to the realist, positivist ontology of the traditional OCB literature. Instead a social constructionist position is adopted which considers the construction of meaning by those who live in the world to be very significant in shaping that world. Consequently an interpretivist approach by the researcher is an appropriate one, because it is designed to access the nature and significance of meaning-construction and contest on the ground. Lobb quotes Cohen, Manion and Morrison (2000, pp. 5-7):

We can identify perspectives in social science which entail a view of human beings responding in a mechanistic or even deterministic fashion to the situations they encountered in their external world. This view tends to be one in which human beings and their experiences are regarded as products of the environment; one in which humans are conditioned by their external circumstances. This extreme perspective can be contrasted with one which attributes to human beings a much more creative role: with a perspective where 'free will' occupies the centre stage; where man [sic] is regarded as the creator of his environment, the controller as opposed the controlled, the master rather than marionette. In these two extreme views of the relationship between human beings and their environment, we are identifying a great philosophical debate between advocates of determinism on the one hand and voluntarism on the other. While there are social theories which adhere to each of these extremes, the assumptions of many social scientists are pitched somewhere in the range between.

Clearly Lobb is approaching her research from within the second camp identified in this quote, and examining the consequences of a literature so far homogenously rooted in the first. This debate permeates her responses to all three of her research questions and constitutes lens through which she interprets her data.

Component 3: The epistemological position adopted

As noted above, an interpretivist position is adopted in this thesis. The key data to be collected pertained to the perceptions of 'normal' work, to the professional role and interpretations of work which is discretionary, and how it came to be done. What it is important to know, here, is the different ways in which reality is seen and shaped by the participants in the study, and what they consider to be shaping their behaviour.

Component 4: The domains of literature chosen for review

Chapter 3 of the thesis, the literature review, covers a lot of ground. The OCB literature is set out and analysed, as is literature on leadership, member exchange theory, nomothetic approaches, the OCB literature as it is applied in the education field (a small part of the general OCB literature), social practice theory and, finally, the significance of studies set at the meso level of analysis. Because the research questions are tightly defined and the parameters of the study are clearly set out, it is very apparent what the relevant literatures are, and they are all addressed in an appropriately evaluative way.

Component 5: The context/s of study selected

Two colleges of further education were selected for research, with three work groups from each site comprising the units of analysis. The manager and 5 lecturers were interviewed in each of these workgroups. The total sample of individuals thus comprised 6 managers and 30 lecturers (this excludes a pilot study interviewing one manager and 3 lecturers). The types of departments within which these groups worked were: business, public services and ICT in one college and catering/hospitality, business and graphics in the other.

Further education was selected because it had not previously been studied in relation to OCB and because it was of direct interest to Lobb, who worked in that sector and understood it well.

Component 6: The 'sample' selected from within that context or contexts

As noted above, a total of 36 people were interviewed. The focus on the workgroup as a unit of analysis was decided because: a) the meso level of analysis was largely absent from the OCB literature to date and b) social practice theory stresses the significance of work groups (called "activity systems" and "communities of practice" in different strands of that literature) in the social construction of reality as they work together on a common project over time.

Clearly one could critique the selection made on a number of grounds. The 36 were predominantly male, and in one case the manager pre-selected the five people in his/her department for interview by Lobb. Other categories of staff (not lecturers or managers) were not studied and the types of departments from which data were collected did not cover the whole range of disciplines.

Component 7: The types and extent of data collected and analysed

Only interviews were used as a source of data. These were semi-structured in form. Because groups of 6 responded belonged to the same workgroup there was an opportunity to compare and contrast different world views, sets of meanings, assumptions and responses in the same context and with similar stimuli. This allowed a depth analysis of the nuanced nature of meaning construction and of the roots and significance of social practices as they are played out, including discretionary practices.

Component 8: The theoretical lens through which the data are viewed

As noted above, the theoretical lens was explicitly one rooted in social practice theory. This shaped the research design (the workgroup as a unit of analysis), the interview schedule and the shape of the analysis. Traces of it can found across all three research questions, but most specifically in the third.

This can be criticised on the grounds that researchers find what they are looking for, and with such a minutely-specified lens the outcomes of the research will largely be determined by these preconceptions. In this case however an explicit aim of the thesis is to re-balance the literature on OCB, offering a counter-weight to the predominantly positivist, realist and essentialist perspective found elsewhere.

Component 9: How the outcomes of data analysis are presented

The data analysis chapter is presented in terms of several themes which emerge from the data, which had been presented in the previous chapter. These themes and sub-themes are:

Disparities and Different Realities:
    Power Relations
    Ambiguity
    Underground Working Practices
    Time, Space and Discretionary Practice
Economies of Performance:
    Identity and Individualism
    Impression Management
The Role of Rhetoric in Discretionary Practice

Component 10: Conclusions drawn and claims made

The concluding chapter begins:

My principal conclusion is that the use of the OCB construct lulls the researcher into a false scientificity which unites the image that discretionary behaviour can be captured and consequently controlled. Instead, what has emerged from the social practice approach adopted for this research is a much more nuanced understanding of discretionary behaviour which neatly illustrates how the OCB construct is insufficiently fine-grained to explore such a dynamic phenomenon, especially within the complex profession of teaching. Whilst OCB researchers are often blinded by the subtleties of discretionary behaviour this approach has examined the motivations and calculations which often lie behind these elusive acts, making it stand in stark contrast to the existing nomothetic literature which is, at times, a highly incomplete account of what actors do. Admittedly, this research, like the existing OCB research relies heavily on retrospective accounts of interpreting behaviour, however, unlike the existing accounts on OCB, this study explicitly recognises the complexity that this entails. Whilst the existing body of work offers an abundance of explanatory mechanisms often focusing on socialized elements around leadership or the more calculative social exchange, this research elucidates how these explanatory mechanisms are not as significant as the literature would have us believe. The nomothetic approach not only disregards the complexity and messiness of human behaviour but also the in-between-ness of discretionary acts which consequently cannot be synthesised like a recipe. (Lobb, 2015, pp. 263).

Lobb then goes on to draw the reader's attention to the significance of the data and the argument in terms of responses to the research questions, spelling out the deficiencies of the OCB literature to date, what an improved approach might look like in a further education context and the ways in which social practice theory helps us to see the situation differently.

I said earlier that no thesis is bulletproof and no research design is perfect. That is true of Lobb's work, which has self-acknowledged deficiencies. However in achieves alignment across the 10 key components in an impressive way.

4.4 Achieving Alignment

For readers of this book the key issue is about ensuring alignment across the 10 components in *their* study or proposed study. So far the chapters have been about understanding the nature of the components and giving examples of them and their alignment and misalignment. This chapter is designed to help you apply this way of looking at doctoral research to your own work.

The chapter begins with an exercise for you, giving you practice in identifying the 10 components and evaluating their alignment. The chapter then moves on to some questions for you to reflect on about your own doctoral work. Finally I offer a narrative about the process of moving from a sketchy idea for a PhD project to a more developed scheme that hangs together reasonably well.

Deconstructing and Evaluating a PhD Abstract

First, then, I ask you to consider a doctoral thesis abstract (and some extra details about it) and to reflect on how far the study appears to be aligned (as far as you can tell only from the abstract). In effect I am asking you to do what I did to the research projects discussed in chapters 2 and 3: to deconstruct the study into its 10 components and to evaluate it in terms of their alignment.

I have chosen this abstract, which comes from Irving (2012) because it is helpfully detailed. The title of the study is: *Leadership in Higher Education: A Longitudinal Study of Local Leadership for Enhancing Learning and Teaching.*

- Of course an abstract does not really contain all the information you need to do this exercise, even this detailed one. However I want to keep this exercise down to manageable proportions for you. You can find a video of my comments on the abstract at the following web address: http://tinyurl.com/k4egkq2. You will need a DropBox account to access this and if you don't have one you can get one for free at: http://tinyurl.com/kqguhh8. There is also a transcript of the video in Appendix 1 at the end of this book. Because the thesis is embargoed I, like you, do not have any more information about the research than is available in the abstract.

> Local level leadership for the enhancement of learning and teaching in higher education is an under-researched area in the leadership literature. The growth of the 'quality agenda' in HE over the past 20 years has led to an increase in the number and range of local leadership roles. These posts, although not usually requiring the exercise of management responsibility, have the potential for considerable influence on practice in local academic communities.
>
> This study aimed to explore local leaders' experience of their role and to examine the barriers and opportunities they faced, in order to determine the optimum conditions for the conduct of this work. The study was focused on one regional HEI in NW England, CountyUni. A subset of data was obtained from another HEI, MetroUni, for comparative purposes. The research design adopted employed an interpretive, ethnographic approach, generating qualitative data from 29 interviews and three focus groups over the course of six years.

The majority of the participants were HE staff in local level leadership roles at department or faculty level. Additionally, 8 staff in managerial roles were interviewed. Data collection focused on the characteristics and practice of local level leadership in the context of learning and teaching. Purposive sampling was used to identify participants.

An iterative process was used to generate interview questions, so that significant themes could be tested for 'saturation' as the study progressed. Data was analysed thematically, based on the approaches of Grounded Theory.

A model of the features of local leadership at department level was generated from the data. The discussion of results incorporated contributions from a number of theoretical strands in social science: structuration theory; communities of practice; networks; academic culture. The nature of local level leadership was contrasted with other extant models of leadership.

The findings showed that, although leadership was demonstrated by local level leaders, there was a low level of recognition and uncertainty of the leadership aspects of these roles, with individuals often feeling that they had "responsibility without power". The importance of leadership for learning and teaching at all levels of the institution was identified as critical to the effective implementation of local enhancement activities.

It was concluded that local level leadership in this context has characteristics in common with leadership elsewhere. The absence of managerial responsibility but the presence of significant responsibility for establishing links between local academic communities and the policy development tiers of an organisation, provides particular challenges. It was shown that success was dependent upon leadership and commitment at all levels of the institution. The roles provide valuable experience for career development. Opportunities for further avenues of investigation were identified.

Once you have done the deconstruction and evaluative work, please do go the video mentioned above and compare your findings with mine (http://tinyurl.com/k4egkq2).

Questions for Reflection

In this next section I ask you to reflect on the answers to a series of questions about your proposal, research, or near-complete thesis. The questions are:

- Do my research questions and my 'sample' mesh properly?

- Are the types and extent of data 'collected' appropriate to my research questions?

- Is the 'sample' selected appropriate in relation to the overall context of the study?

- Does my literature review cover all the areas necessitated by my research questions?

- Are the methods used and the consequent extent and types of data collected adequately addressed in my literature review?

- Do the ontological position and the epistemological position hang together?

- Are my theoretical lenses and my ontological and epistemological positions well-aligned?

- Do my conclusions rest firmly on the data obtained?

- Are the ontological and epistemological positions set out in the thesis compatible with the research questions asked?

- Do the types of data, and what I want to do with them, align with the ontological and epistemological position I have adopted?

- Do my conclusions and my research questions fit? Are there questions unanswered or conclusions not asked about?

- Are my conclusions sufficiently delimited in relation to my research design?

From Sketchy Idea to Aligned Design

Finally in this chapter I want to simulate the process of developing an aligned research project by offering a narrative account of the process of moving from a general area of interest to a reasonably well-specified design. This is about a (fictional) project concerning higher education heads of department (HoDs) and the forms of knowledge they require and deploy.

> Sharon has worked in higher education for 15 years. She has also served three years as HoD in an arts faculty. She now wanted to undertake her PhD and so began thinking about a topic that would continue to interest her for around five years, as she would be doing the PhD part-time while continuing at work.
>
> She reflected on her time as HoD and on the training for that she had received. What she had found at the time was that the training really didn't cover what she needed, instead a lot of that was learned on the job, acquired by talking to others, reading and researching, and in several other ways. She also remembered how she had begun to see things differently as Head of Department than she had previously. So she reflected on the kinds of knowledge and ways of seeing that HoDs in universities need, and usually eventually acquire, and also about how those are best learned.

Next she began to read around in the areas of leadership and management knowledge and skills, management training, and generally in the area of knowledge and frames of reference. She concluded that a useful and interesting PhD study would look in detail at the daily work of university HoDs, the knowledge resources they mobilised in their work, and their own accounts of how they acquired the skills and knowledge they need, together with their reflections on how being a middle manager had changed the way they perceive professional life in higher education.

Her initial set of research questions, then, were:

1. In their daily work practices, what knowledge resources and skills are needed and used by a selection of heads of department in universities?
2. What accounts do these heads of department give of their needs in relation to knowledge and skills, and of the manner of their acquisition?
3. What is their account of changes to the ways in which they frame professional life as they became more experienced in middle management?
4. As a result of the findings, what improvements can be made in the way we conceive and interrogate knowing and seeing among middle managers?
5. How can the findings be applied to enhance middle management preparation in higher education?

These were good enough for the time being, Sharon thought, but would no doubt be refined as the research progressed. The next question concerned research design. Her thinking had led her to see that she would need to gain different types of data. There would need to be observational and other types of data about the actual work practices of middle managers, and this suggested some kind of non-participant observation, perhaps supplemented with analysis of secondary data such as meeting minutes etc. She would also need to gather accounts of HoDs' work and training and of the way they see the world. This suggested interviews as one data collection method, perhaps supplemented by a survey of larger numbers of HoDs to check that she had not missed anything.

Gathering observational data in particular raised difficult questions of access and ethics for her: would she be allowed to observe heads of department at their work, and what would possible sensitivities mean ethically? There were also questions of context and sampling: which heads of department, in which disciplines, in which types of institutions would be best? Clearly she needed rich data to come from the observational work and so the core of the study would be in-depth case study research, meaning just a small number of managers' work lives would be studied. But the interviews, being less challenging ethically and in terms of her resources, could be larger in number, supplemented by an even larger online survey.

So, a multi-method nested research design seemed the most appropriate to access both knowledge-in-action and accounts of the acquisition and deployment of knowledge and skill types. There would be three in-depth case studies of HoDs in context, up to 30 interviews with HoDs in similar areas to the case studies, and a much more open on-line survey. The findings would relate primarily to the types of departments and institutions represented in the case studies, but would be illuminating for further research in other contexts. The truth claims would therefore be limited, but the conceptualisation of the knowledge resources of HoDs and the theorisation of appropriate acquisition methods would be of real professional use in universities. The study would therefore have both academic value and considerable potential impact.

Sharon began the study influenced by her preparatory reading on knowledge, knowing and activity theory. Key influences were Blackler, Schön, Nonoka and Engestrom. She found these theoretically stimulating, and could see a common ontological and epistemological position across their work, particularly between Engestrom and Blackler. She found much of the work on management education to be practice-oriented and sparse in terms of explicit theory. This was good news for her research because she could make a real intellectual contribution to that area of the literature.

Now she felt ready to put the research proposal together, and also felt she could identify appropriate specialists to supervise her PhD: she was in a position to apply to their departments. She had each of the 10 key components in place and felt that they were appropriately aligned at this stage; the proposal really did hang together. She could now see it in concrete terms and had a really strong feel of what would happen. While the project would no doubt become re-shaped as she progressed with her reading and data collection, she felt it represented a solid foundation which could only be improved rather than fundamentally changed as she continued with the research.

4.5 Research Significance

Achieving alignment is a necessary but not sufficient condition for success. Examiners will be evaluating how ambitious and innovative candidates have been in their research questions and the extent to which they have made an **original contribution to knowledge**. Another way of putting this is, simply: 'so what?' This chapter, then, is about making sure you lift your study beyond simply alignment to significance.

So, the nature of and the links between components 1 (research questions) and 10 (conclusions and claims) are critical ones for doctoral research. Research questions must be set at the right level for achieving significance, and conclusions and claims must find the right balance between significance and defensibility.

Research questions

What does 'an original contribution to knowledge' really mean? It is rarely spelled out at all, but is usually understood to suggest that there is something new and valuable emerging from the research which will take the research in the field forward, even just a little. This advance could include:
- a contribution to theory
- new findings in a novel context about an established academic issue
- the application of a different theoretical approach than that normally taken
- findings that offer a research-based underpinning to the enhancement of professional practice
- critical deconstruction of ideas that have become taken for granted

> new and valuable ways of seeing an old problem
> a contribution to policy content or approaches to policy-making.

This list is by no means comprehensive and complete (for a journal editor's list you might want to look at Selwyn, 2014). If the candidate makes a robust argument that their work constitutes an original contribution in some way not previously thought about by the examiners, they are duty-bound to interrogate it and consider its value.

In my narrative in the last chapter about Sharon's research, you will see that as well as aiming for an aligned study she gave consideration to the answer to the 'so what?' question – the issue of why the study should be considered important. Her answer was threefold:

> An empirically-based contribution to the conceptualization of different knowledge resources required by HoDs in higher education in particular types of settings, informed by an improved understanding of perceptual change among those heads.
>
> Research-based findings on appropriate approaches to their acquisition (including for example training courses, manuals, mentoring, peer-support networks, observation).
>
> Illuminative findings for other settings.

It is therefore important that research questions perform the function of locking into the research issues that have broader significance. The research should have the potential for giving a good answer to the 'so what?' question from the outset. Trivial or context-specific questions are reassuringly easy to answer, but do not lift the research to PhD level. Generally the research questions should move from 'what' questions, that require descriptive answers to 'why' and 'how' questions that require analysis and theory. Often the final question will be about the implications of research for policy, practice, theory or some other area.

Impact

Increasingly there is a requirement to consider the potential social, cultural or economic effects of doctoral research – its "impact". The metaphor of impact is entirely inappropriate because it embodies a simplistic notion of causality, of the easily-measureable nature of effects and of the unitary nature of cause and effect. However the idea that research should have a broader relevance than only to the academic community does have some merit.

The Economic and Social Research Council (ESRC) in the UK says this:

> We do not expect you to be able to predict the impact of your research. However, by considering impact from the outset, we expect you to:
> - Explore who could potentially benefit from your work
> - Look at how you can increase the chances of potential beneficiaries benefiting from your work.

Opportunities for making an impact may arise, and should be taken, at any stage during or after the lifecourse of your research. It is important that you have in place a robust plan for maximising the likelihood of such opportunities arising and your capacity for taking advantage of these.
http://www.esrc.ac.uk/funding-and-guidance/impact-toolkit/what-how-and-why/esrc-expects.aspx

The ESRC offers an 'impact toolkit' for scholarship holders: http://www.esrc.ac.uk/funding-and-guidance/impact-toolkit/.

Component 10, the conclusions and claims you make about the outcomes of your research, is therefore becoming more significant as the requirement for broader impact becomes emphasised, not only in the UK but elsewhere.

Abstracts for Analysis

So in planning your study, and in considering alignment issues, you need simultaneously to consider your own answer to the 'so what?' question.

To help you think about what is, and isn't, a good answer to that question I will now ask you to consider some more PhD abstracts. This time, rather than thinking about the issue of component-alignment, I want you to ask yourself: "what is the claim to be making an original contribution to knowledge here, and is it a robust one?" Of course, again we are only looking at the abstract, not the whole thesis, but a good abstract should make the answer to the 'so what?' question very clear.

There are 8 abstracts presented, and of course you shouldn't do this exercise for all of them. Instead choose perhaps 3 that are of particular interest to you. I have selected the abstracts to get a variety of topics and varying degrees of 'risk' in terms of the apparent answer to the 'so what?' question. To me, some appear to have an obvious response to that question while others are not so clearly making a contribution of broader value. Two of the abstracts are on the same topic; internationalisation. An interesting additional exercise is to compare and evaluate the different approaches the researchers took, and to consider which appears to offer the stronger contribution to knowledge, policy or practice. Again, there is no judgement about the research itself, only about the information in the abstract. (Please note: I have not referenced the citations in the abstracts: normally citations should not contain citations).

I have placed a short video of my comments on two of the abstracts at this address: http://tinyurl.com/m7h8lrx. Those are the abstracts by Sabri and Thurab-Nkhosi. There is also a transcript of the video in Appendix 1 at the end of this book. More abstracts can be found at the British Library's Ethos site: http://ethos.bl.uk/

The assumptive worlds of academics and policy-makers in relation to teaching in a higher education humanities context.
Sabri, D. Oxford D.Phil. 2007.
This thesis seeks to make sense of how academics and policy-makers think and act in relation to teaching in higher education. It pursues this inquiry using the concept of assumptive worlds in three contexts – the University of Oxford's History Faculty, the University of Oxford, and the national policy environment – and explores the relationship between them.

The concept of assumptive worlds (Young, 1979) is situated within a new theoretical framework predicated on Giddens' structuration theory. This framework is utilised to analyse assumptive worlds in terms of individuals' knowledgeability which is expressed in discursive and other kinds of social practice. An ethnographically-informed case study was conducted over two years in the History Faculty. Its selection is based upon its uniqueness and its potential for illuminating our understanding of the relationship between higher education policy and an extreme end of the spectrum of higher education institutions in England.

The University of Oxford and the national higher education policy environment are investigated as contexts within which the Faculty operates. Interviews with university officers and policy-makers in a range of national agencies, and documentary evidence provide the data for this investigation. The thesis argues that an analysis of the characteristics and formation of assumptive worlds in academia and policy-making throws new light on taken-for-granted practices in teaching and policy related to teaching in HE.

The concept extends our understanding of each arena within its own terms, and when each is viewed in relation to the others. Engagement, in relation to teaching in higher education, between policymakers, and university officers and academics is rare. An understanding of the assumptive worlds within the three contexts helps to explain why this lack of engagement is recursively produced.

Towards the development of a quality assurance framework for the UWI Open Campus
Thurab-Nkhosi, D. Sheffield Ed.D. 2010

The focus of this dissertation is quality assurance (QA) processes and procedures for open and distance learning. Specifically, I conducted a case study of the QA processes and procedures of the University of the West Indies Open Campus (UWIOC), which is a newly created virtual campus, forming the fourth campus of the University of the West Indies (UWI). The case study reviewed perceptions of QA among stakeholders in the institution, explored existing processes and procedures, theories on QA, gaps in quality, the impact of these gaps on students and suggestions for QA processes and procedures. Based on the review of existing processes and procedures, a suitable framework for the new institution was recommended. To provide a framework for analysis, this study focused on three strands of thought on QA, namely total Quality Management (TQM), 'McDonaldisation' theory and the theory of transformative learning, and existing frameworks for QA such as the Institute for Higher Education Policy's framework [and other work]. The research reported here is insider, action research, which involves an ethnographic approach. Findings demonstrate that while stakeholders are aware of the common mission of the UWI, there is no consensus on the goals or vision for the UWIOC. The data suggested that there have been efforts to implement QA processes. These efforts seem, however, to be inadequate, resulting in gaps in the system with regard to human resource policies and actions; and effective communication with and among departments and between management of the institution, staff, and ultimately, students. It is recommended that the institution should review and articulate UWIOC's vision and philosophy, and understanding of a culture of quality.

A case study of the institution-wide implementation of a managed learning environment
Alltree, J. R. Sheffield Ed.D. 2008

Recent years have seen a marked increase in the use of Virtual Learning Environments and Managed Learning Environments (MLEs) across the UK Higher Education sector. The university at the centre of this research took an institutional approach to implementation of its MLE. This case study examines that implementation against the backdrop of the increasing use of technology to support learning, the impact of technology upon pedagogy in a range of academic disciplines and the strategic approach to managing change. The case study draws upon semi-structured interviews with 23 teachers from the university's six academic faculties.

The framework for analysis was an adaptation of Bronfenbrenner's ecological model...in which the implementation was examined in different, interconnected settings – the microsetting (the individual teacher's practice), the mesosetting (the institution) and the macrosetting (the sector). At the level of the individual participant, the majority were enhancing the student learning experience by using the MLE to 'extend the classroom'. This did not, however, involve a substantive change to the underlying pedagogical approach. A small minority were, however, using the technology specifically to enhance the face-to-face learning experience of their students – either by 'doing things differently' or 'doing different things'.

At the institutional level, there has been a transformative, second order change in the use of technology by staff and students. This had been achieved through a multifaceted approach to change involving institutionally steered but locally set usage targets, local champions, staff development and an MLE that has been developed with ease-of-use as a high priority. Use of the MLE was more concerned with enhancement of the student learning experience than increasing flexibility in when and where students learn. At sector level, implementation was judged against five of the measures of success outlined in HEFCE's e-learning strategy. In general, it was argued that the institution had performed well in relation to these measures, although reuse of resources remains a challenge.

The third mission: academic and institutional management perspectives and the implications for academic work and organisational practice.
Trimble, R. Lancaster Ph.D. 2003

The requirement that HEIs engage with the business and industry sector for the purpose of knowledge transfer has become a key objective embedded within recent UK higher education policy. These activities have been encapsulated within what has become known as a 'third mission' for the university sector.

This research which is situated within two post-92 institutions has captured that attitudes and perceptions of both academics and institutional management to knowledge transfer activities with business and industry. It shows that a range of academic attitudes exist, which are largely attributable to the nature of discipline work and its perceived relevance to the business sector. In particular, academics from the non-vocational disciplines would appear to be challenged by this mission and expressed a range of fundamental reservations, which potentially limits their involvement.

Aspects of discord between the operational requirements of transferring knowledge to the business/industry sector and the areas of academic work and organisational practice were identified and presented within a 'dissonance' typology. These areas of dissonance are considered as possessing dual implications, (1) as they ultimately present significant challenges to the nature of academic work and organisational practice and (2) as they also act as a constraint upon the successful embedding of the policy within the sector.

The UK Government's policy was reviewed and was considered to not adequately recognise these areas of dissonance, in particular those related to the discipline influence or the funding and resourcing of the mission. Finally, a way forward is suggested, which has the potential to resolve the areas of dissonance relating to time and individual attitudes and which requires that the division of labour model is formally utilised as a means of managing the academic resource.

The impeders of strategy implementation within a higher education context in Iran
Rahimnia Alashloo, F. Salford Ph.D. 2006

The aim of this research is to investigate the impeders and difficulties affecting strategy implementation within a HE complex, and specifically the public sector HE provision in Iran, in order to achieve an in-depth understanding of the nature of and reasons for the problems observed in the implementation process. Based on a comprehensive review of literature, the impeders of strategy implementation in organisations, within different sectors, were identified to gain an overview of the various problems encountered in the implementation stage. From the literature survey, a conceptual framework categorising all the impeders, was developed in order to simplify and visually present them. The impeders were divided into five main areas comprising of the planning consequences, organisational, managerial, individual, and environmental impeders. Moreover, the framework was intended to serve as a basis for the development of data collection, data analysis and discussion of findings. In order to achieve the aim and objectives of this research, a case study university was selected as a research site in which to discover the significant impeders to the strategy implementation. The research findings provided a comprehensive appreciation and in depth understanding of the issues faced in implementation and the barriers to it. Some impeders that were identified in the literature were confirmed, but the study also revealed a number of new issues that were considered as unique impeders encountered within the HE of Iran in the public sector, and which have not been reported in the reviewed literature. The main contribution is a developed framework of the categorised impeders to strategy implementation in the HE context based on the five main areas.

The internationalisation of higher education institutions: a case study of a British university
Al-Youssef, J. Bath Ed.D. 2009

This thesis presents a case study of the understandings of internationalisation of higher education at a UK university. The study elicited views from individuals in diverse management positions at the university, particularly in relation to the university's internationalisation strategy document. Prior research in the field of internationalisation of higher education has largely focused on international students' experiences or patterns of their mobility. As far as policy is concerned, there has been an emphasis on the commercial and diplomatic values of the 'education export industry'. Internationalisation has also been seen in terms of 'international activities', the 'international market' and the expanding mass access to higher education. The research reported herein is particularly important in the sense that it provides insight into how the term internationalisation is understood from diverse positions within the university management and how these interpretations influence approaches to the implementation of the university's internationalisation strategy. As a qualitative study, using in-depth interviews as the key data collection approach, the research is unusual in its challenging of interpretations of internationalisation that have previously been largely researched through surveys and questionnaires. The research and its findings take the concept of internationalisation away from the practices of the institution and into the accounts of the individuals who manage it. Findings include the existence of clear differences in views about the meaning and means of implementation of internationalisation, which is widely seen as a goal or end-state rather than as a process. This poses a challenge for the implementation of the centrally-promoted international strategy in the institution concerned.

Implementing internationalisation –factors and issues: the case of Sweden
Sullivan, K.P.H. Bristol Ed.D. 2010

In 2007 changes in the Swedish Higher Education Act and Ordinance came into force that aligned Swedish higher education with the aims of the Bologna Process. This dissertation examines factors and issues surrounding the internationalisation of higher education in Sweden in general and to the Bologna Process in particular. The dissertation is thematically arranged around a set of studies focused on different dimensions of internationalisation: the lecturer and teaching; language and the academy; the student and assessment; and the Bologna Process and the Swedish academy. A mixture of participant observation, interviews, documents, and a questionnaire were used to examine teaching and assessment in a foreign language, ECTS validity in cultural difference contexts, language competence, and knowledge of and attitudes towards the Bologna Process and its implementation in Sweden. The findings point to a range of issues that could undermine internationalism and the Bologna Process, yet that Swedish academics are positive towards the goals of the Bologna Process. To realise internationalisation via the Bologna Process, the universities would need to (i) inform staff about the implementation and the changes that are entailed so that an understanding of the changes needed can be achieved, (2) to educate their staff so that common understandings and applications of learning outcomes and (ECTS) grading can be achieved, (3) support their staff in terms of time, workshops, information networks and help lines, and (4) train their staff to achieve appropriate competence levels in English to be able to achieve classroom competence in the techniques of teaching in a foreign language to non-native speakers.

The impact of marketisation on the professional lives and identities of black practitioners in UK further education
Sargeant, R. A. Sheffield Ed.D. 2007

The extent to which marketisation has impacted on the professional lives and career development of black practitioners within UK further education has been largely overlooked. Most studies have assumed homogeneity of experience of the managerialism which resulted from the enactment of the Further and Higher Education Act 1992. Using a phenomenological approach, this study explores the experiences of ten black educators within further education, interpreted from their narrated professional life stories. The respondents revealed the clash between race and markets and the impact which this had both on their own careers, and on the opportunities offered to black students within further education. The research reveals the professional identities taken up by the ten respondents in response to marketisation, and develops a new typology of black professional identity which demonstrates the plurality of responses amongst black educators, and the consequences of taking up particular identities on career development. This study also reveals that, despite national initiatives which claim to be designed to increase the diversity of the further education workforce, most respondents were either leaving, or were seeking to leave, the further education sector. This study gives voice to the changes to policy and practice which respondents considered essential if race equality is to be delivered within further education, and seeks to render visible the experiences and concerns of a largely overlooked cohort within the further education workforce.

As noted above, I comment on two of these abstracts in the short video at http://tinyurl.com/m7h8lrx. You may want to compare your responses to mine by going there. There is also a transcript of the video in Appendix 1 at the end of this Section.

4.6 Hybridity, Borderlands and Originality: Being Creative

Creative, complex and artistic endeavours will always have rules and constraints, but in the hands of the skilled these are frequently broken, or at least limits are pushed. As the word suggests, guidelines exist to guide and support the novice, not to limit possibilities and potential arbitrarily. In the strongest hands, they are broken to good effect, as is seen in music, literature and fine art.

There is an argument that in some cases misalignment can do powerful work. For example in two articles (2009 and 2012) Abes suggests that:

> [T]he researcher should consider experimenting with the choice and application of theoretical perspectives, bringing together multiple and even seemingly conflicting theoretical perspectives to uncover new ways of understanding the data. Rather than being paralyzed by theoretical limitations or confined by rigid ideological allegiances, interdisciplinary experimentation of this nature can lead to rich new research results and possibilities. (Abes, 2009, p. 141)

She talks about her bringing together of queer theory and constructivism to better expose power structures which were not apparent to respondents. For Abes, bringing together possibly contradictory theoretical perspectives can shed a stronger and wider theoretical light on the subjects of her study: lesbian college students' perceptions of the relationships among their multiple social identities. Her work, she says, operates in the borderlands between two or more theoretical approaches.

There is certainly merit in this argument. But in practice Abes' work is successful because, despite her statements about conflicting theoretical perspectives, the ones chosen are entirely compatible with each other. Queer theory and constructivism are far from incommensurable, and do indeed strengthen the research perspective when used in combination. The same would be true of other compatible perspectives.

Tierney and Rhoades (1993) and Tierney (1994) combine postmodernism and critical theory, which might be thought to be incommensurable. However they rework both to some extent, and meld them into "critical postmodernism". Tierney writes:

> I use critical theory not in opposition to postmodernism but as a way to give political purpose to the postmodern project. Critical theorists work from the assumption that oppressive relations must be transformed and that these relations are in some way connected to structural and material constructions. I am advertising a method, then, that combines the essential elements of critical theory (i.e., praxis) and of postmodernism (i.e., intersubjectivity) in order to develop the concepts of difference and hope. (Tierney, 1994. p. 100)

So Tierney is not just taking theory, but making theory: he is developing a new position by hybridizing two already-existing ones. This is being creative and original while not stepping into the really dangerous territory of internal contractions.

Similarly mixed methods of data collection can involve the danger of approaching research from two different ontological positions. One can see quantitative data as necessary for establishing correlations as a precursor to identifying causality, the other seeing that as inherently flawed because things are never 'the same' in different contexts. One can see a qualitative approach as accessing only 'soft' data, the other might consider qualitative data to be essential in uncovering meaning and the roots of the social construction of reality.

However these are two highly stereotyped positions, and the careful use of mixed methods can yield valuable insights. Carey's doctoral thesis on student engagement in higher education (2013) deploys mixed methods in his doctoral research and offers a well-argued justification for his approach (pp. 60-67). Carey suggests that a mixed methods paradigm can be adopted to transcend sterile debates about the conflict between quantitative and qualitative approaches, debates founded on a flawed, polarized, view of them. As Greene says:

> [A] mixed methods approach to social inquiry distinctively offers deep and potentially inspirational and catalytic opportunities to meaningfully engage with the differences that matter in today's troubled world, seeking not so much convergence and consensus as opportunities for respectful listening and understanding. (Greene, 2008, p. 20)

The original grounded theory approach of Glaser and Strauss (1967) also deploys mixed methods, often both quantitative and qualitative. It differs from the approach to alignment set out here in that there are no research questions at the beginning of the research (though there is a question, of sorts), and no formally adopted theoretical approach. Both the questions and the theory emerge from the data as it is 'collected', and the researcher's role is quite passive in this: the theory and questions emerge from what already exists in the data, the theory goes.

Following a split between Glaser and Strauss a second approach emerged (Strauss and Corbin, 1990), emphasising qualitative over quantitative data and using a well-defined set of coding categories. This brought grounded theory closer to traditional approaches to qualitative research, though still emphasising the inductive generation of theory. A third approach, associated with Charmaz (2000) moved away from the idea of the 'discovery' of theory in the data, acknowledging that in fact theory was constructed in a creative way by the researcher. Again, in some eyes this was a move away from 'pure' grounded theory in the direction of interpretivist social science as normally understood.

In my view, grounded theory of whatever flavour can be dangerous in a doctoral thesis, as it is frequently mis-handled and is itself subject to some powerful criticisms (see for example Thomas and James, 2006). Each flavour has its own alignment rules, and doctoral candidates can easily slip up with them, inappropriately mixing an explicitly grounded theory approach with others. However, in skilled hands it can itself be a valuable approach with gives room to the data to speak for themselves and (at least in Charmaz's 'constructivist' approach) the scope for creativity for the researcher.

The point of this chapter, then, is to drive home the point that the search for alignment in your doctoral thesis should not result in originality, creativity and inspiration being ushered out of the door. Rather, a considered understanding of the nature of alignment and the reasons for it creates a framework in which originality can be achieved in a low-risk way. Examiners will know that you don't believe that 'anything goes' but that you are instead pushing boundaries in the full knowledge that they are there.

Appendix 1: Transcripts of Videos

First I'll have a look at the Sabri abstract. The first thing is there are a couple of technical issues here. One is the question of why we get the reference to Young, 1979, but not the date of Giddens - and they are close to each other so that question arises. Secondly we are not really given any understanding of what is really meant by 'assumptive worlds' although it is in the title and it's very clear that it is highly significant for this thesis. Having said that, the answer to the "so what?" question is really clear here, and despite the fact that it's a history faculty in one institution in a very particular part of the higher education system in England at the extreme end of the spectrum, as she says - Oxford University - it does have - or at least claims to have - some general significance. So, as it says here, "it throws new light on taken-for-granted practices in teaching and policy related to teaching in higher education". And she is very clear that she is looking not just at the history faculty but the University context that it's in, and at national higher education policy environment. So it's clear what she's trying to do here. She has stated it in this section and right at the end "helps to explain why this lack of engagement is recursively produced". So it's not just about that faculty or even that University.

Now there are some similarities with the abstract from Thurab-Nkhosi. But what we don't have here is the more general answer to the "so what?" question. This is an interesting thesis apparently, at least as far as we can tell from the abstract. It's looking at a virtual campus that has been newly set up, it's looking at the quality assurance systems there, it is getting perceptions from stakeholders and so on. And it's got some findings that are relevant to that institution.

So while stakeholders are aware of the common mission of the institution, there is no consensus on goals or vision. There are some other relevant findings here for the institution. And then finally it says that the institution should articulate its vision and philosophy and understanding of a culture of quality. So the findings here, the conclusions and the answer to the "so what?" question are all to do with the institution.

Now, this is an EdD and the Sabri abstract was a DPhil, so this raises questions of the different criteria, or whether there are different criteria for an EdD compared to the DPhil or a Ph.D. or whatever. If I was examining this the first thing I would do is look at the regulations for the Sheffield EdD and see exactly what it says about the original contribution to knowledge. It may be that this kind of contribution in the Thurab-Nkhosi abstract is adequate, but I would say for a Ph.D. it probably isn't. There needs to be something broader, of significance to a wider audience than simply the management and staff of this particular institution. And you can see how Sabri is doing that and is moving away from the history faculty and even the University of Oxford, but in this abstract at least it's not clear that Thurab-Nkhosi is. So it immediately raises questions in the examiner's mind about what the thesis is doing and about what the answer to the significance issue, and also what the regulations are for this particular EdD.

I am just going to comment on Kate Irving's abstract of her Ph.D. from Liverpool University. We have to infer quite a lot about the study of course from this abstract, but that is one of the reasons I chose it, so that neither you nor I have the opportunity to read the whole thesis. So we're just looking at the 10 components through the abstract itself, and as I say I think this is an admirably detailed one where we have got a fairly good description, a fairly full description, of all but really one of the components.

So let's have a look at the first comment, then, where we see component 1 - the research questions - set out, not in research question form - it's only an abstract - but we can see that there are three things going on in terms of the research questions. First of all Kate is going to explore experiences through the data. She is going to have a look at barriers and opportunities faced by these leaders in their attempt to enhance learning and teaching in institutions. And then finally to look at the optimum conditions for the conduct of the work on enhancement of learning and teaching. So three fairly clear and I think quite appropriate questions their leading from descriptions of experience through to more analytical questions.

Then comment 2 which is actually component 5 she moves onto next, the context. So she has taken two universities, of course we don't know much about them from just the abstract, but it sounds like they are different types of university just from the names, County Uni and Metro Uni, so presumably they are somewhat different and so the comparative purposes she talks about could be quite interesting potentially. The next comment, 3, I am inferring the epistemological position she is adopting from the fact that he says that she says that it is an interpretive approach that she is taking. So we can assume that she's placing great significance on the meanings, sets of meanings held by her respondents, by the views of the world in terms so the way they construct the world and the significance that has for what they do.

Comment 4 is related to that and again we are having to infer because it's only an abstract, but we can understand that the ontological position she is adopting is similarly foregrounding meaning, foregrounding the construction of reality - the social construction of reality - because she is adopting an ethnographic approach which draws cultures.

So she is obviously interested in cultures, sets of meanings, sets of practices and so on as they develop in local contexts. We are also helped a bit because lower down, just here, she sets out her theoretical influences and structuration theory, Giddens' structuration theory tells us that - and also communities of practice theory - that one needs to take into account both agency and structure. Both the social construction of the world and the structural conditions which delimit how far one can actually "create the world". So the ontological position can be reasonably inferred from that.

The next comment refers to my component 6, the "sample", and again we've got quite a good bit of detail here about the number of interviews, 3 focus groups and in addition some 8 staff in managerial roles. So quite a good description of the "sample" there. And also we are told that the data collection took place over six years, which is an impressively long time for this kind of study. It's quite unusual partly because of resources these days to get an ethnographic style study over such a long period of time. So I would look forward to reading this thesis, it could be very interesting, although I can understand why it's been embargoed.

So the next comment is comment 6 and that relates to components 7, the types of data. So the data were focusing on the characteristics on the characteristics and practices of local leadership as that relates to learning and teaching, and we are told that the interview schedule was iteratively constructed over time, so clearly there was a process of thinking about the quality of the data, the types of issues that were coming up and so on. So that develops and presumably became more refined and more focused as time went on.

Then comment 7, we are talking about here my component eight - the theoretical lenses. And there are four theoretical lenses identified: structuration theory; communities of practice; networks; and academic cultures. So again, quite specifically set out. And then there is a long section at the end of the abstract which is my comment 8, and that refers to components 9 and 10: the outcomes of the data analysis and then the conclusions and claims made by the research. And again we have got a good feel of the sorts of findings that Kate arrived at.

So the only component that is missing here is the literature review component, 4, but we can infer I think the kinds of literature that would have been looked at in the literature review chapter if there is one, if there is a separate one. So that would be literature on the four main theoretical strands identified, literature on leadership, leadership theory, models of leadership and so on I imagine, and probably the literature on enhancement of learning and teaching in higher education.

So there we go, we can deconstruct this abstract well because it is so detailed in terms of the 10 components, the 10 key components of a PhD. or an EdD thesis in the area of higher education research. Is it well aligned as far as we can tell from this? Yes I think so, it looks quite impressively aligned. There are a couple of areas that spring to my mind that if I were an examiner of this thesis I would want to explore, and again I haven't seen the thesis itself so it is difficult to know. But those two areas: the first one concerns the relationship or the alignment between component 10, the conclusions and claims, on the one hand. component 1, the research questions, and component 5, the contexts chosen.

So we are told that 6 years, that this is a 6 year longitudinal study, and therefore the contexts are changing over time: the people; the structural context; the kind of organisational components and so on no doubt changed in one or both institutions over that time. So the specifics are changing and I'm wondering how far those sorts of changes over time were analysed, discussed and how far one would need to think about the conclusions and claims made as a result of changes over time. In other words, actually we have not only got 2 contexts here, we've got 2 changing contexts and that longitudinal component I think could be quite important and could be used really well or not used much at all. We don't see much of it in the abstract - it's only an abstract-so that would be one area I would be looking at in terms of how stable the conclusions and claims are over time, and how far they can be sustained through the data that were collected over that time period.

The second area of alignment that I would look at if I were examining this and ask Kate about concerns component 5, the context5, and component 10, the conclusions and claims made. So we've got 2 contexts, of course we don't know much about them from the abstract, but some rather broad claims towards the end of the abstract in terms of both component 9 and component 10. So I would be interrogating those contexts that were studied, interrogating the types of data that came from them, and interrogating also the sample I guess, and asking questions about thinking about other kinds of contexts and how far those claims and conclusions stand up. So: an impressive piece of research, as far as one can tell, but some issues about alignment raised. I would say not significant ones, I wouldn't be - if I was externally examining this - I wouldn't be really concerned, I would just be interested to see whether the quality of data, the quality of conclusions had been abstracted from the research.

Section 5: Doing Insider Research in Universities

About this section

This section is designed to be as helpful as possible for anyone who wants to research the higher education institution (HEI*) in which they are employed or enrolled. It offers guidance on the issues which are *specific* to insider research in universities as particular types of organizations. The section also points the reader to key issues they need to consider and to the best literature resources to explore these further, where they need to. It covers areas such as: good research design; avoiding potential problems; taking best advantage of insider research designs; guaranteeing robustness and value; and dealing with especially problematic issues in insider research, such as ethical and political ones. There is a chapter based on the author's own research work which suggests fruitful theoretical approaches and related insider research agendas. The final chapter suggests further resources for insider research.

5.1 Insider research: a brief overview

What is 'insider' research?

Doing research within the university where one is employed or studying is usually described as 'insider' research. However, 'insiderness' is not a fixed value: the researcher may be investigating aspects of the institution previously unknown to them, collecting data from strangers. What counts as 'inside' also depends on one's own identity positioning; how one sees oneself in relation to the university.

Because of this many commentators suggest that it is best to conceptualise a continuum between insider and outsider research rather than viewing them as binary opposites (for example Carter, 2004; Labree, 2002). Some writers prefer the term 'endogenous research' for similar reasons (Maruyama, 1981). However this is simply another way of saying 'inside'. So, I will largely stay with the term *insider*, but ask the reader to keep in mind these health warnings about the concept.

Challenges and opportunities of insider research

Merton (1972) suggests that the 'Insider Doctrine' (that only insiders can do 'proper' research because of the depth of their understanding) and the 'Outsider Doctrine' (that only outsiders have the necessary detachment for robust research) are both fallacies precisely because we rarely are ever completely an insider or an outsider. What Reason and Rowan (1991) call 'new paradigm' research can, they argue, happily combine more objective research approaches, 'naive enquiry', with those suffused with cultural awareness.

Conversely Titchen and Hobson (2011) believe that researchers need to choose between insiderness and outsiderness in their research design on explicit grounds: for them the two approaches are incommensurable. Whichever position is adopted in this debate, it is always important to be explicit as a researcher about exactly where and how the endogenous character of one's research potentially illuminates the issues of interest, and where it could obscure them or give rise to concerns about the robustness of the findings.

Clearly, insider research carries benefits: there is usually better access both to naturalistic data and to respondents; insiders and their respondents have mutual knowledge (Smith, 1982). As a result there is greater access to the **second record** (Hull, 1985) and **hidden transcripts** (Scott, 1992) and so greater access to actors' implicit meanings; the researcher is better able to produce **'emic'** accounts (ones meaningful to actors), especially using an **ethnographic** approach; the insider researcher is empowered to deploy **naturalistic data, critical discourse analysis** and **phenomenography,** being culturally literate; one can deploy different types of data, which are relatively easily available, in interrogating an argument. Insider research can be more practical: cheaper and easier.

In short the researcher is empowered to offer a thick description (Geertz, 1973) of lived realities, of the **hermeneutics** of everyday life. There may be a better chance of having a beneficial impact on university practices too, especially if the research project involves action research or when research questions address the implications for policy and practice of the project's findings (LSE Public Policy Group, 2011).

In addition, specific groups, previously under-represented or disempowered may benefit. For example Harding (1987) suggests that the specific experiences of women can be obscured in organizational life, and women's knowledge marginalized and occluded. Insider research is one way of addressing this issue by shining a light on experiences and ways of knowing of women and other groups.

More negatively, one's involvement as a participant in the site of research may mean loss of the ability to produce good, culturally neutral, **'etic'** accounts because it can become difficult to 'see' some dimensions of social life; they easily become normalised for the participant (the literature talks about the difficulty for insiders of "rendering the normal strange": Delamont, 2002).

Moreover there may be conflict between the role as a researcher and one's professional or student role in the university. There may be issues of power differentials between the researcher and researched, in either direction, which can be very problematic both ethically and methodologically (see Ryan et al, 2011, for a discussion around this, and see chapter 5 of this book). Finally, respondents who know the researcher personally or by reputation may have pre-formed expectations of their alignments and preferences in ways which change their responses to questions (a form of the effect called 'interview bias').

One proposed resolution of these dilemmas around the pros and cons of insider research is to conduct research with 'polyocularity', involving research teams from several 'inside' and/or 'outside' cultures (Maruyama, 1981), a version of Reason and Rowan's new paradigm research. However this is obviously very resource-intensive and is impossible for the lone researcher doing a PhD, for example. However, a research project with a clear-eyed understanding of the costs and benefits of the approach taken, combined with sensible and practical measures to ensure robustness in the approach and findings, will protect its author from criticism.

The key point though is that an insider approach to researching one's university must be appropriate for and congruent with the research questions and with the truth claims being made about the contribution of the research to knowledge generally. Doing insider research for its own sake, or simply because that is the preferred option, is not the way to go.

5.2 Researching universities

Universities as organizations

An important lacuna in much insider research in higher education is that it rarely reflects on the nature of universities as organizations. This is important because aspects of the research may be planned and implemented on erroneous implicit assumptions about 'what universities are like'. Trowler (2008) offers a summary of alternative perspectives on the cultural characteristics of universities and considers their implications for research design.

While some authors consider it unproblematic to categorise different universities into one of a number of boxes (usually four, for example McNay, 1995, but six for Bergquist, 2008), Alvesson (2002) depicts universities as each having a unique *multiple cultural configuration* and warns against fixed, **nomothetic** and **totalising** accounts of institutional culture (2002: 186-187).

Deciding where one stands on this issue, and being explicit about it, is important precisely to exclude the possibility of tacit assumptions inappropriately shaping research design and data interpretation. It is important to be able to answer questions such as the following on the basis of a clear, explicit, theory of organizations: 'are my data generalizable across the whole university?'; 'what is the nature and distribution of power in this university?'; 'how, and how much, does the university change over time?'; 'what are the important characteristics of this university when offering a contextualising description of it in the research?'.

Researching professional knowledge

Another lacuna in many studies is any attempt to deconstruct the nature of professional knowledge. This is important because much insider research involves exploring such knowledge, yet rarely asks questions such as: 'what different forms does this knowledge take?'; 'how amenable is it to data collection, in its different forms?'; 'what is the status of a research account of such knowledge compared to that knowledge as it is articulated in action?'; 'can knowledge be described as a thing ('it') or should knowledge be seen as a context-dependent process better described as *knowing* or *knowledgeability*?'.

Oakeshott (1962) suggests that the knowledge that underlies teaching, for example, is a form of practical knowledge, the Aristotelian *phronesis*. This is quite different to **propositional knowledge**, what he calls 'technical knowledge', which is easily articulated explicitly. Practical knowledge, phronesis, is acquired through experience, it is quite personal and is hard or even impossible to express. Giddens (1984) talks about *practical consciousness*, and he means something quite close to this, distinguishing it from *discursive consciousness*, which is a form of knowing that *can* be expressed, close to propositional or technical knowledge.

For Thomas (2011) the practical nature of much professional knowledge is significant – it means that insider case study research offers a distinctive form of knowledge: *exemplary knowledge*, which draws its legitimacy from phronesis (the fact that it is corrigible and interpretable in the context of experience) rather than from theory or objective verification or refutation. Ruderman (1997) takes a similar view, arguing that good judgement is based on phronesis rather than a scientistic weighing of variables. Burawoy (1998) does likewise, arguing that the 'extended case method' offers an alternative approach to a positivist one, the extended case method having an emancipatory potential lacking in positivism:

> Positive science realizes itself when we are powerless to resist wider systems of economy and polity....[We] are moving toward a contextless world, made for the social survey. Reflexive science, on the other hand, takes context and situation as its points of departure. It thrives on context and seeks to reduce the effects of power-domination, silencing, objectification, and normalization....Reflexive science valorizes context, challenges reification, and thereby establishes the limits of positive methods. (Burawoy, 1998: 30)

Schön (1983) makes a similar argument against scientism in his discussion of reflective practice, showing that no case is identical in professional practice, and so split second judgements need to be made by professionals on a case-by-case basis. What he calls *technical rationality* is just not up to this complicated job.

But of course there are elements of professional work that *do* require technical rationality and involve forms of knowing that are capable of being made explicit through research data collection procedures.

Blackler (1995) distinguishes between five types of knowledge identified in the organizational literature: embodied; embedded; embrained; encultured and encoded. These terms describe, respectively, knowledge which lies in muscle memory and is seen in skilled physical performances (performative knowledge); that which is located in systematic routines; knowledge which lies in the brain (cognition); that which is located in shared meaning systems; and finally knowledge which is encoded in text of various sorts.

Though this classification has heuristic power (for example it can be used to categorise the forms of knowledge a university head of department needs to manipulate on a daily basis), Blackler considers this view of knowledge to be one which sees it as a timeless, static commodity. In the end, for Blackler, 'knowing' is a better term than 'knowledge', stressing as it does the processual character of the development and refinement of understanding. *Knowing* is, says Blackler, "mediated, situated, provisional, pragmatic and contested" (Blackler, 1995: 1021).

In this revised approach cognition becomes seen as inevitably situated (at least in some respects and to some degree) and associated practices such as discursive use similarly become contextually contingent. Winberg's work (2003) shows that the forms of discourse deployed by architecture lecturers and students vary according to their context. This has significant implications for researchers of educational practices. Eraut comments that...

> to understand any situation involving several people we need to adopt two complementary perspectives. One should focus on the situation itself - its antecedents, wider context and ongoing interaction with its environment - and the transactions of its participants throughout the period of enquiry. The other should focus on the contribution of the situation to the learning careers of individual participants, the learning acquired during their "visit". From a situational perspective

knowledge is already present in established activities and cultural norms and imported through the contributions of new participants. From an individual perspective, some of their prior knowledge is resituated in the new setting and integrated with other knowledge acquired through participation. According to the magnitude of the impact of the "visit", their knowledge can be described as having been expanded modified or even transformed. (Eraut, 2000: 131-132).

Some implicit knowledge may be impossible to describe in general terms in any meaningful way (how to deliver a lecture in a way which is both intellectually rigorous and engaging, for example). Even apparently 'simple' explicit knowledge is often combined with tacit knowing. Eraut (2000) distinguishes between the following forms of knowledge: codified knowledge ready for use; knowledge acquired through acculturation; knowledge constructed from experience, social interaction and reflection; skills; episodes, impressions and images; feelings. He points out that in professional areas these are nearly always combined. Jarvis (1999) also shows how content knowledge, tacit knowledge, process knowledge and beliefs and values form a mix in practitioners' knowing.

Tacit knowing and feelings are very hard to capture through the usual data collection methods. In the discipline called knowledge management the process of 'knowledge harvesting' involves interviewing experts with a view to capturing and then codifying the nature of their knowledge. However this only works well with relatively simple forms of knowing and in areas which are quite clearly delimited.

For the insider researcher this debate is important for some types of research questions, specifically those which investigate issues such as the transfer of knowledge from the academy into work situations by students, or (staying inside the academy), the most appropriate approaches to management training.

But these issues raise general questions too about the status of research data, raising questions such as 'what is the relationship between what my respondents tell me in about their professional practices, and the practices themselves?'. This is a question about the difference between Giddens' (1984) notions of discursive consciousness (what respondents can say) and practical consciousness (how they go about doing things), referred to above. Being clear about how far research data can go in this respect is really important, as Kane et al (2002) remind us. We should be clear, for example, that we can only make statements about respondents' statements about or perceptions of practices from interviews with them, not the practices themselves.

5.3 Research design, data collection and theory

Questions and answers

The key issue in research design is ensuring that the decisions made are guided by the research questions: the data generated by the research must be appropriate and sufficient to provide robust answers to the questions asked. It is also important to ensure that a consistent and defensible approach is taken towards **epistemological** and **ontological** issues: what does the research claim can be known about the social reality under investigation and how is that reality conceived?

A **realist** ontological position will usually mean more positivist research designs utilising predominantly quantitative data generation approaches which yield statements describing correlations of a generalisable nature. On the other hand a social constructionist position is likely to be more qualitatively inclined and quite limited in its claims for generalisability.

There are many excellent textbooks on research design, data collection and the role of theory. Here I concentrate on the key issues of relevance to insider researchers.

Single and multi-site studies

Insider researchers are usually faced with multiple pressures on their time and limited resources to use in the research. Some will be employed by the university and have more financial resources but limited time for the research, others will be full-time students studying their own university, with more time but less cash. In either case the option of doing a single-site case study is attractive for practical reasons, and as the next chapter shows can be valuable in itself. Coleman and von Hellermann (eds, 2011) and their contributors advocate doing ethnographic studies based on anthropological methods conducted on the researcher's own 'turf':

> ...the 'field' has traditionally been conceptualized as being 'out there' (away from the anthropologist's home), enclosed within a definable territory, and best understood through the method of participant observation. Bound up with these practices is the assumption that culture is located 'out there', with **ethnography** being about the unfamiliar 'other'. Participant observation traditionally involves intensive dwelling and interaction with the 'native' in order to understand his or her worldview...Such positing of people, places, and 'culture' is increasingly critiqued on account of the problematic ideological assumptions..." (Mand, 2011: 42)

These assumptions include the notion that 'culture' is something exotic and 'other', amenable only to the distanced and more analytical academic eye, eventually represented through the godlike authorial voice. Insider research which views the local and familiar is at least as valuable, they argue. But as well as seeing the value of single-site insider research, Coleman and von Hellerman explore the problems and possibilities of *multi*-site ethnographies including those conducted 'at home'. However, as Marcus acknowledges (p. 27, in Coleman and von Hellerman), attempting to deploy such a labour-intensive method of data collection as ethnography in multiple sites will "overwhelm the norms of intensive, patient work in ethnography".

So for the individual researcher who is doing a doctorate such a design is usually too ambitious. This means that a multi-site approach which uses mixed methods or less labour-intensive methods than ethnography may have benefits which justify their costs in terms of time and labour. The important issue in making decisions around this is appropriateness in terms of the research questions, which themselves then come into the mix of factors to consider when planning research which is both practicable and valuable.

For the insider researcher developing a project which compares results from their own institution to those elsewhere, a multi-site study (using less resource-intensive methods of data collection) is obviously the way to go - unless other studies have already been conducted elsewhere which are close enough to their own.

Examples of such comparative projects include:

1. The factors influencing the success or otherwise of an innovation (for example around virtual learning environments' deployment and use)

2. Approaches to management and leadership and their effectiveness

3. The implementation of a national policy

4. Compliance (or otherwise) with national quality (or other) guidelines

5. Professional practices in a discipline or field of study

6. Student responses to an innovation

Action research

Bensimon et al (2004: 105) suggest that it is important for practitioners concerned with bringing about change in their context to "produce knowledge in local contexts to identify problems and take action to solve them". The authors in that collection advocate the idea that change agents should be 'practitioners-as-researchers'.

Action research is an emergent enquiry process involving cycles of: actions; enquiry, analysis; planning; changed actions. It has, broadly, an enhancement agenda. But there are ofen different understandings of what 'enhancement' may involve, especially among those on the ground in universities.

Action research can be undertaken with different audiences, beneficiaries and purposes in mind. It can be emancipatory in intent, aiming to identify disadvantaged groups and to rectify structural disadvantage, or it can simply be aimed at making sure policy is implemented effectively, regardless of what it is or its effects.

Useful guides to conducting action research are Coghlan and Brannick (2010) and Koshy (2009).

Evaluative research

Evaluative research in higher education aims to attribute value and worth to individual, group, institutional or sectoral activities happening there (Saunders, Trowler and Bamber, 2011). Because this guide concentrates on insider research, the relevant levels of evaluative activity are the individual, group and university ones. Such research asks questions about the value of long-standing activities or of innovations that the researcher is undertaking, or those of a group to which s/he belongs, or those of the university as a whole.

While evaluative research often deploys similar data generation techniques to those of 'regular' research, and can use theory in similar ways too, there is one key question presented by this kind of research if it is to be lifted beyond the particular. That is – 'what is the value of this in terms of a larger contribution to knowledge in the academic world?' If the research focuses on the value of a particular set of activities, or an innovation, in a particular location at a particular time, then it becomes difficult to answer that question. Furthermore, the chances of getting a study of a particular situation published in a reputable journal are rather small, if that is an aim of the research.

There are three key ways in which evaluative studies can be conducted so that they provide good answers to this 'contribution' question and stand a good chance of being published, at least in part. These are: *theoretical* contribution; *methodological* contribution; *professional* contribution. Often good evaluative studies will offer a combination of these.

The *theoretical* contribution relates to some aspect of the relevant literature, perhaps on implementation theory or the management of change, or some aspect of theory related to the substance of the activity or innovation (information and communication technologies, for example). The later part of this chapter deals with the place of theory in research.

The *methodological* contribution relates to evaluative methodology, the techniques and theories employed in conducting evaluative research, and the study should offer something additional to what already exists in this area. There are a number of different approaches to evaluative research, methodologically and in other ways, so the contribution can be made to one or more of these. In summary they are: technical-rational evaluation; appreciative enquiry (Cooperrider and Srivastva, 1987); utilization-focused evaluation (Patton, 1997); realistic evaluation (Pawson and Tilley, 1997). An overview of these is offered in chapter 2 of Saunders, Trowler and Bamber, 2011.

Finally, the *professional* contribution relates to practice in the area being investigated, and to achieve this it is necessary to expand the truth claims of the research beyond simply establishing the value of the particular activity or innovation to encompass *similar* activities/innovations in similar circumstances. In this third category the issues covered in the next chapter become particularly relevant.

Institutional ethnography

This is an approach to researching what its founder, Dorothy Smith (2005; 2006), describes as the "textually-mediated social organization". Smith says that institutional ethnography begins by locating a standpoint within an institutional order, a particular guiding perspective from which to explore that order.

This raises a set of concerns, issues or problem germane to those people who occupy that standpoint. These "local actualities of the everyday world" (Smith, 2005: 34) are only the starting point however. From here the investigation of institutional processes is launched, and the broader structural forces which impinge on the everyday world are explored. Because of this unfolding from the local it is not always possible to sketch a detailed research design in advance. But Smith argues that the design is not random: "Each next step builds from what has been discovered and invades more extended dimensions of the institutional regime" (2005: 35). Language, and textual objects are very significant in this – for Smith language serves to co-ordinate subjectivities.

Devault (2006: 294) says this:

> Institutional ethnographies are built from the examination of work processes and study of how they are coordinated, typically through texts and discourses of various sorts. Work activities are taken as the fundamental grounding of social life, and an institutional ethnography generally takes some particular experience (and associated work processes) as a "point of entry." The work involved could be part of a paid job; it might fall into the broader field of unpaid or invisible work, as so much of women's work does; or it might comprise the activities of some "client" group.

This examination is conducted through the standard mix of ethnographic approaches; interviews, observation, documentary analysis and so on. But careful attention is paid in particular to the use of textual artefacts, the discursive repertoires employed in them and the causes of effects of these on social relations within organizations.

In Smith's original formulation there is a concern to investigate the ruling relations that are articulated in work processes and instantiated in texts, and she pays particular attention to the ways in which women are subjugated within institutional processes and through texts and discourses. For example in universities 'mothering work' can be a discursively and organizationally embedded in such a way that women academics disproportionately find themselves doing low-status and unrecognised work supporting students in difficulties. And of course what used to be known as 'support staff' are disproportionately female in most universities.

How this has come to be, and how it is perpetuated, are areas that can usefully be explored in a fine-grained way through institutional ethnography. And not only explored. A key tenet of the approach is that it should be *for* people and not just *about* them: the research must illuminate the mechanisms of oppression and disadvantage and suggest ameliorative strategies.

Institutional ethnography sees local practices in terms of the larger picture of structured advantage and disadvantage, despite the fact that it starts from a particular standpoint within the institution. In this it addresses one of the criticisms sometimes made of fine-grained ethnographic research, for example by Hamersley (1993) and Porter (1993), that such research loses sight of the structural constraints on actors and structural conditioning of their behaviour.

It is clear that insider research and institutional ethnography are highly compatible, at least for some kinds of research questions. However as an approach to enquiry it does leave the researcher with some problematic questions. One is: what standpoint should I start from and how do I draw the limits around it?

This is a question of level of analysis: the standpoint might be that of 'students', or 'women students', or 'women students with disabilities'. That last category could itself be segmented further. Another question is: if I start from one standpoint and work outwards, as Smith recommends, what about other standpoints that exist in the university – why should I privilege just this one? These and many other questions need good answers if readers are to be convinced that the study is robust.

Hypothesis testing

Here the purpose of insider research is to test an hypothesis or to replicate a previous study in a different but relevant context in order to test its conclusions. Either qualitative or quantitative approaches may be adopted to do this, or a combination of both.

This research purpose is best illustrated by an example. Such research could involve a study designed to test the hypothesis developed by Arum and Roksa (2011) that universities (at least in the USA) are "academically adrift". Arum and Roksa used the Collegiate Learning Assessment, a standardized test administered to students in their first semester and then again at the end of their second year, as well as survey responses to answer the question: "do students learn the important things that universities claim to deliver?" They conclude that 45 percent of the students included in their data demonstrate no significant improvement in critical thinking, complex reasoning, and writing during their first two years of college.

In addition Arum and Roksa extrapolate from their analysis some explanations: one is that students are distracted from their studies by socializing or by working at the same time. A further cause is the fact that universities and their staff prioritise other things than undergraduate learning, such as research. In addition there is, they claim, deliberate collusion between staff and students not to tax each other too much.

Methodologically this study has come under criticism, most notably from Alexander Astin (2011), and there are many claims in it that are unsubstantiated and which from a UK perspective appear to be just wrong (for example about the findings of the majority of studies on the 'teaching-research nexus').

So, this study could be tested in a different but relevant context. A similar or identical research design could be adopted to test the findings, and the same statistical techniques could be applied to the data. Alternatively the hypothesised causes of this claimed lack of significant learning could be explored. A further alternative is to build on Astin's critique and design a 'better' study.

Theory and insider research

Theory-use is very important in research generally and insider research in particular – it lifts it above mere market research or journalism, and it allows the researcher to step outside generally accepted ways of seeing the social world.

'Theory' is usually portrayed as consisting of six linked characteristics:

> 1. It uses a set of interconnected concepts to classify the components of a system and how they are related.

> 2. This set is deployed to develop a set of systematically and logically related propositions that depict some aspect of the operation of the world.

3. These claim to provide an explanation for a range of phenomena by illuminating causal connections.

4. Theory should provide predictions which reduce uncertainty about the outcome of a specific set of conditions. These may be rough probabilistic or fuzzy predictions, and they should be corrigible – it should be possible to disconfirm or jeopardize them through observations of the world. In the **hypothetico-deductive** tradition, from which this viewpoint comes, theory offers statements of the form 'in Z conditions, if X happens then Y will follow'.

5. Theory helps locate local social processes in wider structures, because it is these which lend predictability to the social world.

6. Finally, theory guides research interventions, helping to define research problems and appropriate research designs to investigate them.

Different levels and types of theory inform decisions, processes and outcomes in research (see Trowler, 2012, for an account of them).

There are also different views on the role of theory, some challenging its fundamental role, as set out above, and seeing it not as part of a 'scientific' process but as creative and emancipatory. Feminist thinkers, among others, tend to adopt this perspective:

> how often their own cherished analytical rationality is broken up by glimpses into the imagination of more provocative thinkers. I have come to the conclusion that it is not so much that we self-consciously assemble all the resources for the making of research imaginaries as those vivid ideas (and frequently their authors) come to haunt us. (Hey, 2006: 439)

Stephen Ball agrees:
> Theory is a vehicle for 'thinking otherwise', it is a platform for 'outrageous hypotheses' and for 'unleashing criticism'. Theory is destructive, disruptive and violent. It offers a language for challenge, and modes of thought, other than those articulated for us by dominant others. It provides a language of rigour and irony rather than contingency. The purpose of such theory is to de-familiarise present practices and categories, to make them seem less self-evident and necessary, and to open up spaces for the invention of new forms of experience. (Ball, 1995: 265-6)

Haraway (1991) takes this point further in elaborating the notion of 'standpoint theory'. Sprague and Hayes, 2000, in discussing the concept, say this:
> Standpoint epistemology argues that all knowledge is constructed in a specific matrix of physical location, history, culture, and interests... A standpoint is not the spontaneous thinking of a person or a category of people. Rather, it is the combination of resources available in a specific context from which an understanding might be constructed. (Sprague and Hayes, 2000: 673).

For Sprague and Hayes, as for Smith (2005), discussed above, it is important to challenge the standpoint of the privileged from the standpoint of the disadvantaged and (as feminists) from that of women. This can bring empowerment and self-determination; it uses theory as a weapon against structures of privilege and structured disadvantage.
> Feminist standpoint theory suggests that an important way to develop this line of research is to build on the standpoints of those who are least empowered in our current relationships. People living in different intersections of gender, class, and race are likely to have different stories to tell. Thus, a good way to start is to

listen to people with disabilities who are also women and/or poor and/or people of color, and the people who nurture them, as they describe in their own ways the constraints on their daily lives... (Sprague and Hayes, 2000: 690).

Insider research presents particular problems in terms of the use of theory and the relationship between theory and data. Insiders conducting emic research are themselves liable to be influenced by tacit theories held by respondents, or even they can even be captured by institutional or by management discourse, as Hammersley argues (see Trowler, 2001, for more on this).

In such cases it becomes particularly difficult to render the normal strange, to move beyond the standpoint of the privileged. But human behaviour viewed through the microscope tends to bring to attention impalpable drivers far more than when it is seen through a telescope and by their nature these are difficult to apprehend through pure empiricism. In fine-grained qualitative insider research knowledgeability and sense-making are foregrounded as explanation is prioritised above simple correlation. In this respect the role of theory in insider research holds both promise and dangers.

An example of research design

My PhD, subsequently published as Trowler (1998)

Sources of data

This was a single-site ethnographic case study of an institution of higher education. The sources of data used in the study were fourfold and included both primary and secondary data. These were: interviews; observant participation; documents generated within and without the institution and other studies of it.

Interviews

A total of 50 interviews were conducted, covering 30 disciplines and domains in total, mainly with two academics from each being interviewed (some individuals were serially or concurrently located in two disciplines or domains and so were able to provide data for both). The interviews took a semi-structured form and generally lasted between an hour and an hour and half. All were tape recorded, except one. The first 5 and the last 14 were fully transcribed with the others being partially (about 50%) transcribed and annotated.

The selection of interviewees was guided by three main considerations: personal characteristics; their 'location' in terms of the credit framework and disciplinary characteristics. I interviewed roughly equal numbers of women and men and included the full range of age groups and degrees of experience both in HE in general and at NewU in particular. Some key respondents were selected on the basis of their commitment to the credit framework, sometimes having been involved in setting it up (eg respondents 3, 33 and 45).

No one above Head of Department level was selected as this was designed to be a study of ground level actors. 4 HoDs were interviewed and one other interviewee was appointed to that post shortly after the interview. I included individuals with a variety of backgrounds: those with PhDs and those without; those with long experience of study in elite higher education contexts and those with other experiences of education and training; those with professional or industrial backgrounds and those who have largely stayed within the education sector. Only academics from Subjects which contributed to the Combined Honours degree were selected for interview.

I did not include staff on short-term, part-time contracts on the grounds that they would have limited contact with the framework, though some of those I interviewed had permanent contracts below 100% or were full-time but on short-term contracts. Areas of study taught 'above' or 'below' degree level were not included in the study. I did not extend the study into the partner colleges, firstly on the grounds of practicality and secondly because other studies of this type had recently been or were in the process of being conducted in NewU's partners.

The choice-criteria concerning the disciplinary characteristics of the sample selected were fivefold. First I wanted a range of 'areas of study' and Clark's (1987) categories (based on the Carnegie classification) were used to ensure a good range. I also included disciplines and domains which have a variety of levels of strength in terms of Bernstein's (1971) categories of 'classification' (the degree of 'boundedness' of study areas) and 'frame' (the extent to which there is an explicit and agreed content to be transmitted to students in a particular study area and how far this is under the control of academics).

I reasoned that these two characteristics may have important implications for academics' attitudes to the credit framework. Likewise the degree of demand for the discipline or domain by students would seem influential in this respect and so I ensured that the disciplinary sample included those able to pick and choose their students, those who could not afford to be so selective and many points between.

Finally I included areas of study which had been previously under-represented in higher education research (which had predominantly concentrated on high status disciplines). In particular I wanted to include domains of study, especially the more recent entrants to the higher education system such as women's studies and development studies. This was done in order to "yield new insights into a relatively neglected but none the less substantial sector of academic activity" as Becher (1989) puts it.

Observant participation

This aspect of the research involved observing and making notes about events and comments people made more or less as they happened. I sought out locations which would give me greater insight into work across the university. During the 'survey stage' of research (Fetterman, 1989) my observation was conducted in a fairly unstructured way. However after completing the literature review and a depth analysis of the first five interviews observation became increasingly focused.

The clear specification of the research questions plus the progressive development of concepts and theoretical approaches led to a far greater sensitivity to what was more, or less, significant for the research. At the same time, however, I was aware of and allowed for the danger of premature cognitive closure. The practice I developed was to jot down observations in a notebook, including verbatim quotes if possible, at the time of observation or immediately afterwards. In the evening I transferred this into my computer file, adding any other comments or observations as necessary as well as the appropriate HyperResearch code (see below). Eventually I accumulated a very large...file of records of observations, thematically organised.

Documentary evidence

Documents produced internally, official and unofficial, were routinely collected to inform the study. Eventually a very large archive of material was accumulated, including anything that appeared even potentially relevant. These documents ranged from formal statements of academic policy to internal memos, from the unofficial staff newspaper (*The New Guardian*) to the official ones (*New Diary* and *Newlook*), from drafts of reports, subsequently amended, to formal and public reports (for example of validation meetings).

The documents were both quantitative (eg the student profile) and qualitative in nature (eg the Vice-Chancellor's review of the year). The observant participation and documentary analysis aspects of the study were intertwined: as one of the respondents noted, the institution is "paper bound" and inevitably attendance at any formal event involved a number of documents: usually a very large number.

Using both official and unofficial documents made me very aware of the various 'stages' of public performance (Goffman, 1959; Bailey, 1977; Becher, 1988), as did observant participation. Comparing, for example, the public utterances of the Vice-Chancellor on the sexual harassment policy of the university, comments about it in the editorial and letters columns of *The New Guardian* and the discussion of staff over coffee highlighted the distinctions between and the importance of front-of-stage, backstage and under-the-stage discourse and made me think more clearly and critically both about received notions of organisational culture and the interpretation of data in the analytical phase.

Previous studies of the institution

The final element of data collection was the use of other studies of the University. Here I include both 'academic' and non-academic studies. The latter included HEQC and HEFCE reports. With these in particular, however, the analysis was conducted with care because of the issue about the 'stages' of action. For example in a memo of the 15th January 1996 circulating the HEQC Quality Audit Report on Collaborative Provision the Pro-Vice Chancellor states that:

> I am very pleased to note that the HEQC have taken into account most of the comments which were made to them regarding the draft report... (NewU PVC, 1996, p 1).

The Director of the HEQC's Quality Assurance Group, Peter Williams, in a letter to the Vice Chancellor about the report acknowledges the essential negotiability of its contents and its public function:

> I am grateful for your comments on the draft audit report of your University, and have taken them carefully into account in the preparation of the final version....In accordance with HEQC policy, we shall be publishing

the report four weeks after the date of this letter. The four week 'embargo' period is to allow you time to consider whether you wish to prepare a press release or commentary on the report before it is released for general publication... (Williams, P. 1996, p 1).

Where I had access to both draft and final versions, I tended to give analytical priority to the former because of the more 'negotiated' character of the latter, particularly where the HEQC was concerned.

This was less of a problem, though by no means absent, in the academic studies of the institution and its work which I used. I cannot cite them here to retain the anonymity of the institution but they included two historical studies of the institution, three commissioned reports on equal opportunities issues, one other study of equal opportunities issues, three studies of collaborative provision, one internal study focusing on issues around values and ethics, one PhD thesis concerning mature students' experiences.

Even these academic reports needed to be treated with some caution too. Of one of the commissioned studies of equal opportunities in the institution, for example, respondent 27 warned me that:

> There was a secret version which [was]...produced for [the Director's]...eyes alone." (27).

Neither that respondent nor I ever gained sight of this alleged secret version: ethical considerations prevented me from making an attempt to do so (I eschewed attempting to obtain any confidential documents throughout the research on these grounds). However I did make some fruitless tentative enquiries among those who might have knowledge of it with the intention of gaining a view about the status of the data and conclusions in the publicly available report.

Similarly a careful reading of another (uncommissioned) report suggested that its results also needed to be treated cautiously: comments made within it suggested that the researchers had been 'captured' by senior management's perspective as a result of the researchers' dependence upon them for access.

This suspicion was strengthened by the fact that one of my respondents (10) had read the report and been an insider during a particular series of events described in detail in it. His interpretation was that the report both reproduces the management perspective of events and is inaccurate in its account of some of the facts. The final grounds for doubt were that the report's account of the role and reception of the work of an equal opportunities officer within the university is also at odds with the under-the-stage currents on this issue which I accessed.

Rather than not use these studies, however, I decided to extend the application of Stenhouse's (1979) notion of the 'second record' (the use of a detailed understanding of meaning systems to 'read' interview data) to this kind of secondary data about the institution. Thus I not only used the data and results of other studies to check my own understandings and interpretations, but also the reverse.

Methods of data analysis

Analysis of the interview transcripts was done partly using the qualitative data analysis package HyperResearch and partly through more traditional means. A total of 157 codes were developed, around 40 of which related to the characteristics of the respondents: their gender, discipline and age, while the rest were thematic. Passages were coded and the software permitted the retrieval of passages on the same subject and some limited cross tabulation.

The computer package proved invaluable as a database for retrieving comments and reading the reports it produced often led to new analytical ideas. My early fears that the holistic nature of the data would be destroyed, the individual lost, as a result of this kind of vertical slicing proved groundless: I made frequent reference back to the original interview transcript, and sometimes the audio-tape itself. There were issues however about the effect on the analysis of using qualitative data analysis software. I explore these in Trowler, 1997.

The analysis of the fieldnotes and secondary data, however, was much less structured. I read through the notes from time to time, reminding myself of what they contained and consulted them during the analysis and write-up phases. Later I checked them again to ensure that nothing of value had been missed and that there was nothing that contradicted my interpretation. This analysis procedure can be summed up as familiarisation, selection and later checking for missed or contradictory data.

The sheer amount of data collected presented a considerable problem for the data analysis phase. Although theoretically it was possible to engage in a highly systematic procedure as had been done with the interview data, in reality this presented too many practical problems, particularly in the amount of time involved.

5.4 'Value' and robustness in insider research

Beyond the particular

Researching one's own university will almost always be a form of case study research, about which there is a large literature base (to dip into it see Gomm et al, 2000; Simons, 2009; Yin, 2009).

Case study researchers may find their work subject to the following criticisms (Flyvbjerg, 2006): it only yields concrete, practical knowledge rather than the supposedly more valuable general, theoretical and propositional knowledge; generalization from one case is not possible and so the research does not contribute to the development of knowledge; the research can generate hypotheses, but other methods are necessary to test them and build theory; case study design contains a bias toward verification, i.e., a tendency to confirm the researcher's preconceived notions.

Both Flyvbjerg (2006) and Yin (2009) refute these criticisms, but those who research their own universities need to be clear about precisely what their research questions are, what the rationale behind the research design is, and what the truth claims are. This advice holds for any kind of research, but other designs tend to draw less critical fire.

Thomas (2011) takes a different line; that case study research offers a distinctive form of knowledge: 'exemplary knowledge', which draws its legitimacy from phronesis (the fact that it is corrigible and interpretable in the context of *experience*) rather than theory. This is a significant argument for those who research their own university because judgements about the robustness of data analysis and conclusions drawn from data are made on the basis of 'insider' knowledge. This is true of the acting agent (lecturer, student, administrator), of the researcher and also of the reader. The acting agent makes "calculations of probability based on an insider's knowledge" (Hirsch, 1976: 18) and learns to make subtle judgements based on largely tacit knowledge about the context (Eraut, 2000): s/he is, in short, a reflective practitioner (Schön, 1983).

The culturally literate researcher in a university can also make such judgements, as I noted above, reading between the lines and accessing the 'second record'. But the reader too is significant in using the exemplary knowledge presented in the report of endogenous case studies – readers actively make judgements about how significant a study *for them*, and of its value, based on their own knowledge of the area of practice being discussed.

This argument requires the clear differentiation between the sorts of research questions which are and are not suitable for the development of exemplary knowledge, between more and less appropriate research designs, and between audiences who can and cannot apply phronesis.

Bamber et al (2009) take and apply an approach similar to Thomas' in their positioning of the significance of the insider case studies of learning and teaching enhancement. They use exemplary knowledge developed from case studies in their book to develop Frameworks for Action for readers. These rely on readers' phronesis, about which they say:

> We are very keen to stress the great significance of *context* in change processes. For these reasons we strongly caution against the fallacy of *secundum quid* – the mistake of attempting to learn direct, general, lessons from individual cases. Translation, reconstruction and bridging are more likely to succeed than attempts to transfer learning between contexts. (Bamber et al, 2009: 5).

Sayer (2010) distinguishes between research which aims to establish 'truth' and that which seeks to offer 'practical adequacy'. He says that naive objectivist ontological positions would propose that the former is possible, but this misses the complexity of social life and the significance of interpretation in the social world: "Thought objects and their material referents are utterly different, and yet we can only consider the latter via the former" (p. 66). But recognising this leaves us in a dilemma about the value of the findings of research. For Sayer one resolution to that dilemma is to establish practical adequacy: meaning that knowledge should be judged as more or less *useful* rather than more or less true.

Another approach to dealing with the issue of complexity of social life and the limited degree to which one can generalise from findings to is follow Bassey's approach (Bassey, 1999; Bassey, 2000; Bassey, 2001). For him "fuzzy generalization" is one way of rendering value to research given the complexity of social life. He writes:

> The problem of generalisation has long been a stumbling block for researchers in the social sciences. In terms of research into learning strategies, for example, teachers and policy-makers have wanted clear statements like, "do x in y circumstances and z will be the result". But researchers have been unable to make such predictions because of the complexity of the notion of "circumstances". Putting it another way, there are too many uncontrolled variables in most social settings for

straightforward statements like this to be made. (Bassey, 2000: 1)

For Bassey the solution, put at its simplest, is to conduct research which renders statements of the form "do x in y circumstances and z may be the result in between w and z% of cases". This is what he calls a *fuzzy prediction with best estimate of trustworthiness*. To make such a statement goes beyond what the data themselves can support and into the realms of professional and tacit knowledge: the researcher (not the audience this time) needs to make estimates of who may use the findings and in what circumstances.

For Hammersley (2001), while Bassey's concept has much to offer educational researchers there are some important conceptual problems with it, and I agree with him. The concept of "y circumstances" in particular is a problematic one – it is not easy to draw lines between circumstances which are, or are not, 'similar'. In addition, this use of fuzzy generalizations and predictions might apply in some areas of university life but certainly not in others. Many circumstances in higher education and professional life in general are characterised by wickedity (Bore & Wright, 2009) – that is they are *one-off* issues or problems in unique circumstances that have no algorithms to follow to solutions. They are ill-understood or understood in multiple, perhaps conflicting, ways and are fundamentally complex in character (Trowler, 2012).

When faced with wicked issues of this sort, fuzzy generalizations need to be so fuzzy as to be virtually useless to the manager or other professional – they might indicate where danger lies or where achieving desirable outcomes is almost impossible, but not much beyond that. At best they might indicate potentially more fruitful approaches to tackling a specific issue.

This does not mean though that conducting research with the intention of enhancing practice in complex, 'wicked', circumstances is a hopeless task, as the notion of Frameworks for Action, outlined above, illustrates. It simply means that the work should empower professionals on the ground to make good choices and to themselves decide where situations described in the research are, and are not, analogous to their own situation. Professionals must be able to decide when, and when not, to implement ideas in research reports, to determine relevance for their own situation. The important location for phronesis lies with those professionals, not only with the researcher as Bassey argues.

Questions for the insider researcher

The following questions are useful stimuli for reflection on the quality and rigour of proposed design for insider research. Thinking them through should uncover flaws in the approach and so enhance the robustness and value of the research.

1. In designing the research, how do I know that my planned approach will answer the questions I have more fully than any other?

2. How do I design the research to take best advantage of the benefits of insider research while avoiding its pitfalls as far as possible?

3. Conceptually, how do I represent my organization, its culture and its practices? (And how does this representation shape my design?)

4. How and from whom will I secure access to the data I need? (Why them and why not others?)

5. Whom should I inform about the project, and how should I describe it, when I seek 'informed' consent? (And how might this affect my data?)

6. How will I ensure that the project is run ethically so that all participants and institutional bodies are protected? (While at the same time being as transparent as possible to readers so they can judge the robustness of my approach and conclusions?)

7. If I am using participant observation, what are the ethical issues in relation to the people I observe in natural settings? (And how might my answer to that question affect my data?)

8. If using interviews, what measures should I take to deal with interview bias? (And will they assure a sufficient degree of robustness?)

9. What should the balance be between collecting naturalistic data and formally 'collected' data? (And how can I offer assurances of robustness about conclusions drawn from both?)

10. How should I analyse the different forms of data I have, given that there will almost certainly be a large amount of various sorts? (And how do I ensure that sufficient and appropriate weight is given to each form of data in generating conclusions?)

11. How, and how much, will I communicate my findings to participants to ensure that they are happy with what I intend to make pubic? (And will this affect the way I present my conclusions to other audiences?)

12. Generally, in what other ways can I satisfy the reader about the robustness of my research and its findings?

5.5 The ethics and politics of insider research in universities

Ethics

There are excellent discussions of ethical issues in general in the BERA online resources (referenced in the Resources chapter), but this chapter deals with the particular ethical issues that insider research gives rise to. This kind of research foregrounds the problem of institutional and personal anonymity. It also makes it difficult to cite and reference information from reports on, or commissioned by, the university (because the institution is usually named in titles).

Participant observation, often deployed as part of ethnographic studies by insiders, raises its own ethical challenges. Homan (1991) for example suggests that, as in areas where pickpockets are active, there should be warning signs posted as a constant reminder, in this case: "Beware! Participant observers at work". In medical research the notion of 'rolling consent' echoes this – the practice of obtaining consent from participants at every new stage of the research. The view underlying this practice is that 'informed consent' needs to be specifically given for each new phase, and in Homan's view it needs to be renewed again and again because in participant observation other participants quickly forget about the dual role of the researcher, or are confused about the relationship between their two roles (participant and researcher).

There are well-understood steps to assist in anonymising organizations and people: creating pseudonyms; obscuring identifying details; laying false trails in descriptions – changing small, but unique, details of history, geography and characteristics in a way which does not alter details of the research (the reader must however always be aware that the author has done this, and why). But these have limited value when the significant fact that the researcher is known by the audience to be a member of the university in which the insider research has been conducted. This is always the case in conference presentations, for example. One option is to obscure the institutional location of the researcher too, but this breaks the important principle of transparency in methodology (so that the reader to assess its robustness) and transparency about and reflection on oneself and one's position as a researcher (Ezzy, 2002).

Because of these issues the insider researcher needs to take special ethical measures and to make different assumptions than would be the case in other research designs. It is normally best to assume that the reader will be able to identify the researched institution, should they wish to. Therefore in the ethical clearance process and in information given to respondents, the researcher cannot guarantee institutional anonymity.

This has a number of corollaries in terms of the decisions to be taken. Senior managers and others will want assurance that the research will not damage the reputation of their organization (increasingly significant in a very competitive HE environment).

Individuals will need assurance that neither they nor their job role will be traceable, if their university is identified. Insider data collection can raise ethical issues around disparities in power: interviewing the powerful (Walford, 1994); collecting data from those who lack power relative to the researcher or to others (Scott, 1992; Rubin and Rubin, 2005); and even interviewing peers (Platt, 1981). These each raise political, ethical and methodological issues. Especially strong ethical measures need to be taken, then, to offer these kinds of assurances.

One significant possible measure is to offer respondents sight of drafts of all outputs from the research so that they can assess whether the anonymising measures taken and the false trails laid adequately obscure their identity and role. Another is to ask an independent reader to assess potential research outputs for any 'traceability' they may contain – and to guarantee this measure to the researched university and its respondents. A third is to change details of publications relating to the organization (having informed the reader of this). Given the usual measures to protect, limit access to and eventually destroy raw data, the key ethical question concerns the outputs of research: how they are written; what their circulation is; and how robust they are at protecting institutions and people. Transparency in the approach taken to this is very important.

Halse and Honey (2007) note that universities have tended to adopt an institutional discourse to describe ethical research that represents research practice as an ordered, linear process with objective principles and rules that inform and direct ethical decision making and moral action. By contrast feminists, for example....

> have proposed an ethical orientation of care that privileges relationality, care, vulnerability, and responsibility and asserts the importance of active concern for others and for community. (Halse and Honey, 2007: 342).

For Halse and Honey the ritualized technologies and practices of ethics review which reflect the technical-rational discourse of ethics constrain the possibility of this orientation of care by delimiting what is constituted as research. Again, the insider researcher needs not simply to undertake the routinised ethical processes required by their university, but also to think critically about their potential effect on the research itself.

Politics

The choices one makes in designing an insider research project quickly become infused with political judgements and have political consequences. In choosing to study academic staff, for example, one is choosing **not** to study whole categories of other staff: administrators, secretaries, cleaners and the rest. In focusing on the ground level of social practices one brackets out perspectives from senior managers, and the reverse is obviously also true. In researching students and learning one backgrounds academic teachers and teaching. In a political context, research **focus** becomes a political issue.

A second and related issue can be summed up in the question 'whose problem?' Dale (1989) and Ozga (2000) distinguish between three research 'projects':

> A. The *social administration* project is reformist, with research efforts aimed at improving the lot of the 'clients' of policy.

> B. The *policy analysis* project treats policy-making as the preserve of government and managers. The role of the researcher is not to question policy but to ensure that social policies are delivered effectively, regardless of content, of who benefits and irrespective of the priorities that have been selected.

C. The *social science project* treats 'the problem' separately from those conceived by either the client or the policy-maker. Instead it is to some extent defined in terms of theory and the literature in the area. Its concerns involve a mix of attempting to gain a better understanding of how things work, contributing to theory and perhaps 'making' rather than 'taking' problems in the area of investigation – in other words the social science project proposes new issues and concerns that neither policy-makers nor clients have identified.

While both the social administration and policy analysis projects are, in different ways, technicist, the social science project is more conceptual in character. So, for the insider researcher in a university, a key question is – 'whose concerns are being framed in my research questions and design?'

A third issue arises from the power structures within universities and the subordinate position of some categories of people. This has implications in terms of data collection: the consequences of being too forthcoming in revealing sensitive information about the university can be very serious for those in more vulnerable positions. Not all respondents have equal latitude in respect of what they say and how they say it. Scott (1992) talk about "infrapolitics" which he describes (p. 19) as "a wide variety of low-profile forms of resistance that dare not speak in their own name." He writes:

The recovery of the nonhegemonic voices and practices of subject peoples requires, I believe, a fundamentally different form of analysis than the analysis of elites, owing to the constraints under which they are produced. (Scott, 1992: 19)

Finally, the role of the researcher and what s/he is doing in the university, the choices made and the interpretation put on data are political issue. This further reinforces the importance of being transparent about oneself as researcher, one's location in the institution and the motivations for conducting the study. The reader needs to be as fully informed as possible to be able to judge for themselves the degree of robustness of the study and any ulterior agendas that may be driving its shape, direction and conclusions.

5.6 Social practice theory applied: a research agenda

Researching social practices

Social practice theory (SPT) derives from the work of Bourdieu (2000), Foucault (1984), Giddens (1979, 1984), Reckwitz (2002) and Schatzki *et al.* (2001). This strand of theory offers illuminative concepts, explanatory power and insights into probable outcomes of behaviour. SPT also offers value as a 'sensitising theory' - it gives fresh perspectives on habitual practices, rich ways of conceptualising the world (Sibeon 2007).

SPT lies within the broad category of 'cultural theory' which emphasises the significance of the symbolic structures of meaning in the social world, both their construction and their enactment by people. These symbolic structures condition behaviours, enabling and constraining them in particular ways.

SPT also has links with actor network theory which looks beyond simply human agency, taking cognisance of the power of *things* (Lefebvre, 1984). It is interested in the relationships between humans and artefacts and how the two co-exist and 'use' each other in the enactment of practices. Artefacts in use can configure human behaviours, scripting them, but at the same time recurrent practices shape the way artefacts are deployed.

Social practices always consist of patterned relations between humans and things, including those things that together create the physical context of practice: buildings, furniture and spatial organisation. Spatiality theories explore the latter aspects in detail (see for example Löw, 2008; Tissen and Deprez, 2008). So the single human agent is 'de-centered' in this view. Rather each of us is part of a network of things and other people that operate relationally, and do so as part of a temporal flow.

For SPT specifically the significant unit of analysis for the researcher lies in *practices*, what is enacted. Reckwitz defines these social practices as follows:

> forms of bodily activities, forms of mental activities, 'things' and their use, a background knowledge in the form of understanding, knowhow, states of emotion and motivational knowledge. A practice, a way of cooking, of consuming, of working, of investigating, of taking care of oneself or of others, etc. forms so to speak a 'block' whose existence necessarily depends on the existence and specific interconnectedness of these elements, and which cannot be reduced to any one of these single elements. (Reckwitz, 2002: 249)

Because of this focus on practices, knowledge is also seen in a particular way in SPT. Knowing, or knowledgeability, is situated in practices, so that knowledgeability and emotionality is a constituent of a practice. Intentionality, knowing, desiring and behaving are all tied into social practices. They are situationally contingent, therefore, and are distributed among the people and things engaged in the relations which make up the practice. Again, the individual is de-centred in this view: knowledge lies not in a single person's head, but is distributed and situated.

Pulling these comments together, for me the key characteristics of a social practice approach to understanding universities and change that I want to emphasise and draw on are as follows:

1. People are carriers of practices: they enact in specific ways a reservoir of ways of behaving, understanding and responding in ways which are to a certain extent particular to them in a social field (Bernstein, 2000, distinguishes between 'reservoir' and 'repertoire to describe this process of individuation from structural characteristics). Individuals thus articulate repertoires of recognisable practices: 'patterns of bodily behaviour and routinized ways of understanding, knowing and desiring' (Reckwitz, 2002: 250). The focus on analysis is therefore best located in the practices, not the individuals involved.

2. People in universities, departments and work groups engage in clusters of practices in different locales, and in so doing develop partly unique sets of recurrent behaviours and meanings about the world they are dealing with, ones that are particular to their location. Universities end up with a *multiple cultural configuration*, with different clusters of social practices in different locales within them usually departments as well as many commonalities.

3. In their practices clusters perhaps in developing a new syllabus, teaching face-to-face in a lecture, or researching in a laboratory, doing bedside rounds in a teaching hospital or a 'crit' in an art studio human agents use artefacts and tools of various sorts which themselves influence the social reality in particular ways. Patterns of understanding, feeling and wanting are involved in this, it is not simply a technical tool-use. The use and manipulation of artefacts to achieve goals involves 'knowing' those artefacts in specific ways, interpreting rather than just using them. They are cultural symbols. Meanwhile the process of contextualisation shapes the ways in which tools and artefacts are used. New initiatives such as those aimed at sustainability often involve changes in tool use, and so this interaction is significant for them. Another way of putting this is that artefacts can configure activity, inscribing relations between people (Latour, 2000; Harman, 2009), but usually there is co-adaptation between people and artefacts: the reproduction of everyday life involves *actively* and effectively configuring complex assemblies of material objects, often in new ways. Thus, for example, the use of PowerPoint can shape the way classes are taught and content is presented (Adams, 2006), but there is space too for active manipulation of the technologies involved.

4. Discourses the particular forms of production of 'text' (talk, writing, etc.) which are mediated by reservoirs of deeper, historical, social forces and social structures express social reality and also operate to constrain and delimit it. Discursive practices and the social construction of reality work together. Thus 'managerialist' discourse expresses a particular view of the nature of universities and works to bracket out other views and other discourses. There is an interplay between discursive and other practices. However, from an SPT perspective discourse is not privileged above other forms of practice: it is simply one among many.

5. Individual identity, or subjectivity, is intimately involved in the process of contextualisation both shaping and being shaped. People and things operate to shape and reshape context, and each other. There is a process of contextualising, decontextualising and recontextualising (Nespor, 2003) in which identity is intimately involved. As people engage in social practices they shape their own identities and those of others, though they may also defend their identities from this process. However, identity is a lifetime project and people bring with them relatively permanent aspects of identities as they follow their lifecourse. This is one source of difference, even conflict, within sites of social practice.

6. So, the historical background of individuals and also of the group is important. History, and narratives about history, have significant influences on social life in the present. These may be stories about academics' disciplines, about the institution, about other institutions or about the higher education system as a whole. Whatever they are, these histories and stories about the past will impact on change initiatives such as sustainability in the present: practices have an evolving trajectory, rarely a revolutionary one. However, narrativity is not privileged to the extent that 'voice' theories foreground it. There are semiotic trajectories too, trajectories of evoked meanings. Additionally the temporality of practices, and differing temporalities for different actors in the same practice, are significant in affecting the trajectories of practices (Nespor, 2007).

7. A corollary of all of the above is that the process of context generation, with the particularities it creates, is a very significant factor in changing organisations. There are special features in every university, and every university department, every discipline, that mean that initiatives will be received, understood and implemented in ways which are, partly at least, unique. So, any attempt to generalise advice on how to change things is fraught with danger. Leaders on the ground need to understand their own situation well, and what will work and not work there. This needs good ways of seeing.

8. The social practice perspective stresses the significance of the *knowledge resources* individuals and groups access in order to engage in routine or emergent practices. These resources are of different kinds and can include examples such as the following: self knowledge; knowledge of tools and artefacts and their interactions; 'readings' of prevailing pressures and strategic imperatives historically derived but contemporaneously experienced; the way the cultures of disciplines help structure our activities and behaviours. Knowledge and interpretations of these imperatives and their implications help reconstruct new configurations or 'repertoires' of practices. They may result, for example, in new emphases in the way curricular designs evolve, the discourses in use develop and professional identities change.

9. Finally, practices are conditioned by the operation of power in various ways. I understand 'power' to have both a solid and a fluid character: power is located in structures and in positions for example in university governing bodies such as Senate and Council, or in committees as well as in people who occupy senior roles and it has a moment-by moment character in which it ebbs and flows between social actors and things for example within committee meetings. These different articulations of power, the 'faced' and the 'de-faced' (Hayward, 2000), can constrain agendas, limit actions, imbue preferred readings and actions in situations and, of course, punish and reward in different ways.

Ontological and epistemological consequences

So what does this mean for doing insider research in universities? At a fundamental level it has ontological and epistemological implications which affect the research design. From this perspective universities consist of multiple, interlocking, constellations of practices. In each area of practice different identities, discourses and contextual concerns (Archer, 2007) are mobilised.

Bodily activities, forms of mental activities, forms of understanding, knowledge, states of emotion and sets of motivations are very differently configured and mobilised in, for example, teaching, research or university meetings of different sorts. Individuals carry, and carry out, a multitude of routines, practices even though some are derived from social structures and are simply enacted and so can gain a perspective upon them. "The individual is the unique crossing point of practices, of bodily-mental routines" (Reckwitz, 2002: 256). Texts of all sorts are manipulated by literate individuals who "read situations and understand what is required to participate effectively in particular practices" (Wolfe and Flewitt, 2010: 389).

For SPT social interaction and the development of meaning, ways of seeing and ways of doing are key drivers of both social order and sometimes social change. As Warde (2005: 141) says:
> practices also contain the seeds of constant change. They are dynamic by virtue of their own internal logic of operation, as people in myriad situations adapt, improvise and experiment...In addition, practices are not hermetically sealed off from other adjacent and parallel practices, from which lessons are learnt, innovations borrowed, procedures copied.

The trajectories of practices are inherently unstable because they depend upon of the recurrent assembly and integration of artefacts, meanings and forms of competence by groups of practitioners who 'carry' practices.

SPT sees people as carriers of routinised bodily behaviours that are underpinned by socially situated and acquired knowledge, ways of understanding, feeling and wanting. They 'carry out' practices which are recurrent, often taken for-granted and founded in socially acquired sets of meanings developed and learned through social interaction. These practices can be both quite distinct and as in a university interconnect in institutional complexes: a nexus of practices or a 'social field' in Bourdieu's language.

Research design and topics

In more practical terms, for the insider researcher, all this means:
> 1. That the focus of research is on the characteristics of practice (as defined above) in particular situations, and the effects of these characteristics.
>
> 2. That both 'things' and people should receive attention

3. That care should be taken not to lose sight of the structural influences on practices (the danger being that the researcher is over-focused on the practices-as-presented rather than on the forces that shape them).

4. That truth claims need to be carefully delimited to the areas of practice being discussed.

The research agendas that stem from an SPT point of view will often concern issues around change and changing practices. My earlier work (Trowler, 2008) on this has suggested that change initiatives work best when they are grounded in current sets of practices and build on them. They are likely to succeed when there is *salience, congruence* and *profitability* for people who will be most affected by proposed changes. The outcomes of change initiatives will be strongly influenced by the history of the context and its previous configuration. People 'domesticate' initiatives so that there is a better fit between previous practices and the new situation; reshaping and selective retention and use occurs. The result is that the outcomes of initiatives will be different in different locations, depending on the previous practices in place there.

All this means that establishing an anthropological understanding of context is vitally important in researching change, as is developing a keen awareness of the nature of the initiative and the proposed change and, crucially, the relationship between the current situation and the envisaged new one.

Again, in earlier work (Trowler, 2008) I have suggested ways of looking at university contexts, particularly in relation to teaching and learning. I have suggested that one can 'unpick' different teaching and learning regimes (TLRs) that are in place and use that process to think about the likely consequences of change initiatives.

TLRs consist of eight 'moments'; interconnected characteristics which shape contextual concerns and which depict the social practices in place. These are:

1. Recurrent practices

2. Tacit assumptions

3. Implicit theories of teaching and learning

4. Discursive repertoires

5. Conventions of appropriateness

6. Power relations

7. Subjectivities in interaction

8. Codes of signification

These suggest ways in which data-generating methods can be adopted which will offer insight into change processes.

5.7 Resources for insider research

5.8 Literature

There is a considerable literature on researching organizations, but most of this work concerns research within a commercial context (eg Buchanan and Bryman, 2009; Ybema et al, 2009; Broussine, 2008). That is not to deny their utility for research on universities: Buchanan and Bryman's book contains many useful chapters, including ones on using digital archives, conversation analysis, interviews, mixed methods, discourse analysis, visual methods and autoethnography. These offer more specific, organizationally-oriented, advice than that found in more general (but excellent) books on educational research methods such as Cohen, Manion and Morrison (2011).

There are journals devoted to that topic, for example *Research in Organizational Behavior* and *Organizational Research Methods*. These too are mostly concerned with commerce, the first favouring more qualitative approaches, the latter more quantitative.

The literature dealing with *insider* organizational research, particularly that within universities, is rather sparser. Mercer (2007) for example found just four studies looking at the "unique epistemological, methodological, political, and ethical dilemmas (Anderson and Jones, 2000, p. 430) that insider research into higher education management presents. These were: Preedy and Riches (1988); Anderson and Jones (2000); Hockey (1993); Labaree (2002).

More recently a wider literature has begun to develop, some of which also looks at insider research in universities (eg Foreman-Peck and Winch, 2010), but more often examines *practitioner* research, adopting a view of 'insiderness' as referring to a professional area rather than to organizations (eg Drake and Heath, 2011). There is meanwhile an expanding literature on endogenous research in organizations generally, not specifically universities (eg Coghlan and Brannick, 2010; Costley, Elliott and Gibbs, 2010).

While insider higher education research is often characterised by limited reflectivity about context or approach there is a considerable, and increasing, amount of it around the world. The rising number of EdD's in the UK has led to a growth in this type of research. While most higher education research generally has been conducted in a few European countries, the USA and Australia, analysis of consecutive issues of the journal *Abstracts of Research into Higher Education* shows increasing numbers of papers from new regions, most notably South Africa (Shay, Ashwin and Case, 2009). Many of these are insider studies (eg Shay, 2008). As a result there are increasing numbers of papers describing the author's experience of doing insider research in their university. These can be useful for the researcher new to this. Two examples are Roland and Wicks (2009) and Rabbitt (2003)

The *European Association for Institutional Research* (EAIR) and its North American equivalent (AIR) has members who conduct research into higher education administration, often as 'insiders', much of which is professionally-oriented. Their membership numbers have been growing, as have those of the *Society for Research into Higher Education* (SRHE) which has a network dedicated to 'Close Up' research.

Educational development centres and those concerned with planning and implementing technology-enhanced learning also engage in a considerable amount of endogenous research. Much of it is focused on areas of concern which include: orientations to and the enhancement of teaching and learning; the implementation of technology-enhanced learning; discursive issues; management and new managerialism; the student experience; course design; academic work and knowledge (this list draws on but does not reproduce information in Tight, 2007; 2008).

Common research methods or methodologies used in higher education research generally are: documentary analysis; comparative analysis; interviews; surveys; multivariate analyses; conceptual analyses, phenomenography; critical/feminist perspectives; and auto/biographical and observational studies (Tight, 2007). Some of these are more easily deployed in endogenous research, but none are excluded: the limitations are mostly related to one-person research conducted within a single HEI rather than to do with endogenous research per se. Both Sage and Routledge have an extensive list of excellent textbooks covering these areas.

Online resources for insider research

ALL WEBSITES CITED LAST ACCESSED 25.1.2016
Association for Institutional Research: http://www.airweb.org
BERA online resources on ethical issues in research: http://www.bera.ac.uk/bera-resources/ethics/
European Association for Institutional Research: http://www.eair.nl/
Higher Education Close UP JiscMail list: https://www.jiscmail.ac.uk/cgi-bin/webadmin?A0=HIGHER-EDUCATION-CLOSE-UP

Organizations and Journals interested in endogenous research: https://www.academia.edu/20060426/Organizations_and_Journals_Interested_in_Endogenous_Research

Peter Reason on action research/human inquiry/participative inquiry: http://www.peterreason.eu/Papers_list.html

Trowler (1998) on accessing the 'second record' and deploying different types of data to interrogate an argument: https://www.academia.edu/20060452/Interpreting_Data

Trowler (1997) on his use of qualitative data analysis software in an endogenous study of his university: https://www.academia.edu/12432374/From_Technological_Somnambulism_to_Epistemological_Awareness_reflections_on_the_impact_of_computer-aided_qualitative_data_analysis

Section 6: Frequently Asked Questions about Doctoral Research into Higher Education

About this section

In this section I address questions that my doctoral supervisees often ask. I point to readings that are accessible, both stylistically and in terms of getting hold of them. The word 'supervisor' is used throughout, which is the English term for the role that is elsewhere called 'advisor' or equivalent. The section divides the questions it addresses into 9 different aspects of doing a doctorate.

6.1 Research Questions

6.1.1 How do I write good research questions?

The issue of research question formulation is probably the issue that most frequently divides doctoral students on the one hand and their supervisors and examiners on the other. Supervisors and examiners consider them very important, generally, and give them very close scrutiny. Examiners use them to assess how far and how well a thesis has met its declared intentions. Supervisors use them to help students navigate their progress in the research. Doctoral students and candidates often take a more relaxed approach to them, perhaps because formulating good ones is harder than it seems, or because they don't want to close off possibilities in their research by specifying it too precisely, or for other reasons.

However research questions are very important and should be one of the top issues on the agenda in early meetings with your supervisor. They are important precisely because, well-specified, they have some of the features of both map and compass.

Like a map, research questions set out the territory to be covered and, by implication, what will not be covered – what is off that map. In giving a feeling for the topography of the area being covered, one can also infer from them the best way to approach the journey – not by train, car, bike or on foot but in terms of aspects of the research design which might work best in that terrain. Like a compass, good research questions indicate when you are going off course, and which direction you should go next. They also help you locate how far you've got when combined with the map function.

Of course you may decide that being off the original course has taken you to more interesting places, in which case you can consider changing the questions themselves.

So, what makes "well-specified" research questions? Your questions should:

1. Be answerable: it must be possible to know when a question has been answered
2. Be specific, that is set clear boundaries in terms of what is being studied, and what is not
3. Include at least one analytical question which goes beyond the descriptive
4. Be capable of operationalisation; that is, use concepts that can be turned into measureable, observable, describable phenomena
5. Be bounded in what they require, that is they can be realistically answered given the resources available
6. Be significant; that is, they should provide an answer to the '**so what?**' question - the issue of offering wider interest to a larger audience

One role of research questions is to guide research design, and there needs to be congruence between that design and the questions. This means that the research design chosen must be capable of answering the research questions.

There are common errors made in formulating research questions, which I have characterised elsewhere as the "seven deadly sins". They are:

1. Too descriptive – "What are the management styles in place in Saudi Arabian universities?" (This is also too ambitious, as well as only requiring a descriptive answer).
2. Too narrow – "How can the use of e-portfolios at the University of Bentham be improved?" (Who cares – apart from people at Bentham?).

3. Too ambitious – "What teaching and learning approaches are in place in UK higher education and how can they be improved?" (Impossible to answer).
4. Only focused on perceptions – "In what different ways do Accountancy lecturers at the University of Bentham view the merger of their Department with the Department of Statistics there?" (So what?).
5. Too vague – "How does the higher education system in Chile differ from that in Argentina"? (How long have you got?).
6. Normative – "What are the benefits of linking research and teaching in universities?" (What about the dysfunctions?).
7. Too prescriptive – "Why does the modular system in UK higher education need to be changed?" (Makes an unsubstantiated assumption).

Note how the deadly sins are rarely found alone – problematic research questions often combine two or more of them.

You can find more information elaborating on the above in my short Kindle book *Doctoral Research into Higher Education: Thesis structure, content and completion* (Trowler, 2012c), on which the comments above are based.

6.1.2 Do I really need research questions right now?

You need to draft some research questions right at the start of your research, from the moment you begin to formulate your topic. They will change, at least in subtle ways, right to the very moment of submission. So, yes, if you have any idea at all of what your research topic is, then you need explicit research questions.

The process of writing research questions, like the process of writing an early abstract, helps you to identify exactly what it is you are looking at. At least as important, though, is the fact that the writing process also helps you to clarify exactly what it is you are *not* looking at. It helps you to think through what the important dimensions of your study will be and what your ambitions are in relation to making an original contribution to knowledge.

Doctoral students using some specific methodologies sometimes say that it is not appropriate to have research questions; that these will emerge during the course of the study. The grounds for this claim for exceptionalism often rest on the fact that the research will be undertaken using the lens of institutional ethnography (Smith, 2005), standpoint theory (Allen, 1996) or grounded theory (Charmaz, 2009). The rationale used frequently revolves around the 'emergent' nature of the significant issues, or data, or theory. My view is that for doctoral research this "research question-free" approach is very high risk indeed, and is rarely justified.
Research question formulation can be itself 'emergent' in the sense of adapting the specifics of the questions over time as the research progresses, but there do need to be explicit draft research questions of some sort right at the beginning. In addition any research design choice must itself be founded on some kind of question or hypothesis, however ill-defined and tacit.

The upshot is that you need to talk the issue through in detail with your supervisor/advisor if you really do not want to formulate research questions, even at an early stage, and for whatever reason.

6.1.3 How many research questions should I have?

A convention appears to have developed that somewhere between 3 and 6 questions is about right. Some candidates have an overall research 'aim' which they then break down into researchable questions. My view is that this adds unnecessary complication and could confuse the issue. The research questions must be able to stand alone; it is those that the thesis addresses.

Normally the questions move from relatively simple ones which require only a descriptive response to more complex questions which require answers which are analytical and explanatory, usually informed by theory. This 'gear shift' through the questions is probably the reason why most people have between 3 and 6 – there are perhaps two questions requiring a descriptive response and then two, three or four which incrementally shift the complexity of type of response from description to analysis, explanation and implications.

6.1.4 What are good examples of research questions?

Let's imagine a doctoral student who is highly motivated to research how the attitudes of 'ground level' academic staff in a single institution affect the implementation of a new policy there. That policy might involve extending and enhancing the use of virtual learning environment (VLE) across all disciplines and levels of study there. This is their own institution and top management are keen to make full use of its VLE and to expand the number of students it has studying at a distance from the campus.

This raises three significant issues that need to be thought through before research questions can be formulated:

1. What might the general contribution to knowledge be? In other words, what is the answer to the 'so what?' question that a PhD must provide.
2. How can the idea of 'attitudes' best be conceived, theorised and researched?
3. How can 'effects' be captured, and how can the effects of 'attitudes' be separated out from other causal factors?

The doctoral researcher might decide that the answer to number 1 lies in drawing and contributing to an already-existing literature – say the literature on 'followership' which has developed out of the literature on 'leadership' in recent years. The answer to number 2 may lie in that literature or could come from elsewhere – for example in the notion of **'assumptive worlds'.**
He or she might, on reflection, want to broaden the idea of 'attitudes' to include 'practices', which are underpinned by attitudes and emotions but include recurrent behaviours. Or s/he may want to take a phenomenographic approach and talk about 'orientations' within an **outcome space.** The answer to number 3 might lie in a highly granular research design which traces the trajectory of causality in a forensic manner, and if so this will have consequences for the scope of the research questions.

So, decisions about the wording of the initial set of research questions (which will usually be adapted as the research progresses) is predicated on a number of important considerations.

Now let's imagine that the thinking has been done. A starting position on the research questions for this study might be:

In relation to learning and teaching issues and the use of virtual learning environments in a higher education context:

1. What regularities, if any, can be identified in the assumptive worlds of academics in four disciplines in a single English university?
2. In what ways do the identified characteristics of assumptive worlds manifest in practices generally and in the implementation of relevant policies in particular?
3. How do these findings relate to what is already known about 'followership' in organizations?
4. What are the implications of the findings for policy and practice in the case study institution?
5. To what extent do the findings make a contribution to a body of knowledge and to policy and practice more broadly?

These questions have the advantage of immediately indicating a research design which would be appropriate and adequate to answer them. They also point to bodies of literature that will be relevant. They also show an awareness of where the answer to the 'so what?' question might lie. Finally, they help the student draw parameters around the study, indicating what is 'in' and what is 'out' in terms of what they need to research.

There are still problems, particularly with the last question, but this set of questions will do for a start. As the research progresses these questions will no doubt be refined, but they provide a working compass and a rough map to get going.

6.2 Research Design

6.2.1 How many interviews is 'enough'?

In quantitative research there are clear guidelines on this, and if your study is quantitative you will already be skilled and knowledgeable about how to calculate sample size. You will need to take into account a number of statistical considerations in order to assess the trustworthiness of any generalisations you make from the sample. The most important are the size of the population, its heterogeneity, the degree of sampling error you are willing to allow and so the level of precision and degree of confidence you can have in the results. Fox, Hunn and Mathers (2009) have put together a useful resource pack about doing this. The answers to the questions are a matter of judgement, and like so much else in doctoral research this judgement needs to be informed by (and inform) the research questions.

In qualitative research, the decision about the number of participants also depends on consideration of a number of factors, but only some of them are quantitative in character. They include:

> The quality of data, the scope of the study, the nature of the topic, the amount of useful information obtained from each participant, the number of interviews per participant, the use of **shadowed data** and the qualitative method and study design used. (Morse, 2000, p.3).

Morse has missed some other key factors in determining participant numbers: the precise nature of the research questions; the scope of the **truth claims** intended to be made; whether the notion of **'saturation'** is being applied; and how significant theoretical development is in the thesis compared to its **empirical** dimensions.

In the end, the doctoral researcher must make a careful judgement about the numbers of respondents, and feel confident that s/he will be able to defend that judgement convincingly to the examiners. Examiners will also be making a judgement, bringing their experience to bear to assess the rationale for the design in general and they will make a judgement about the number of participants in particular. They will be asking themselves something like: "is this selection adequate and appropriate to answer these research questions?"

You may want to use the following contrasting sets of points to help you think about respondent numbers in your own study:

INDICATES MORE RESPONDENTS
1. Single burst of data gathering.
2. Research questions demand limited information from/about respondents.
3. Truth claims involve broad generalisation of findings.
4. Research is investigating a large social field.
5. Data are characterised by simplicity and clear definition.
6. The study relies heavily on the data from respondents.
7. The development, refinement, application or testing of theory plays a small role in the research outcomes.
8. The idea is to reach 'saturation' in relation to data collection.
9. Data from respondents represent the focus of the study. In other words, the respondents are the primary unit of analysis.

10 There is plenty of time and enough resources for data 'collection'.

INDICATES FEWER RESPONDENTS
1. Extended longitudinal design.
2. Research questions demand depth understanding of perspectives, values etc.
3. Truth claims are limited to the study itself or a very defined and limited broader set.
4. Research is investigating a small social field.
5. Data are characterised by complexity and nuanced variations.
6. Data from respondents form only part of the research design.
7. The development, refinement, application or testing of theory plays a large role in the research outcomes.
8. The idea is to collect data from a purposively-selected group of respondents.
9. Data from respondents are only the locus of the study. The respondents are not the primary unit of analysis.
10. Time and resources are restricted.

A final point on this is that while the notion of 'sample size' comes from and is used in quantitative research, in qualitative research the term should be used with caution. This is because it rests on assumptions about a 'sample' being able to represent to some extent the wider 'population' from which it is drawn. Many traditions which use qualitative research would challenge this assumption as itself resting on a flawed positivist view of the nature of social reality.

Useful websites on sample size: http://blogs.cmdn.dundee.ac.uk/meded-research/2013/06/samplesize/
http://www.qualitative-research.net/index.php/fqs/article/view/1428/3027
http://www.quirks.com/articles/a2000/20001202.aspx

6.2.2 How many case study sites should I choose: one, two or more?

As with the question of the number of interviews, there are various factors to balance in making this decision in research which is predominantly qualitative. Many of those factors are the same or analogous to the ones set out in the sets of contrasting points in the previous question.

However because of the different level of analysis involved, there are some additional issues to think about. Yin (2009) helpfully sets out three situations in which adopting a single-site case study design would be appropriate. I have renamed the first two and extended Yin's rationales beyond the first three.

1. The 'test bed' rationale. Here a single case is chosen because it is particularly appropriate for testing different possible answers to the research questions. In other words, the site chosen has unique characteristics, and their presence means the site is a particularly good one in which to collect data for *your* research questions.
2. The 'critical case' rationale. Again, there is something special about the location, but this time because it is extreme or unusual in some way. Freud used his work with patients who had unusual conditions to develop theories about the normal. Neuroscience likewise has made discoveries about the brain's functioning by studying individuals with brain injuries.
3. The 'revelatory case' rationale. Here the single site is chosen because it has special characteristics not present anywhere else and so it can reveal new information or highlight problems or issues not so far recognised.

4. The 'second record' rationale. When you research a single site which is the institution in which you are employed or are a student you have access to the **'second record'** (Hull, 1985) and **'hidden transcripts'** (Scott, 1992). There are a number of other advantages and disadvantages to this choice.
5. The 'generative case' rationale. Here the research questions themselves emerge from studying the site.

Multiple-site case study design has advantages. They result in data which can be compared across the sites and they can allow questions to be pursued in different contexts (for example different disciplinary specialisms or different types of universities). It is sometimes possible to select case study sites as a form of natural experimental method, comparing sites which are similar except in one important respect, something that the research questions focus on. Of course it is not possible to control all variables in terms of other differences between them, but the results can be illuminative.

To repeat, there are a mix of factors to be taken into account when determining the specifics of research design, but the over-riding factor is the logic that flows from the research questions. Though these can be amended in the light of other factors that affect what is possible and desirable in research design, in the end the design must flow from the logic of the questions.

6.2.3 Can I use mixed methods?

Mixed (or multi-) methods research uses two or more data collection methods, including both quantitative and qualitative approaches. The question 'can I use both?' comes up because candidates are worried about falling into the trap of using incommensurable approaches – that is, ones which rest on contradictory assumptions about the nature of social reality (see below). However, as long as care is taken in the uses the different methods are put to, there is nothing to worry about. This is for two main reasons.

Firstly, so called 'qualitative' approaches usual have a simple quantitative element to them anyway, and always have done. Secondly mixed methods have become mainstream – there is a Sage journal called *The Journal of Mixed Methods Research*, founded in 2007. Johnson et al (2007) refer to mixed methods approaches as the 'third research methodology', one which frees research from polarized ontological and epistemological approaches. From this point of view mixed methods can liberate the researcher from the limitations of both paradigms – quantitative/positivist on the one hand and the qualitative/constructionist one on the other.

Mixed methods research can involve using different types of data sets in a variety of combinations. Data can be treated separately so that the research questions are addressed in different ways. Alternatively, both methods can be used together in a 'nested' way, with both quantitative and qualitative data collected (for example in surveys). Another alternative is to connect the approaches in a linear way with one data set building upon the findings of another. In addition, Carey (2013, 62) notes:

> [Q]ualitative data can be analysed quantitatively (such as the auditing of key word repetition) and quantitative data considered qualitatively (e.g. through the use of data in individual profiling) (Rocco et al, 2003)....[The] study can be a single design, where the qualitative and quantitative elements are completed and reported together, or a multiple design, with the phases reported separately and adding to each other as the project progresses (Creswell and Plano Clark, 2007). What is needed is something to bind all of this together. This, it can be argued, is through mixed methods research being grounded in a distinct ontological and epistemological vision.

Some writers have qualms about the use of mixed methods however (see for example Giddings and Grant, 2007). For PhD researchers the main piece of advice is to think carefully about what each approach is doing, and how they fit together. The main danger is that in using the different methods sloppily the candidate is adopting incommensurable ontological and/or epistemological positions in the way the different data types are used. This means that the fundamental assumptions about the nature of social reality shift around in the thesis, as do the assumptions about what can be known and said about that reality.

To illustrate this kind of error I will take the fictional example of a thesis that concerns student engagement amongst non-traditional students. The thesis begins by saying that previous attempts to identify the characteristics of 'non-traditional' students by age, ethnicity etc are flawed. This is because the non-traditionality is contextually contingent (what is non-traditional at Oxford and at the University of the West of Scotland is very different). But it is also at heart a **phenomenological** issue – it is about self-definition, about feelings and perceptions. If the thesis then goes on to apply quantitative methods to map different 'types' of student it would be moving into very dangerous territory, because of those earlier statements about the nature of the non-traditionality. So, mixed methods approaches need to be handled with care.

6.2.4 What are good ways of answering the 'so what?' question?

In some kinds of doctoral research there can be an issue about answering the **'so what?'** question. This can be the case where the research is predominantly evaluative – looking at the effectiveness and outcomes of a single initiative, project or approach to something. It can also be a concern in single-site research projects, perhaps an ethnography or insider research looking at a particular issue in the researcher's own higher education setting. The issue is about what the wider significance is for anyone not concerned with the project or with that institution. It's also about longevity: if the research gives a snapshot at a particular time, what is its long-term significance? Why would the readers of, say, *Studies in Higher Education* have any interest in it in five years' time?

Yin (2009) talks about "generalisation to theory" which he contrasts with any claim to generalisation to a wider population than that studied. The contribution is thus a theoretical one, developing theoretical resources for the wider academic community. This can take a number of forms, for example: testing a theoretical approach in a new situation; using data from the research site to refine a theory; deploying a theoretical perspective to illuminate what is going on (beyond the obvious) at the research site.

Another, more radical way, of looking at this is to talk about using the *sociological imagination* to look at the local in relation to broader issues. That term is C Wright Mills' and he says this about it (his ideas are worth a lengthy quote – though I have made very slight amendments to this version of the original):

> Perhaps the most fruitful distinction with which the sociological imagination works is between 'the personal troubles of milieux' and 'the public issues of social structure.' This distinction is an essential tool of the sociological imagination and a feature of all classic work in social science.
>
> *Troubles* occur within the character of the individual and within the range of his or her immediate relations with others; they have to do with one's self and with those limited areas of social life of which one is directly and personally aware. Accordingly, the statement and the resolution of troubles properly lie within the individual as a biographical entity and within the scope of one's immediate milieu - the social setting that is directly open to her personal experience and to some extent her wilful activity. A trouble is a private matter: values cherished by an individual are felt by her to be threatened.

> *Issues* have to do with matters that transcend these local environments of the individual and the range of her inner life. They have to do with the organization of many such milieux into the institutions of an historical society as a whole, with the ways in which various milieux overlap and interpenetrate to form the larger structure of social and historical life. An issue is a public matter: some value cherished by publics is felt to be threatened. Often there is a debate about what that value really is and about what it is that really threatens it. This debate is often without focus if only because it is the very nature of an issue, unlike even widespread trouble, that it cannot very well be defined in terms of the immediate and everyday environments of ordinary people. An issue, in fact, often involves a crisis in institutional arrangements, and often too it involves what Marxists call 'contradictions' or 'antagonisms.' (Mills, 1959, 8)

> The sociological imagination enables its possessor to understand the larger historical scene in terms of its meaning for the inner life and the external career of a variety of individuals...The sociological imagination enables us to grasp history and biography and the relations between the two within society. That is its task and its promise. (Mills, 1959, 5-6, adapted).

So Mills goes beyond Yin's more technicist approach, saying research can and should use insights about the way aspects social life work to address local problems. Other classic writers make the same point in different ways: Schön's discussion of the reflective practitioner (1983) stresses the significance of applying broader understanding to very particular, local, problems that are not amenable to algorithmic solutions or the application of 'best practice' learned from elsewhere.

John Dewey (1920, 169) was clearly a source for both Mills and Schön:

> But the value of ...systematization is intellectual or analytic. Classifications suggest possible traits to be on the lookout for in studying a particular case; they suggest methods of action to be tried in removing the inferred causes of ill. They are tools of insight; their value is in promoting an individualized response in the individual situation.... Generalized science provides a man as physician and artist and citizen, with questions to ask, investigations to make, and enables him to understand the meaning of what he sees.... Just in the degree in which, no matter how great his learning, he subordinates the individual case to some classification of diseases and some generic rule of treatment, he sinks to the level of the routine mechanic.

Dewey's distinction between 'mechanics' and 'artists', between simply applying ideas and categories and being creative with them, is replicated in Schön, Mills and elsewhere, although the language can change. Ball (1995) for example contrasts 'intellectuals' with 'technicians', while Schön talks not about artistry but 'reflection' and Mills about 'imagination'. Whatever the language, the general point is that the researcher should be playful, creative, imaginative. He or she should go beyond the palpable, the everyday, the immediately apparent, and look for wider significance.

So, to misuse Blake, the researcher looks for aspects of the world in a grain of sand, and uses theoretically-informed understandings about the world creatively to unpick what is happening at the granular level, and so perhaps change it.

Exactly which analytical frameworks, theoretical perspectives and conceptual categories could be fruitful depend very much on the topic of the research: this is something to discuss with your supervisor. But thinking of the research site as to some extent only the locus of research rather than its focus can shift thinking away from the particular and towards a wider view which offers answers to the question; 'so what?'

The following table summarises the different ways in which one might argue for the significance of one's research:

"So what is the wider significance of this research to the academic community generally and/or to the economy, society or culture?"

"Conceptual"
1. Contribution to an academic debate
2. Illuminates a concept
3. Brings ideas from outside the discipline to illuminate an issue within it
4. Elaborates on theory, critiques it, replaces it
5. Develops conceptual models which illuminate some aspect of social reality
6. Critiques current positions in literature, policy or practice
7. Develops new approaches to research
8. Brings together and building on previous research findings

"Applied"
1. Lessons learned of professional significance but rooted in research
2. Significance of contextual factors in shaping outcomes (in the light of previous debates)
3. Social complexities of tool use (not the tool itself)
4. Significance for policy-making or policy enactment

5. Offering new insights into significant issues relating to making a difference
6. Building a basis for new policy or practice in wider contexts
7. Offering new data which sheds light on policy – but it has to be more than just evaluation
8. Meta-analysis of previous findings for policy implications – the key thing is the analysis part, not just an overview summary

"Replication"
1. Testing previous research findings in a new context
2. Approaching questions previously addressed by other research using new methodological or new theoretical tools – or both
3. Applying an established research approach in a new area of research
4. Attempting to exactly replicate a study

6.2.5 What is the significance of ontology and epistemology?

Simply put, ontology refers to our understanding of the nature of reality, while epistemology refers to what we think we can know about reality. An ontological position might be a *foundationalist* one which sees an objective reality as existing in a palpable way. This is also sometimes called *realism*, and social realism in particular refers to a solid and very influential set of social structures which affect behaviour in important ways. An alternative ontological position is *relativism*, which sees reality as malleable, constructed and contextually contingent. This is also sometimes referred to as *constructionism*. It is important to be explicit in doctoral research about one's ontological position because it has consequences for what the research is trying to do: it might involve a search for particular regularities, the influence of social structures and so on. Alternatively the researcher might consider that to be something of a wild goose chase and instead look at contextual factors influencing behaviour and how behaviour shapes context.

Clearly, a particular ontological position will have consequences for one's epistemological position: the view what can be known about the world. For example it might be thought possible to establish law-like propositions about the world, to make large generalisations about whole populations and to design very robust research, which is replicable, to get a more and more accurate representation of reality. Such objectives would be founded in a realist ontological position. From a constructionist or relativist perspective, though, this kind of knowledge at least in the social sciences is not possible and instead research can eliminate social processes, the social construction of reality, the life-worlds of social groups and so on. From a social constructionist position interpretivism is really important: understanding the social world of research subjects. Although ideas, beliefs, assumptions and frames of reference are of course subjective, they are often real in their effects.

These distinctions also have significance for how we assess research. From a scientific or positivist point of view, founded on realism, notions such as validity and reliability are important. They ask questions about how well designed the research is in seeking to apprehend reality, and whether another researcher using the same methods would discover the same information, for example. From a phenomenological point of view these questions are not appropriate in evaluating the robustness of research because findings will be contextually and temporally contingent. Instead one should ask how convincing the research is (plausibility), how tight the rationale is for the decisions made and generally how trustworthy the research is.

So a number of polarised concepts are significant when we think about the positions we take on ontology and epistemology. These include:

agency	structure
relativism/ constructionism	realism/foundationalism
phenomenology/ interpretivism	positivism/science
voluntarism	determinism
illumination/explanation	generalization/correlation

Cohen, Manion and Morrison (2000, pp. 5-7) sum up a few of these issues:

> We can identify perspectives in social science which entail a view of human beings responding in a mechanistic or even deterministic fashion to the situations they encountered in their external world. This view tends to be one in which human beings and their experiences are regarded as products of the environment; one in which humans are conditioned by their external circumstances.

This extreme perspective can be contrasted with one which attributes to human beings a much more creative role: with a perspective where 'free will' occupies the centre stage; where man [sic] is regarded as the creator of his environment, the controller as opposed the controlled, the master rather than marionette.

In these two extreme views of the relationship between human beings and their environment, we are identifying a great philosophical debate between advocates of determinism on the one hand and voluntarism on the other. While there are social theories which adhere to each of these extremes, the assumptions of many social scientists are pitched somewhere in the range between.

One of the traps that researchers can fall into is inadvertently developing what's called *incommensurability* between their positions, so their ontological position and the epistemological position that they are adopting may be misaligned or unstable. An example of a misaligned the design would be, for example, a project which takes an ontological position which stresses the social construction of reality in local contexts, but an epistemological position which claims it is possible to generalise from the study's findings to other contexts.

What follows is an example of this from draft Ph.D, which needed to be re-written before submission to avoid the errors indicated in the sections of it quoted below.

At one place in the draft thesis the candidate says:

> ...I did not wish to limit the data to one single case study as this would offer a poor representation of the population. I believed that eight departments in total would be both sufficient and adequate coverage to meet the initial research objectives. I believed that the four case study universities, with two departments in each would enable me to make some naturalistic generalisations about the topic under exploration.

If you think about it, that kind of statement it is rooted in strongly in a realist ontological position with a corresponding epistemological one. The candidate is saying there is a reality out there and if we can establish its nature through a good robust sample then we will be able to generalise from this because it will be the same situation in other contexts.

However, towards the end of the draft thesis the candidate says this:

> [A] limitation [of this study] is the case study approach where there may be criticism that the four case study universities are not representative of the sector. I have stated elsewhere in this thesis that universities will differ depending on a number of variables such as their local community, leadership as well as their financial situation. This exploration explicitly recognises that the findings and interpretations are within the four organizational contexts and I do not attempt to make claims for other organizations. However, with this limitation in mind, I have attempted to reference the wider literature pertaining to the HE sector to highlight either linkages or variances.

So there is a feeling of apology there, but also a shift along the spectrum towards a voluntarism/constructionism perspective. Epistemologically there's been a shift. So there is something of a contradiction between those two statements. And this despite the candidate quoting from Denscombe's book (2010):

...Denscombe (2010:118) points out that realists regard the social world as existing 'out there' and having properties which can be objectively measured just like in the natural world. This ontological position fits with the quantitative research paradigm where there is great emphasis on the processes of observation and measurement in the process of building knowledge. This contrasts with the ontological position of many qualitative researchers who consider the social world to be socially constructed, in part at least, and that contextual factors locally are intimately involved in this constructive process. Knowledge about people's behaviours and understandings that is true for every context is very hard to come by, from this perspective.

The question is, then: "if this candidate believes that and is convinced by that, why apologise for it not being generalisable? Why not take on the logical corollary of the ontological and epistemological position that is being taken up in the second quote from the draft?"

Clearly this prevarication, this unstable positioning epistemologically and ontologically, has led to incommensurable perspectives on the aims and significance of the research being articulated in different places in the thesis.

6.3 Literature Review

6.3.1 How do I find relevant literature?

Nowadays there are very easy ways to find literature as bibliographical search engines have become more sophisticated and can agglomerate a number of different sources. Lancaster University library's OneSearch engine (http://tinyurl.com/m9kkaop) is an example. This largely obviates the necessity of using different databases, such as the British Education Index, the Education Resources Information Centre (ERIC) and so on. Nonetheless I have compiled some of the sources for finding literature on my research resources web page (the top left box):

http://paul-trowler.weebly.com/for-doctoral-students.html

However, while the mechanics of finding appropriate literature have got easier, the intellectual work of determining what is relevant, and what is most important remains. The twin issues of the *salience* and *significance* of areas of literature and of particular works for your research need careful thought. In order to address this you need to be clear about what the literature review is doing. Normally it will map the relevant area to date, it will critique areas of work, identify gaps in the literature and identify common themes and approaches.

The basic idea here is to *position* your own research in different ways in relation to the literature. The types of literature you look at will probably be substantive (that is, relate to the area you are studying – for example "internationalisation of higher education"), but they will also be theoretical (that is, to do with the particular lens you are adopting, theoretically, for example *actor network theory*), and they will also be methodological (to do with **phenomenography**, for example, if that is the approach you are taking). Your research questions should be the initial guide as to salient literature, but you also need to think about your research design and theoretical angle.

As to significance, you must determine which are the most important strands and pieces of literature for you. It is often a good idea to read a general overview of your area, perhaps in the introduction to a relevant edited book, a textbook or an article which maps the field. In doing this you will be looking for authors' names that are frequently repeated and particular texts that have been seminal, or perhaps a strand of work started by one person and developed by others over time. Another tool at your disposal is to look at the number of citations received by an author or by particular articles or book – Google Scholar is valuable for this (http://scholar.google.co.uk/), or the free software Publish or Perish (http://www.harzing.com/pop.htm) which uses Google Scholar data in an easily-accessible way.

In suggesting you should look for the most commonly cited works I am not suggesting you should not challenge the existing orthodoxy or the dominance of a particular approach or author in your field. On the contrary; effectively critiquing an approach that has become taken-for-granted can be a valuable contribution to the literature. However you must not be in ignorance of the tradition that has developed, and you must be able to distinguish important (in whatever sense) from less significant work.

6.3.2 What key issues are involved in literature reviews?

The first purpose of your literature review is to map the research that has already been done on your topic. You want to set out what is already known, what perspectives and approaches predominate and whether there are any gaps in the literature. You also want to know how your study will fit. Will it challenge and critique? Will it add to a tradition? Will it replicate in order to test an approach and its findings? Will it take a completely new approach? Your thesis must have a thorough grounding in what has already been done: you must be a top specialist in your own small area.

A second purpose is to assemble the *theoretical* resources that you need in order to conduct the study. This aspect of the review will explore previous elaborations of the theory and concepts are being used. Here you should set out your own definitions and accounts of issues. A common mistake is simply to describe the work of others. The point here is to **make** as well as **take** concepts, definitions, approaches.

In a section above I set out the "seven deadly sins" of literature reviews. These are common errors that doctoral candidates make. I reproduce them here:

Literature reviews: the seven deadly sins
1. There is little or no attempt to organize the literature – a 'listing' approach is taken. It is important to impose a relevant organizing schema on bodies of literature - they are usually very chaotic in their content and approaches. In order to do this a good feel for the relevant literature is necessary as it enables the categorisation of different types of work in a way which makes sense for the argument of the thesis. It is often best to start with work that itself tries to offer an overview of the literature, even with a textbook, and then work back to the specific articles and books.

2. There is little or no attempt to relate the discussion to the research questions/argument or the thesis generally. It is important to regularly show how the discussion of the literature is significant to the argument of the thesis, to tell the reader why this or that book or chapter is worth discussing, what light it sheds on the research questions being addressed by the doctoral thesis, or how it relates to them.

3. The discussion of the literature is descriptive rather than critically engaged. Make sure that the review doesn't just offer a description of the literature - this is, after all, the job of a textbook, not a postgraduate thesis. Rather it should engage in a dialogue with authors, and contrast one approach against another. The review is searching for deficiencies and strengths in the argument, areas that have not been covered, consistent bias in the approach taken as well as comparing and contrasting sets of approaches and findings.

Dunleavy (2003: 30) argues that one should beware of being too critical of existing literature for fear of raising unrealistic expectations in readers' minds about one's own contribution, and particularly in the minds of the examiners. While this is a fair warning, my own experience is that doctoral candidates generally are not critical enough. Certainly one should resist the urge to make claims about going far beyond the state reached by the current literature if such claims are not realisable. A doctorate need only make small steps into previously unknown territory, not undertake an armed invasion.

4. There is too much or too little material included. It is sometimes difficult to know what to include and exclude in the literature discussed. The key thing is to make clear decisions about this, to plan the different sections of the chapter (with word limits) and to make the rationale for those decisions explicit in the thesis. The guiding principle is alignment with the argument of the thesis. There will be areas of literature that are peripheral to that argument but still significant, and so judgement is required about how much attention to give them. One way to think about this is to remember that it is acceptable not to have a literature review chapter but instead to engage in a dialogue with the literature within other chapters (usually most significantly in the data analysis chapter and subsequently). When this route is taken it is necessary to engage with different literatures in different chapters as they become pertinent to the discussion, and thinking this through can be helpful in deciding what literature to include. In practice it is usually easier to have a separate literature review chapter, even if this gives a slightly disconnected feel to the argument as a whole.

5. Literature is selected according to criteria which are too restricted or oriented in a particular direction. Unfortunately journal articles and books are not written into neat categories and where keywords are selected, they often fail to yield comprehensive results. Thus, for the researcher seeking to review the literature in a field it can be quite tricky ensuring that all of the relevant literature has been identified. So, for example, in a review of the literature on 'student engagement' in higher education (Trowler, V. 2010) it was necessary to limit the work discussed to that which was defined *by its authors* as concerning that topic. This was because the term 'student engagement' covers a multitude of issues and practices and not setting this criterion for inclusion would have resulted in a huge review. But because authors do not necessarily tag their paper with the 'right' terms, arguably quite a bit of relevant literature was missed. The worst form of this fifth sin is to deliberately cherry-pick literature which suits the argument of the thesis, ignoring more difficult areas entirely.

6. Consistently taking an overly-critical or too-forgiving approach. Finding the right balance between recognising the strengths of previous work and being critical of deficiencies is difficult. And it can be made harder when one's own views on the topic interfere, so that some authors receive more critical fire than others simply because their position is some distance from or opposed to that of the review author. One solution to this is to ask another person who knows something about the field to assess whether this sin has been committed; and of course the doctoral supervisor is a suitable person for that task.

7. There is a disconnection between the review of the theoretical resources to be deployed, as set out in the literature review chapter, and what actually happens in the rest of thesis. Sometimes big claims are made in the literature review chapter which are not fulfilled later, either because the theoretical resource is not really applied, or is not taken as far as it could go. Another variation of this sin is to attempt to take theoretical perspectives to places they were not designed to go (for example using actor network theory in an explanatory way). My article on the relationship between theory and data (Trowler, 2012a) covers this in more detail.

To conclude: a literature review should:

1. Give an overview of the main perspectives, traditions or schools in the area (and explain why some are excluded, if they are).

2. Identify commonalities, differences and debates present in the literature.

3. Identify any gaps in the literature, including alternative perspectives or methodologies that have not been employed.

4. Explore any differences in methodological approaches found in the literature and their implications.

5. Relate the significance of the review for the topic of the thesis, and offer a position on the account of the literature, a perspective on it.

6.4 Collecting Data

6.4.1 Can I do a PhD without primary data?

Yes of course. A non-empirical PhD uses only secondary data, including the literature on the topic. It investigates an area in the same way as an empirical PhD does but is desk-based. These PhDs are often rooted in the disciplines of philosophy or history, but they can be entirely theoretical in nature, developing sociological theory for example.

Such a PhD can be more challenging because it has to meet the same criteria as an empirical one, but does so without being able to present original primary data. It usually requires the ability to handle theory adeptly, and the candidate has to become a real specialist in their chosen area in order to add something new of publishable standard.

Clearly a literature review on its own is not enough; this forms only a part of a PhD. There needs to be an additional contribution in terms of new insights, new ways of seeing an issue. Often there will be implications for practice arising from the argument in the thesis.

An example is Professor Ron Barnett's PhD thesis: *The Legitimation of Higher Education*. The abstract includes the following passages:

> Drawing on modern debates in epistemology, social theory, and the sociology of knowledge, it is argued that we cannot escape to a presuppositionless or socially independent position. The only option available is the development of critical reflection on what counts as knowledge – in short a metacritique. Higher education embodies these features: it consists of discourse about discourse. (Barnett, 1984, p. 2)

Another example is Dr. Lynn Patricia Edwards' PhD: *Women Students at The University of Liverpool: Their Academic Careers and Postgraduate Lives 1883 To 1937*. In the main this drew on historical records of different sorts. However some limited primary data were collected in the form of 30 questionnaires and 2 interviews with women to gather their recollections. Edwards writes:

> The thesis provides evidence of the students' previous schools, social class and academic success, and of the reasons to account for the withdrawal of students before the completion of their degree courses. It shows how the University served the interests of its women students in many different ways, and argues that women both made progress in academic terms, and enjoyed a harmonious relationship with their male colleagues in their social activities.

If you are thinking about doing a PhD using only, or primarily, secondary data then it is worth having a look at the British Library's Ethos database and searching for analogous ones that have been completed.

6.4.2 What is 'saturation' and how do I know when I have it?

Saturation of data has come to mean the point at which no new ideas or information emerge from the data-'gathering' process, that new respondents or other sources are simply reiterating data already 'gathered'. Having reached saturation is frequently offered as a reason to cease 'gathering' data.

However it did not originally mean this. O'Reilly and Parker (2013, p. 192) cite Green and Thorogood (2004) to show that in grounded theory it originally meant that: "categories are fully accounted for, the variability between them are explained and the relationships between them are tested and validated and thus a theory can emerge." This is at the same time a more specific and wider use than simply, essentially, "there is nothing further of any interest or value to be wrung out of this research site".

Ajjawi (2013) says the following in criticising this new and somewhat impoverished use of the term 'saturation':

> How many articles have you read that claim saturation as the defense for their sample size? I know I've made that claim in at least one of my published articles (cringe). What does it mean – that no themes 'emerge' (another pet-hate – last I checked data analysis was a very active interpretive process? but I digress) from the data. Saturation is used as a 'marker for sampling adequacy' (O'Reilly and Parker 2013). Can you achieve saturation in qualitative research? Perhaps the next person you sample would have a very different experience? Perhaps a different lens or deeper analysis could identify other understandings and meanings related to the experience?

So 'saturation' hides a particular ontological view – a **foundationalist** one which understands reality has being always amenable to capture, and accounts of it being closer or further away from accuracy. It has much in common with the idea of 'gathering' data in this respect. In many areas of social life, however, 'capturing' reality is not filmic in this way: there are multiple ways of seeing the complexity of what is going on, with multiple accounts possible of the 'same' occurrences. This, together with the Ajjawi's point that it is impossible to know that something new will not crop us, means that the notion of 'saturation' should be handled with care. Other rationales for decisions made about research design and data 'collection' are usually better than ones invoking the idea of saturation.

6.4.3 How long should semi-structured interviews last?

Generally they seem to have a natural span of between 45 and 75 minutes. This length of time is very frequently described as being the norm in doctoral and other types of research. If the interview schedule is well-constructed and the interviewer is skilful this is plenty of time to 'gather' rich data, regardless of whether the person being interviewed is being treated as an informant, a respondent or something of both. It can be quite a tiring business for the interviewer, who has to stay very focused indeed on what is being said and making moment-by-moment decisions based on continuing reflection on the schedule, the words spoken, their potential significance for the argument of the thesis and other factors.

Interview transcription is also a tiring and very lengthy process. Some estimates suggest that one hour of an interview recording takes six hours to transcribe. However sometimes it is not necessary to fully transcribe every interview (this needs to be discussed with your supervisor), and an alternative is to pay a professional to do some or all of the transcription. Again, there are issues around that which need to be discussed with your supervisor.

My own approach is to use voice recognition software such as *Dragon Naturally Speaking* and *Dragon Dictate*. At the time of writing these cannot accurately transcribe the natural speech of a recorded interview so I use the technique of **re-speaking**. This results in a written transcript produced in about double the actual length of the interview. It is far less tiring and frustrating than typing, though it takes about half an hour to get used to the technique.

6.5 Using Theory

6.5.1 Do I really need to use a theory?

The short answer is that you will be using a theory whether you recognise and acknowledge it or not, so it is better to use an explicit, carefully-considered one rather than a tacit theory that influences your thinking in an unacknowledged way.

The long answer to this and other questions about the use of theory is set out in the Section above concerning theory use. Reasons to deploy theory include the fact that, used well, it can do these things:

* Illuminate reality – showing how causal connections work and what the significance is of otherwise rather opaque phenomena.
* Bring to the surface sets of propositions and so render them amenable to critique (something not done if theory is left tacit).
* Generate hypotheses which can then guide questions, methodology and methods.
* Take research beyond what appear to be 'simply' descriptions - though even the simplest description is infused with tacit theory of a sort.
* Avoid a 'market research' approach which is rooted in one context only and describes correlations but offers no explanations.
* Help answer the 'so what?' question by adding layer to a thesis involving theory testing or theory development, beyond simply dealing with empirical results.
* Shift the level of analysis and bridge different levels of analysis, illuminating links between them.

* Link the everyday life with the broader social structures which condition it.
* Help us imagine a different world, rather than just analysing this one.

Without deploying explicit theory your thesis risks being pedestrian, descriptive, empiricist and contextually-bound.

6.5.2 How do I choose which theory to use?

Fundamentally the answer to this, like the answer to the question 'should I use a qualitative or a quantitative approach?' lies in your research questions.

Theory may *drive* your research questions, and in that case you begin with questions about theory which lead to the development of your research questions. So your research may be motivated to challenge an existing theory or to see whether it applies in a context where it has never been applied before. One of my research students looked at the theory of Organizational Citizenship Behaviour (OCB), critiquing many aspects of the way it has developed and been applied in the literature to date. Secondly, she researched the extent to which any redeeming features apply and are useful in a further education context.

More usually however doctoral research begins with primarily substantive issues which need a theoretical lens to avoid being simply descriptive and contextually-bound.

Another of my students wanted to evaluate an organization with significant policy-making powers in the area of higher education in her country. Of course such an evaluation alone would not be suitable for a PhD – it would only be of interest to that organization, and it would be a snapshot in time; probably out of date as soon as the thesis was ready. What concepts and theory could be brought to bear to lift it from that state? Together we concluded that the literature around learning organizations and organizational learning could have considerable purchase in this research, offering a set of conceptual tools around which data-gathering could be aligned. This led to a reformulation of the initial set of research questions to address issues raised in those twinned literatures. Later, as the research progressed, it became clear that the management literature around 'followership' (as distinct from 'leadership') would also be of value, as would macro social theory around social practices. Together these offered a valuable lens for looking at that single organization and added value to the thesis, giving it a clear answer to the 'so what?' question.

That case illustrates a recurrent sequence in doctoral research:

1. An initial broad idea or motivating question that in itself leads to research questions which are not-quite-adequate at the doctoral level.
2. Reflection on what research design flows out of those research questions and what kinds of data that design would provide.
3. Development of the research questions via the injection of theoretical and conceptual sophistication in order to make the data do more 'work'.
4. Revisions to draft data collection instruments and perhaps research design in the light of these changes.

Sometimes (more rarely) the decision is made about an appropriate theoretical lens only once data have been collected. There can be good reasons for approaching it this way, though it is a higher-risk approach. Grounded theory approaches of different sorts (but not all of them) do this explicitly.

It is impossible to provide a list of the theoretical resources available to you from which you could choose: that list would be different for different broad topics and trying to cover and explain everything would necessitate a multi-volume encyclopaedia (this Cmap tool illustrates the scope of the problem just in terms of learning theories: http://cmapspublic3.ihmc.us/rid=1LGVGJY66-CCD5CZ-12G3/Learning%20Theory.cmap).

There would be theories about the operation of capitalism to theories about personal and professional identity. And there would be learning theories to theories about the behaviour of organizations. And again, there would be theories about the nature of social reality to theories of gender inequalities. In addition there would need to be theories about discourse to theories about disciplinary differences, marketing theory to theories of media effects…and so on, pretty much *ad infinitum*. Your supervisor is the first contact to help you think about what is right for your research. The second is the relevant literature in your field and the theoretical and conceptual resources being brought to bear there. This latter is a starting point rather than an answer, however: as noted above it is often beneficial to depart from dominant approaches altogether.

6.6 Writing the Thesis

6.6.1 Should I use "I" when writing about the research?

The short answer is yes.

The long answer is that to do otherwise is usually an attempt to hide the subjectivity of the writer. The more sophisticated way of hiding yourself is to use the passive voice throughout the thesis to the complete exclusion of any reference to your agency, decisions and so on (as in: "were interviewed"; "were identified"; "were encouraged" etc). The less sophisticated way is to retreat to a meta-level, commenting on actions and choices as if they were not yours but those of some un-named other (as in: "the author took the step of"; "the researcher selected"; "on the basis of the evidence, this author answers"). This is worse because it not only tries to hide the subjectivity of the writer in plain sight, but is stylistically pretty clunky.

It was originally feminist writers who insisted on the unapologetic insertion of the writer into the text, pointing out that the 'godlike' voice of the invisible author was usually a male voice inserting a gendered perspective on research, an androcentric one, as if it were unchallengeable. Some took the further step of adding a second layer to the text, revealing the 'workings' so to speak; the viewpoint of the author on the issues in the text in the writing of it and in the research underpinning it.

This second text revealed the author's feelings, decisions, challenges, sometimes ambivalence and insecurities. Feminist standpoint theory took this further, situating the different standpoints of the researcher and the researched, of men and women, as meaning that research must be grounded in the lives of those involved. With these **epistemological** insights 'the author' had become an intimate part of the text, empowering the reader to approach it with new perspectives and insights.

There was a further impetus to the move away from the impersonal in academic texts in social science; its 'discursive turn'. This turn marked a recognition that talk, writing and production of 'text' (broadly understood) are highly significant social actions in themselves. Talk is not 'just talk', it is a framing of the world, an articulation of a hegemonic world view as well as potentially a reconstruction of that. The text scripts the speaker as well as the converse, in a strong version of this. Following this social science turn, the production of text of any sort became highly significant.

> [T]here is always a sense in which both the researcher and the research participant are "being had" - in which they are made captive to the story line, the expression, the images, the metaphors, the emotions that rise up in the telling, in the writing, and in the listening (Davies and Davies, 2007, p. 1141).

Many social scientists, including non-feminists and those critical of standpoint theory, took the point and changed their writing practices. There are exceptions, including some researchers who primarily deploy quantitative approaches and those located in traditions untouched by this insight.

However for the doctoral researcher there is a clear rationale available for the insertion of the 'I' in the thesis, should it be challenged. You can find further comments on this in my account of being special editor of a journal number where this issue became a major point of contention: https://www.academia.edu/15238501/Paul_Trowler_s_Introduction_to_HEQ_Special_Number_from_HECU7_The_excised_parts.

6.6.2 What structure should a programme's assignments take?

Every taught doctoral programme will have different assignment tasks and different assessment criteria. On the Higher Education Research, Evaluation and Enhancement (HEREE) PhD programme at Lancaster the three main assignments essentially involve writing a 7,000-8,000 word equivalent to a journal article. Some candidates assume that there needs to be a formal structure, perhaps one like this:

- Introduction
- Literature Review
- Research Methodology and Ethical Issues
- Findings and analysis
- Conclusion

However there is no formal requirement of this sort because different journals and different academic articles have different structures. To have a formal literature review, as a thesis often does, would be too costly in terms of word-count.

Similarly any discussion of methodology and ethics needs to be very brief and designed to give the reader a quick overview of what was done so that they can make a number of judgements about the piece. The key thing in a journal article, and hence the HEREE assignments, is to give the reader an early overview of what you are about, including research questions, to get quickly to the point, to present the data (if any) and make the argument. The criteria on that programme concern the coherence of the assignment and the quality of the research, not the structure of the paper.

However, common errors in doctoral do involve issues about the way the paper is structured. They include:

1. Not giving the reader enough information at the beginning about what the assignment is about and so what the significance is of early contextual descriptions.
2. Related to this: presenting the research questions several pages into the assignment rather than at the beginning.
3. Treating the abstract as an introduction rather than ignoring it in the assignment itself.
4. Not signposting the structure of the chapter by making clear links in the argument, using headings and so on.
5. Not telling the reader how different parts of the discussion relate to the research question.
6. Writing a conclusion which is nothing more than a précis of what has gone before rather than encapsulating the key contribution of the assignment and its findings.

6.7 Examiners Examining

6.7.1 How can I know whether my thesis is ready to submit?

Your supervisor will give you advice about this. However your opinion may be different from the advice you get. Leonardo da Vinci is quoted as saying that "art is never finished, only abandoned", and the same is true of a thesis. Usually the candidate feels that it is not quite perfect; there is a constant nagging feeling that various things about it could be improved. If you really can't bring yourself to 'abandon' it, then you do need advice from someone with experience to tell you whether it is at the stage to submit.

More rarely candidates feel that it is definitely ready to go when actually major issues remain to be addressed. In the UK, at least, it is normally the candidate's decision as to when they submit. There are rumours that some institutions and departments accede to this, hoping that the examiners will give detailed advice and so provide a quick route to completion. However this is both dangerous and unethical: dangerous because they may simply fail the candidate, unethical because it turns to the examiners into supervisors: this is not their role and not what they agreed to.

Before you ask your supervisor whether your thesis is ready to submit you should address the questions in the next section (7.2), slightly rephrased:

* Have I made it clear why this is a significant-enough topic for a PhD, and is my argument for this convincing?

* Do the data, as presented and analysed, properly link to my answers to the research questions? Are those questions comprehensively answered?

* Have I given the examiners a good-enough overview of the thesis and insight into the details of the research so that they can make informed judgements about robustness, absence of bias and so on?

* Have I engaged with the literature in a critical, constructive way and is my account comprehensive and adequate?

* Have I applied, developed or tested theory in a way which adds value to the thesis?

* Does the thesis hang together as a whole – are its different parts well-articulated?

* Have I provided an adequate rationale given for the choices made and the options rejected?

* Have I avoided the trap of having incommensurable ontological and epistemological positions?

* Are my conclusions convincingly robust?

* Have I made claims for the significance of the thesis that I can defend?

* Are my findings significant enough to be publishable in that they add something valuable to what is already known?

6.7.2 What are the key things examiners will be looking for?

In the Section above about thesis structure, content and completion I quoted from empirical research into this question by Trafford and Leshem (2002), and I suggested some additional items. I won't repeated that here, but will indicate that the following are key issues that often come up when examiners consider a thesis on higher education:

* Is this a significant-enough topic for a PhD? (Does it go beyond just local interest in a single institution, for example, and is it more than just a one-off evaluative or action-research study?)

* Is the research design appropriate and adequate to answer the research questions?

* Are we, the examiners, given a good-enough overview of the thesis and insight into the details of the research to be able to make informed judgements about robustness, absence of bias and so on?

* Does the way the literature is addressed involve engagement, critique and use rather than just description?

* Is theory applied, developed or tested in a way which adds value to the thesis?

* Does the thesis hang together as a whole – are its different parts well-articulated?

* Where critical decisions have been made about methodology, the parameters of the study and so on, is an adequate rationale given for the choices made and the options rejected?

* Is there alignment between the ontological and epistemological positions of the candidate, on the one hand, and the way s/he uses data and the claims s/he makes about them, on the other?

* How robust is the thesis? How can we, the examiners, be confident that the conclusions have been arrived at in a reliable way?

* How far does the thesis claim its findings can stretch – and is that claim sustainable?

* Are the findings significant enough to be publishable in that they add something valuable to what is already known?

6.7.2 How can I convince examiners that my research is robust?

"Robust" here means a number of things:

1. That the research is comprehensive in terms of the literature it has taken into account – there are no gaps left which mean that the thesis only partially covers its topic and so is weak.
2. That the logic of the argument is free from one-sidedness or tendentiousness – the thesis has not taken a skewed direction because of **cognitive closure**.

3. That the design has resulted in data which are appropriate, adequate and trustworthy – that the data themselves are strong enough to be the foundation of answers to the research questions.

4. That the process of data analysis, which involves reducing and organizing the raw data, has retained their significance – that there has been no loss of significant results through a sloppy, partial or one-sided analytical approach.

5. That the conclusions are well-founded in the data and argument – that what is said does not stray beyond what can be said from the evidence and argument presented.

Examiners will certainly be evaluating how successful you have been in establishing and applying appropriate criteria for reliability in your research. In a predominantly statistical study there are well-discussed ways of establishing degrees of confidence, touched on in Section 2 above. In qualitative research there is much discussion in the textbooks about the different ways of establishing validity and reliability. You certainly need to be familiar with these and to decide, and give a rationale for, which you have decided to apply.

As noted above, one error that is sometimes made by doctoral candidates is to apply approaches to reliability that are incommensurable with the overall ontological and epistemological approach of the thesis. For example the concepts of validity and reliability themselves derive from a positivist ontological and epistemological position – one which considers it possible for research to get closer or further away from an 'accurate' account of reality.

So 'reliability' is often used to mean stability of results across different cases or when different researchers investigate exactly the same phenomenon. But a constructionist view of reality would challenge whether this: different cases involve different realities and are never 'the same' in social life. And reality can be perceived and described in multiple ways, from multiple perspectives, so it is inevitable that there will be different accounts. Some years ago a special number of the *Journal of Contemporary Ethnology* in 1992 explored this in depth using one example, Whyte's *Street Corner Society* (1943)– an ethnographic study of 'Cornerville'. Denzin (1992) and Troyna (1994) comment on the ontological issues involved and show how debates about whether Whyte's account of Cornerville was "accurate" or not are fruitless because they are rooted in a foundationalist ontology which does not apply.

Meanwhile "validity" is often used to refer to the robustness of the data collection approaches in measuring what is claimed to be measured. There is a lack of validity, for example, if respondents and researchers are using different conceptual categories, interpretations and meanings around what they are discussing. This raises numerous questions about the mutuality of meanings generally. These issues mean that it is really important to consider the congruence between the ontological and epistemological position taken in the research and the guarantees of robustness offered. Qualitative researchers often reject notions of reliability and validity and move instead to ideas like 'trustworthiness', 'robustness', 'credibility' or 'dependability'.

In the UK the viva examination is very important in convincing examiners that your work is robust. In preparing for the viva it is a really good idea to think carefully about the five bullet points above: the different dimensions of robustness. Practise talking around each one in a way that convincingly shows your work is free from the potential weaknesses in each.

6.8 The Viva Experience (in the UK)

6.8.1 What is likely to happen in the viva?

Though the details vary from university to university in the UK, the procedure for the viva is usually something like this:

1. Supervisor and candidate discuss possible internal and external examiners and settle on one or more options for each. The supervisor approaches them informally.
2. The two examiners (sometimes more for internal candidates and other cases) are formally appointed.
3. They each write a pre-viva report based on their reading of the thesis, usually with some guidance from the university as to headings they should write to. This must be done independently of each other, usually, and they are often asked to say at this stage what the expected outcome might be.
4. On the day of the viva the examiners meet and share their pre-viva reports. They spend around an hour discussing their views and constructing an agenda for the viva, including a likely sequence of questions and which of them should lead on successive areas of questioning.
5. The candidate and supervisor (the latter in a non-speaking role) are invited into the examination room. After introductions the chair (if there is one) sets out what will happen and what the broad agenda will be. They will usually spell out what the range of possible outcomes is.
6. The viva proper will usually begin with a broad question to the candidate to allow them to settle and to talk in general terms about the research and the thesis. After that the sequence of detailed questions begins.
7. Likely broad areas of questioning are as follows (see also Section 7.2, above):

a. Conceptualisation of the project – theories and concepts deployed.
b. Research design.
c. Research methodology.
d. Research methods.
e. Sampling.
f. Conceptual and other conclusions.
g. Issues around robustness of the thesis.
h. The contribution made by the thesis.
i. The roads not travelled and the areas that would be addressed differently if done again.

8. At the end of the viva the candidate is usually asked if they have any comments, questions or additional points they wish to make. Candidate and supervisor are then asked to leave the room.

9. At this point the examiners confer about their evaluation of the defence of the thesis given by the candidate and the extent to which s/he addressed the issues they raised. They decide on the outcome and the feedback to be given.

10. The candidate and supervisor are invited back into the examination room and the outcome is communicated verbally, as well as an outline of further work to be done on the thesis, if any. The supervisor takes notes at this point for the subsequent discussion with the candidate, if needed.

11. The outcome and any requirements are communicated in writing at a later point to both supervisor and candidate as well as being officially recorded by the university.

6.9 Post-Award

6.9.1 Should I accept a publisher's approach to publish my thesis?

Usually the answer is no. Think of the difference between being cold-called by someone wanting you to buy shares in a bargain company and going to a reputable financial adviser to help you decide where to invest. There are very many 'publishers' whose aim is simply to charge people for 'publishing' their work, though some may hope to accidentally discover a best-selling author too. The 'publishing' that happens, if any, has no value and is not underpinned by any marketing or distribution networks. These are 'predatory publishers' (or, 'sham publishers') and their journals and company names usually sound very reputable and often extremely similar to real publishers and journals.

There is a list of predatory publishers in Beall's list: http://scholarlyoa.com/publishers/. Beall's list also offers advice to those considering a publisher.

6.9.2 To which journals should I submit articles from my thesis?

In making this decision you need to bear two important criteria in mind:

1. **Alignment of your topic to the interests of the journal.** Here you can look again at the journals that are most frequently cited in your thesis, and the journals used by the main authors you have drawn from. Look at journal websites to read the description of what their field of interest is, but pay at least as much attention to the topics of the articles actually published.

2. **How confident you are in the quality of your article**. Some journals are extremely selective, others are less so. Generally the value of getting published is proportional to the selectivity of the journal and the rigour of its peer review process. This selectivity and rigour is indirectly related to the esteem in which the journal is held, though some low-esteem journals are extremely rigorous. How can you judge the extent of selectivity, rigour and esteem of a journal? The answer is "only indirectly" – and the indirect measure is the citation index of the journal. This is measured in different ways and over different time periods, but the easiest way to do it using Publish or Perish software: http://www.harzing.com/pop.htm.

Click on 'journal impact' on the left hand side and then type in the names of some journals you are considering. The higher their H index, the more likely they are to be selective, rigorous and of high esteem. But remember, this is only an indirect measure. Another way to find the esteem of general education journals (i.e. not specialising in higher education) is to go here: http://www.scimagojr.com/journalrank.php?category=3304.

The work of finding citation indices of different journals has been done by others and summarised on this page. Several other websites do this sort of thing – to find them type "rank of education journals" into Google.

One tactic is to submit first to a highly esteemed journal and then work your way down the rank order until one accepts your article. This is, however, an extremely slow and potentially dispiriting process. It is usually better to aim your first article somewhere in the middle or lower ranked journals and aim higher for subsequent ones.

Don't forget that there are frequently calls for special numbers of journals focused on a particular topic. You have a better chance of publication there if your subject is on-topic. Publishers' email alerts will let you know when relevant journals have special calls. Similarly special journal numbers or edited books on a theme arising from a conference are fairly good bets when your piece is on-topic. Conference symposia are much easier to get into but have limited value in terms of appointments, promotions or (in practice if not in theory) the UK research exercises.

A list of relevant journals (in no particular order) is available on this web page (the lower right hand box):
http://paul-trowler.weebly.com/for-doctoral-students.html
This is not comprehensive, however. The best place to look is in the references of your own thesis.

References

Abell, P. & Reyniers, D. (2000) Review Article: On the failure of social theory. *British Journal of Sociology*, 51, 4, 739-750.

Abes, E. S. (2009) Theoretical Borderlands: Using Multiple Theoretical Perspectives to Challenge Inequitable Power Structures in Student Development Theory. *Journal of College Student Development*. 50, 2, 141-156.

Abes, E. S. (2012) Constructivist and Intersectional Interpretations of a Lesbian College Student's Multiple Social Identities. *The Journal of Higher Education*. 83, 2, 186-216.

Adams, C. (2006) Powerpoint, Habits of Mind and Classroom Culture. *Journal of Curriculum Studies,* 38, 4, 389-411.

Adams, J., Cochrane, M. & Dunne, L. (2011) *Applying Theory to Educational Research: An introductory approach with case studies*. London: John Wiley & Sons.

Adler, P. A., Adler, P. and Johnson, J. M. (1992) Street Corner Society Revisited: New Questions About Old Issues. *Journal of Contemporary Ethnology*. 21, 3-10.

Ajjawi, R. (2013) *Sample Size in Qualitative Research*. Medical Education Research Network. http://blogs.cmdn.dundee.ac.uk/mededresearch/2013/06/samplesize/.

Allen, B. J. (1996) Feminist Standpoint Theory: A black woman's review of organizational socialization. *Communication Studies*. 47, 4, 257–271.

Altbach, P. G. And Rapple, B. (2012) Anarchy, Commercialism, and "Publish or Perish". *International Higher Education*. 67, 5-7. http://www.bc.edu/content/dam/files/research_sites/cihe/pdf/IHEpdfs/ihe67.pdf

Alvesson, M. (2002) *Understanding Organizational Culture*. London: Sage.

Anderson, G. L. and Jones, F. (2000) Knowledge Generation In Educational Administration From The Inside Out: The promise and perils of site-based, administrator research, *Educational Administration Quarterly,* 36, 3, 428–464.

Andreski, S. (1972) *Social Sciences as Sorcery.* London: Deutsch.

Anyon, J. (2009) Introduction. In Anyon, J., Dumas, M. J., Linville, D., Nolan, D., Perez, M., Tuck, E. & Weiss, J. (2009), *Theory and Educational Research: Toward critical social explanation.* New York and London: Routledge. Pp-pp 1-23.

Anyon, J., Dumas, M. J., Linville, D., Nolan, D., Perez, M., Tuck, E. & Weiss, J. (2009), *Theory and Educational Research: Toward critical social explanation.* New York and London: Routledge.

Archer, M. (2000) *Being Human: The problem of agency,* Cambridge University Press, Cambridge.

Archer, M. (2007) *Making Our Way Through the World.* Cambridge: Cambridge University Press.

Arum, A. and Roksa, J. (2011) *Academically Adrift: Limited learning on college campuses.* Chicago: University of Chicago Press.

Ashwin, P. (2013) How Often Are Theories Developed Through Empirical Research into Higher Education? *Studies in Higher Education* 38, 1, 1-15.

Ashwin, P. (2009) *Analysing Teaching-Learning Interactions in Higher Education: Accounting for structure and agency.* London: Continuum.

Astin, A. (2011) In 'Academically Adrift,' Data Don't Back Up Sweeping Claim. *The Chronicle of Higher Education*, February 14. Available at: http://chronicle.com/article/Academically-Adrift-a/126371/

Backhouse, J. P. (2009) *Doctoral Education in South Africa: Models, pedagogies and student experiences.* Johannesburg: University of Witwatersrand. https://www.academia.edu/820332/Doctoral_education_in_South_Africa_Models_pedagogies_and_student_experiences

Bailey, F. G. (1977) *Morality and Expediency.* London: Blackwell.

Baker, S. E. and Edwards, R. (2012) *How many qualitative interviews is enough? Expert voices and early career reflections on sampling and cases in qualitative research.* National Centre for Research Methods Review Paper. http://eprints.ncrm.ac.uk/2273/4/how_many_interviews.pdf

Ball, S. J. (1995) Intellectuals or Technicians? The urgent role of theory in educational studies. *British Journal of Educational Studies*, 43, 255-271.

Ball, S. J. (2006) *Education Policy and Social Class: The selected works of Stephen J Ball.* London and New York: Taylor and Francis.

Bamber, V., Trowler, P., Saunders, M. and Knight, P. (eds) (2009) *Enhancing Learning, Teaching, Assessment and Curriculum in Higher Education: theories within practices.* Open University Press/SRHE.

Barnes, B. (2001) Practice as Collective Action. In T. Schatzki, K. Knorr Cetina K,. and E. Von Savigny, (eds) *The Practice Turn in Contemporary Theory.* London: Routledge. Pp. 25-36.

Barnett, R. (1984) *The Legitimation of Higher Education.* PhD Thesis, University of London.

Bassey, M. (1999) *Case Study Research in Educational Settings.* Oxford: Oxford University Press.

Bassey, M. (2000) *Fuzzy Generalisations and Best Estimates of Trustworthiness: A step towards transforming research knowledge about learning into effective teaching practice.* http://www.tlrp.org/pub/acadpub/Bassey2000.pdf

Bassey, M. (2001) A Solution To The Problem Of Generalization In Educational Research: Empirical findings and fuzzy predictions. *Oxford Review of Education*, 27, 1, 5-22.

Becher, T. (1988) Principles and Politics: An interpretative framework for university management. In A. Westoby (ed). *Culture and Power in Educational Organizations.* Buckingham: Open University Press/SRHE, 317-328.

Becher, T. (1989) *Academic Tribes and Territories: Intellectual enquiry and the cultures of disciplines*. Buckingham: Open University Press/SRHE.

Bell, J. (1999, 3e) *Doing Your Research Project*. London: Open University Press.

Bensimon, E. M., Polkinghorne, D.E., Bauman, G. & Vallejo, E. (2004) Doing Research that Makes a Difference. *The Journal of Higher Education,* 75, 1, 104-126.

Bergquist, W. H. (2008) *Engaging the Six Cultures of the Academy: Revised and expanded edition of The four cultures of the academy*. San Francisco: Jossey-Bass.

Bernstein, B. (1971) On the Classification and Framing of Educational Knowledge. In Young, F.D. (ed.) *Knowledge and Control: New directions for the sociology of education*. London: Collier-MacMillan, pp47-69.

Bernstein, B. (1999) Vertical and horizontal discourse: an essay, *British Journal of Sociology of Education*, 20, pp. 157-173.

Bernstein, B. (2000) *Pedagogy, Symbolic Control and Identity: Theory, research and critique*. Revised Edition. Oxford: Rowman and Littlefield Publishers.

Beverungen, A., Böhm, S. and Land, C. (2012) The Poverty of Journal Publishing. *Organization.* 19, 6, 929–938.

Blackler, F. (1995) Knowledge, Knowledge Work And Organizations: An overview and interpretation. *Organization Studies* 16, 6, 1021-1046.

Bore, A. & Wright, N. (2009) The Wicked and Complex in Education: Developing a transdisciplinary perspective for policy formulation, implementation and professional practice. *Journal of Education for Teaching*, 35, 3, 241-256.

Bourdieu, P. (1990) *The Logic of Practice*. Cambridge: Polity Press.

Bourdieu, P. (2000) *Pascalian Meditations*. Translated by R. Nice. Cambridge: Polity Press.

Broussine, M. (2008) *Creative Methods in Organizational Research*. London: Sage

Brown, A. (2006) Languages of Description and The Education of Researchers. In R. Moore, M. Arnot, J. Beck, & H. Daniels (eds) *Knowledge, Power and Educational Reform: Applying the sociology of Basil Bernstein*. London: Routledge.

Buchanan, D. and Bryman, A. (eds) (2009) *The Sage Handbook of Organizational Research Methods*. London: Sage.

Burawoy, M. (1998) The Extended Case Method. *Sociological Theory*, 16, 1, 44-33.

Carey, P. (2013) *Student Engagement in University Decision-Making:Policies, Processes and the Student Voice*. PhD, Lancaster University. Available at: http://eprints.lancs.ac.uk/67667/.

Carter, J. (2004) Research Notes: Reflections on interviewing across the ethnic divide. *International Journal of Social Research Methodology*, 7,4, 345-353.

Castells, M. (2000) The Rise of the Network Society: Economy, society and culture v.1 London: WileyBlackwell.

Charmaz, K. (2000) *Constructing Grounded Theory: A Practical Guide Through Qualitative Analysis*. Thousand Oaks, CA: Sage.

Clark, B. (1987) *The Academic Life: Small worlds, different worlds*. The Carnegie Foundation for the Advancement of Teaching, Princeton.

Clegg, S. (2007) Extending the Boundaries of Research into Higher Education. In *Enhancing Higher Education, Theory and Scholarship, Proceedings of the 30th HERDSA Annual Conference*, Adelaide, 8-11 July 2007: pp 10.

Coghlan, D and Brannick, T. (2010) *Doing Action Research in Your Own Organization*. (3rd edition). London: Sage.

Cohen, L. Manion, L. and Morrison, K. (2011) *Research Methods in Education*. (7th edition). London: Routledge.

Cohen, L., Manion, L. and Morrison, K. (2000) *Research Methods in Education*. London: RoutledgeFalmer.

Coleman, S. and von Hellermann, P. (2011) *Multi-Sited Ethnography: Problems and possibilities in the translocation of research methods*. London: Routledge.

Cooperrider, D. L. and Srivastva, S. *(1987)* Appreciative Inquiry in Organizational Life. *Research in Organizational Change and Development,* 1, 129-169.

Costley, C., Elliott, G. and Gibbs, P. (2010) *Doing Work Based Research.* London: Sage.

Creswell, J.W. & Plano Clark, V.L. (2007) *Designing and Conducting Mixed Methods Research.* Thousand Oaks, CA.: Sage.

Dale, R. (1989) *The State and Education Policy.* Buckingham: Open University Press.

Dale, R. (1992) Recovering from a Pyrrhic Victory? In M. Arnot and L. Barton, (1992) (eds) *Voicing Concerns: Sociological perspectives on contemporary education reforms.* Wallingford, Oxfordshire: Triangle.

Davies, B. and Davies, C. (2007) Having, And Being Had By, "Experience". Or, Experience in the Social Sciences After the Discursive/Poststructuralist Turn. *Qualitative Inquiry.* 13, 1139-1159.

De Certeau, M. (1984) *The Practice of Everyday Life.* Berkeley: University of California Press.

Delamont, S. (2002) *Fieldwork in Educational Settings: Methods, pitfalls and procedures,* Falmer: London, (Second, expanded edition 2002).

Deming, W. E. (1993) *The New Economics for Industry, Government, Education.* Cambridge, MA: MIT Centre for Advanced Engineering Studies.

Denscombe, M. (2010) *Ground Rules for Social Research.* London: Open University Press.

Denzin, (1992) Whose Cornerville is it Anyway? *Journal of Contemporary Ethnology.* 21, 120-132.

DePaolo, P. (nd) *Sample Size for Qualitative Research.* Quirks Marketing Research Media. http://www.quirks.com/articles/a2000/20001202.aspx

Devault, M. L. (2006) What is Institutional Ethnography? *Social Problems*, 53, 3, 294-298.

Dewey, J. (1920) *Reconstruction in Philosophy*. New York: Henry Holt. http://archive.org/stream/reconstructionin00deweuoft/reconstructionin00deweuoft_djvu.txt

Dimitriadis, G. (2009) Series Editor's Introduction. Anyon, J. et al, *Theory and Educational Research: toward critical social explanation*. New York and London: Routledge.

Dobson, I. (2009) The Journal of Higher Education Policy and Management: An output analysis. *Journal of Higher Education Policy and Management*, 3, 1, 3-15.

Drake, P. and Heath, L. (2011) *Practitioner Research at Doctoral Level: Developing coherent research methodologies*. London: Routledge.

Dressman, M. (2008) *Using Social Theory in Educational Research: A practical guide*. London: Taylor & Francis.

Dunleavy, P. (2003) *Authoring a PhD: How to plan, draft, write and finish a doctoral thesis or dissertation*. London: Palgrave.

Edwards, L. P. (1999) *Women Students at The University of Liverpool: Their Academic Careers and Postgraduate Lives 1883 To 1937*. PhD Thesis, University of Liverpool.

Eraut, M. (2000) Non-Formal Learning and Tacit Knowledge in Professional Work. *British Journal of Educational Psychology*, 7, 1, 113-136.

Ezzy, D. (2002) *Qualitative Analysis: Practice and innovation*. London: Routledge

Fenwick, T., Edwards, R. & Sawchuk, P. (2011) *Emerging Approaches to Educational Research: Tracing the socio-material*. London: Routledge.

Fetterman, D. M. (1989) *Ethnography Step by Step*. Beverley Hills: Sage.

Fine, M. (2009) Epilogue. In Anyon, J., Dumas, M. J., Linville, D., Nolan, D., Perez, M., Tuck, E. & Weiss, J. (2009) (eds), *Theory and Educational Research: Toward critical social explanation*. New York and London: Routledge. pp-pp 179-196.

Flyvbjerg, B. (2006) Five Misunderstandings About Case-Study Research. *Qualitative Inquiry*, 12, 2, 219-245.

Foreman-Peck, L. and Winch, C. (2010) *Using Educational Research to Inform Practice: A Practical Guide to Practitioner Research in Universities and Colleges.* London: Routledge.

Foucault, M. (1977) *Language, Counter-Memory, Practice: Selected interviews and essays.* Edited by D. F. Bouchard. New York: Cornell University Press.

Foucault, M. (1984) *Le souci de soi. L'histoire de la sexualité,* Vol. III. Paris: Gallimard.

Fox, N. Hunn, A. and Mathers, N. (2009) *Sampling and Sample Size Calculation.* The NIHR RDS for East Midlands and the NIHR RDS for Yorkshire and the Humber http://rds-eastmidlands.nihr.ac.uk/resources/doc_download/9-sampling-and-sample-size-calculation.html

Geertz, C. (1973) *The Interpretation of Cultures: Selected essays.* New York: Basic Books

Giddens, A. (1979) *Central Problems in Social Theory. Action, structure and contradiction in social analysis.* London: Macmillan.

Giddens, A. (1984) *The Constitution of Society.* Cambridge: Polity Press.

Giddings, L.S. & Grant, B.M. (2007) A Trojan Horse For Positivism?: A critique of mixed methods research. *Advances in nursing science, 30,* 1, 52-60.

Glaser, B. G. & A. L. Strauss (1967) *The Discovery of Grounded Theory.* Chicago: Aldine Publishing.

Glover, J. (2011) What is the Government's 'Nudge Unit'? The work of the Behavioural Insights Team is one of the under-discussed elements of creative coalition thinking. http://www.guardian.co.uk/commentisfree/2011/sep/19/government-nudge-unit-behavioural-insights-team

Goffman, E. (1959) *The Presentation of Self in Everyday Life.* New York: Doubleday.

Gomm, R., Hammersley, M. and Foster, P. (2000) *Case Study Method.* London: Sage.

Gouldner, A. (1970) *The Coming Crisis of Western Sociology.* New York: Avon.

Green, J. and Thorogood, N. (2004) *Qualitative Methods for Health Research*. London: Sage.

Greene, J. C. (2008) Is Mixed Methods Social Inquiry a Distinctive Methodology? *Journal of Mixed Methods Research*. 2, 7-22.

Halse, C. and Honey, A. (2007) Rethinking Ethics Review as Institutional Discourse. *Qualitative Inquiry*, 13, 3, 336-352.

Hammersley, M. (1993) On The Teacher As Researcher. In M. Hammersley (ed) *Educational Research: Current issues*. Buckingham: Open University Press.

Hammersley, M. (2001) On Michael Bassey's Concept Of Fuzzy Generalisation. *Oxford Review of Education*, 27, 2, 219-225.

Haraway, D. J. (1991) *Simians, Cyborgs and Women: The reinvention of nature*. New York: Routledge.

Harding, S. (1987) *Feminism and Methodology: Social science issues*. Bloomington: Indiana University Press.

Harman, G. (2009) *Prince of Networks: Bruno Latour and metaphysics*. Available at http://re-press.org/books/prince-of-networks-bruno-latour-and-metaphysics/

Harvie, D., Lightfoot, G., Lilley, S. and Weir, K. (2012) What Are We To Do With Feral Publishers? *Organization*. 19, 6, 905–914.

Hayward, C.R. (2000) *De-facing Power*. Cambridge: Cambridge University Press.

Hesse-Beber, S. (Ed.) (2012) *Handbook of Feminist Research*. London: Sage. Second edition.

Hesse-Biber, S. N., & Leavy, P. (2006) *The Practice of Qualitative Research*. Thousand Oaks, CA: Sage.

Hey, V. (2006) The Politics of Performative Resignification: Translating Judith Butler's theoretical discourse and its potential for a sociology of education, *British Journal of Sociology of Education*, 27, 4, 439-457.

Hirsch, E. D. (1976) *The Aims of Interpretation*. Chicago, University of Chicago Press.

Hockey, J. (1993) Research Methods: Researching peers and familiar settings, *Research Papers in Education*, 8, 2, 199-225.

Homan, R. (1991) *The Ethics of Social Research*. London: Longman.

Horsburgh, D. (2003) Evaluation of Qualitative Research. *Journal of Clinical Nursing*, 12, 307-312. http://www.fctl.ucf.edu/ResearchAndScholarship/SoTL/creatingSoTLProjects/implementingmanaging/content/evaluation%20of%20qualitative%20research.pdf

Huisman, J. (2008) Higher Education Policy: The evolution of a journal. *Higher Education Policy*, 21, 2, 265-274.

Hull, C. (1985) Between the Lines: The analysis of interview data as an exact art. *British Education Research Journal*, 11, 1, 27-32.

Irving, C. (2012) *Leadership in Higher Education: A Longitudinal Study of Local Leadership for Enhancing Learning and Teaching.* uk.bl.ethos.569243 (Thesis embargoed until 2017).

Jansen, J. (2008) The Challenge of the Ordinary. In I. Bogotch, F. Beachum, J. Blount, J. Brooks, F. English & J. Jansen, (2008) *Radicalizing Educational Leadership.* Sense Publishers; Rotterdam, pp-pp 147-156.

Jarvis, P. (1999) *The Practitioner-Researcher: Developing theory from practice.* San Francisco: Jossey-Bass.

Johnson R.B., Onwuegbuzie A.J. & Turner L.A. (2007) Toward a Definition of Mixed Methods Research. *Journal of Mixed Methods Research.* 1, 2, 112-133.

Johnson, R. (2012, 2nd edition) Resources in the Management of Change in Higher Education. In Trowler, P. (ed) (2012*) Higher Education Policy and Institutional Change: intentions and outcomes in turbulent environments.* Amazon Kindle edition.

Kane, R., Sandretto, S. and Heath, C. (2002) Telling Half the Story: A Critical Review of Research on the Teaching Beliefs and Practices of University Academics. *Review of Educational Research*, 72, 2, 177-228.

Kettley, N. (2010) *Theory Building in Educational Research.* London: Continuum.

Koshy, V. (2009) *Action Research for Improving Educational Practice: A step-by-step guide.* London: Sage (second edition).

Labaree, R. V. (2002) The Risk of "Going Observationalist": Negotiating the hidden dilemmas of being an insider participant observer. *Qualitative Research*, 2, 1, 97- 122.

Latour, B. (2000), When Things Strike Back: A possible contribution of 'science studies' to the social sciences. *British Journal of Sociology.* 51, 1, 107-123.

Lave, J. & E. Wenger (1991) *Situated Learning. Legitimate peripheral participation.* Cambridge, Cambridge University Press.

Lefebvre, H. (1984) *Everyday Life in the Modern World.* New Brunswick: Transaction Books.

Lincoln, Y. S. & Guba E. G. (1985) *Naturalistic Inquiry.* Thousand Oaks: Sage.

Lobb, R. (2015) *Organisational Citizenship Behaviour in the Further Education Sector – Deconstructing a Managerialist Positivist Paradigm.* PhD, Lancaster University.

Lodico, M. G., Spaulding, D. T., and Voegtle, K. H. (2010) *Methods in Educational Research: From theory to practice.* London: John Wiley & Sons.

Löw, M. (2008) The Constitution of Space: The structuration of spaces through the simultaneity of effects and perception. *European Journal of Social Theory*, 1, 11, 25-49.

LSE London School of Economics (nd) *Maximizing the Impacts of Your Research: a handbook for social scientists.* Available at: http://www2.lse.ac.uk/government/research/resgroups/LSEPublicPolicy/Docs/LSE_Impact_Handbook_April_2011.pdf

LSE Public Policy Group (2011) *Maximizing the Impacts of Your Research: A handbook for social scientists.* London: LSE. Available at: http://blogs.lse.ac.uk/impactofsocialsciences/the-handbook/

Lukes, S. (1973) On the Social Determination of Truth. In R. Horton & R. Finnegan (eds) *Modes of Thought.* London: Faber.

Mand, K. (2011) Researching Lives in Motion: Multi-Sited strategies in a transnational context. In S. Coleman and P. von Hellermann (2011) *Multi-Sited Ethnography: Problems and possibilities in the translocation of research methods.* London: Routledge.

Mann, L. (2009) *Research Methods: Phenomenography*. http://aaee-scholar.pbworks.com/w/page/1177079/Research%20Method%20-%20Phenomenography

Marcus, G. E. (2011) Multi-Sited Ethnography: Five or six things I know about it now. In S. Coleman and P. von Hellermann (2011) *Multi-Sited Ethnography: Problems and possibilities in the translocation of research methods*. London: Routledge.

Marshall, M. N. (1996) Sampling for Qualitative Research. *Family Practice*. 13, 6, 522-525.

Marton, F. and Booth, S. (1997) *Learning and Awareness*. Hillsdale, NJ: Lawrence Erlbaum.

Maruyama, M. (1981)Endogenous Research: Rationale. In P. Reason & J. Rowan (eds) *Human Inquiry: A sourcebook for new paradigm research*. Chichester: John Wiley & Sons, 227-238.

Mason, M. (2010) Sample Size and Saturation in PhD Studies Using Qualitative Interviews. Forum Qualitative Sozialforschung / Forum: Qualitative Social Research 11, 3. http://www.qualitative-research.net/index.php/fqs/article/view/1428/3027

Maxwell, J. A., & Mittapalli, K. (2008) Theory. In L. Given (ed), *The SAGE Encyclopedia of Qualitative Research Methods* (pp. 876-880). Thousand Oaks, CA: SAGE Publications.

Mayer, R. (2007) *Learning and Instruction*. 2nd edition. New Jersey: Pearson Education.

McNay, I. (1995) From Collegial Academy to Corporate Enterprise: The changing cultures of universities, in T. Schuller (ed) *The Changing University?* Buckingham: Open University Press/SRHE, 105-115

Mercer, J. (2007) The Challenges of Insider Research in Educational Institutions: Wielding a double-edged sword and resolving delicate dilemmas. *Oxford Review of Education*, 2007, 33, 1, 1-17.

Merriam, S. B. (2009) *Qualitative Research: A Guide to Design and Implementation*. London: Wiley and Sons.

Merton, R. (1949) *Social Theory and Social Structure.* New York: Free Press.

Merton, R. (1972) Insiders and Outsiders; A chapter in the sociology of knowledge. *American Journal of Sociology*, 78, 1, 9-47.

Meyer, J. H. F. and Eley, M. G. (2006) The Approaches to Teaching Inventory: A Critique of its Development and Applicability. *British Journal of Educational Psychology.* 76, 633–649.

Mills, C. W. (1959) *The Sociological Imagination.* Harmondsworth: Penguin.

Morse J. M. (2001) Using Shadowed Data. *Qualitative Health Research.* 11, 3, 291-292.

Morse, J. M. (2000) Determining Sample Size. *Qualitative Health Research.* 10, 1, 3-5.

Munby, H. (2003) Guest Editorial: Educational Research as Disciplined Inquiry: Examining the Facets of Rigor in Our Work. *Science Education.* 87, 2, p.153-60.

Murray, R. (2011) *How to Write a Thesis.* 3rd edition. London: Open University Press.

Nespor, J. (2003) Undergraduate Curricula as Networks and Trajectories. In R. Edwards and J. Usher *Space, Curriculum and Learning.* Charlotte, NC: Information Age Publishing, 93-122.

Nespor, J. (2007) Curriculum Charts and Time in Undergraduate Education. *British Journal of Sociology of Education*, 28, 6, 753-766.

NewU Pro-Vice Chancellor (1996) HEQC *Quality Audit Report: Collaborative provision. Memorandum to Management Team*, 15 January. Newtown: NewU.

O'Reilly, M., & Parker, N. (2013) 'Unsatisfactory Saturation': a critical exploration of the notion of saturated sample sizes in qualitative research. *Qualitative Research.* 13, 2, 190-197.

Oakeshott, M. (1962) *Rationalism in Politics.* London: Methuen.

Ozga, J. (2000) Policy Research in Educational Settings: Contested Terrain. Open University Press, Buckingham.

Pang, M. F. (2003) Two Faces of Variation: On Continuity in the Phenomenographic Movement. *Scandinavian Journal of Educational Research.* 47, 2, 145-156.

Patton, M. Q. (1997) *Utilization-Focused Evaluation: The new century text* (3rd edition). Thousand Oaks: Sage.

Pawson, R. and Tilley, N. (1997) *Realistic Evaluation*. London: Sage.

Platt, J. (1981) On Interviewing One's Peers. *British Journal of Sociology*, 32, 1, 75-91.

Popper, K. (1945) *The Open Society and its Enemies*. London: Routledge and Kegan Paul.

Popper, K. (1957) *The Poverty of Historicism*. London: Routledge and Kegan Paul.

Popper, K. (1963) *Conjectures and Refutations*. London: Routledge and Kegan Paul.

Porter, S. (1993) Critical Realist Ethnography: The case of racism and professionalism in a medical setting. *Sociology*, 7, 4, 591-609.

Preedy, M. and Riches, C. (1988) Practitioner Research in School Management: An analysis of research studies undertaken for an Open University course. In: J. Nias and S. Groundwater-Smith (Eds) *The Enquiring Teacher: Supporting and sustaining teacher research* (Lewes, Falmer Press).

Prosser, M. and Trigwell, K. (1999) *Understanding Learning and Teaching*. Buckingham: SRHE and Open University Press.

Rabbitt, E. (20003) Insider Research: The implications of conducting research in your home locale. Paper to AARE Conference, 30 Nov-3 Dec, Auckland. Available at http://www.aare.edu.au/03pap/rab03740.pdf

Reason, P. and Rowan, J. (eds) (1981) *Human Inquiry: A sourcebook of new paradigm research*. Chichester: Wiley.

Reckwitz, A. (2002) Towards a Theory of Social Practices: A development in culturalist theorizing. *European Journal of Social Theory*, 5, 2, 243-63.

Rhoades, G. (2007) Technology-enhanced Courses and a Mode III Organization of Instructional Work. *Tertiary Education Management,* 13, 1, 1-17.

Rocco, T.S, Bliss, L.A, Gallagher, S. & Perez-Prado, A. (2003) Taking the Next Step: Mixed Methods Research in Organizational Systems. *Information Technology, Learning, and Performance Journal.* 21, 1, 19-29.

Roland, D. R and Wicks, D. A (2009) Qualitative Research in the New Century: Map points in insider research. Paper to CAIS conference, May 28-30, Ottawa. http://www.cais-acsi.ca/proceedings/2009/Wicks_Roland_2009.pdf

Ross, A. (1992) Two Decades of Higher Education. *Higher Education,* 23, 99-112.

Rubin, H. J. and Rubin, S. (2005) *Qualitative Interviewing: The art of hearing.* Thousand Oaks: Sage.

Ruderman, R. S. (1997) Aristotle and the Recovery of Political Judgement. *American Political Science Review,* 91, 2, 409-420.

Ryan, L., Kofman, E. and Aaron, P. (2011) Insiders And Outsiders: Working with peer researchers in researching Muslim communities, *International Journal of Social Research Methodology,* 14, 1, 49-60.

Saunders, M., Trowler, P. and Bamber, V. (eds) (2011) *Reconceptualising Evaluation in Higher Education: The practice turn.* London: Open University Press.

Sayer, A. (2010) *Method in Social Science.* London: Routledge.

Schatzki, T. R., Knorr-Cetina, K. and von Savigny, E. (eds.) (2001) The *Practice Turn in Contemporary Theory.* London: Routledge.

Schön D. (1983*) The Reflective Practitioner.* London: Basic Books.

Scott, J. C. (1992) *Domination and the Arts of Resistance: Hidden transcripts.* New Haven and London: Yale University Press.

Selwyn, N. (2014) 'So What?'... A Question that Every Journal Article Needs to Answer. *Learning, Media and Technology.* 39, 1, 1-5.

Shaw, I. and Crompton, A, (2003) Theory Like Mist on Spectacles Obscures Vision. *Evaluation,* 9, 2, 192-204.

Shay, S. (2008) Researching Assessment As Social Practice: Implications for research methodology. *International Journal of Educational Research,* 47, 3, 159-164

Shay, S., Ashwin, P. and Case, J. (2009) A Critical Engagement with Research into Higher Education. *Studies in Higher Education*, 43, 4, 373-375.

Shove, E. and Southerton, D. (2000), 'Defrosting the Freezer: From novelty to convenience - A narrative of normalization', *Journal of Material Culture*, 5, 3, 301-319.

Shove, E., Pantzar, M. and Watson, M. (2012) *The Dynamics of Social Practice: Everyday life and how it changes*. London: Sage.

Sibeon, R. (2007) *Contemporary Sociology and Policy Analysis*. Eastham: Tudor Business Publishing.

Simons, H. (2009) *Case Study Research in Practice*. London: Sage.

Smart, J. C., & Paulsen, M. B. (2011) *Higher Education: Handbook of Theory and Research, volume 26*. Dortrecht: Springer.

Smith, D. E. (2005) *Institutional Ethnography: A sociology for people*. Oxford: Altamira Press.

Smith, D. E. (ed.) (2006) *Institutional Ethnography as Practice*. Lanham, MD: AltaMira.

Smith, N. V. (1982) *Mutual Knowledge*. Michigan: Academic Press

Sprague, J. and Hayes, J. (2000) Self-Determination and Empowerment: A feminist standpoint analysis of talk about disability. *American Journal of Community Psychology*, 28, 5, 671-695.

Stenhouse, L. (1979) *The Problem of Standards in Illuminative Research*. Lecture given at the Annual General Meeting of the Scottish Educational Research Association, Glasgow: University of Glasgow, mimeo.

Strauss, A. L. And Corbin, J. (1990) *Basics of Qualitative Research: Grounded Theory Procedures and Techniques*. Thousand Oaks, CA: Sage (1990)

Tan, H. K. and Prosser, M. (2004) Qualitatively Different Ways of Differentiating Student Achievement: A Phenomenographic Study of Academics' Conceptions of Grade Descriptors. *Assessment and Evaluation in Higher Education*. 29, 3, 267-282. Available (on 12.11.2014) here: http://tinyurl.com/p6rmpju

Thomas, G. & James, D. (2006) Re-inventing grounded theory: some questions about theory, ground and discovery. *British Educational Research Journal*, 32, 6, 767–795.

Thomas, G. (2011) The Case: Generalisation, theory and phronesis in case study. *Oxford Review of Education*, 37, 1, 21-35.

Tierney, W. G. (1994) On Method and Hope. In A. Gitlin (Ed.), *Power and Method: Political Activism and Educational Research*. London: Routlege. Pp. 97-115.

Tierney, W. G. and Rhoades, R. A. (1993) Postmodernism and Critical Theory in Higher Education: Implications for Research And Practice. In J. C. Smart (Ed.), *Higher Education: Handbook of Theory and Research*, v. 9. New York: Agathon Press. Pp. 308-343.

Tight, M. (2003) *Researching Higher Education*. Maidenhead: Open University Press.

Tight, M. (2004) Research into Higher Education: An a-theoretical community of practice? *Higher Education Research & Development,* 23, 4, 395-411.

Tight, M. (2007) Bridging the Divide: A comparative analysis of articles in higher education journals published inside and outside North America. *Higher Education*, 53, 235-253.

Tight, M. (2008) Higher Education Research as Tribe, Territory and/or Community: A co-citation analysis. *Higher Education*, 55, 593-605.

Tight, M. (2011) Editorial: Eleven years of Studies in Higher Education. *Studies in Higher Education*, 36,1, 1-6.

Tight, M. (2012a) Higher Education Research 2000-2010: Changing journal publication patterns. *Higher Education Research and Development.* 31, 5, 723-740.

Tight, M. (2012b 2e) *Researching Higher Education*. Maidenhead: Open University Press, second edition.

Tissen, R. and Deprez, F. L. (2008) *Towards a Spatial Theory of Organizations: Creating new organizational forms to improve business performance.* NRG Working Paper 08-04. http://www.nyenrode.nl/FacultyResearch/research/Documents/Research%20Paper%20Series/2008/08-04.pdf

Titchen, A. and Hobson, D. (2011) Understanding Phenomenology Through Reverse Perspectives. In B. Somekh and C. Lewin, (eds) *Theory and Methods in Social Research* (2nd edition), 121-130.. London: Sage.

Tooley, J. & Darby, D. (1998) *Educational Research: A Critique: A survey of published educational research.* London: OFSTED.

Trafford, V. and Leshem, S. (2002) Starting at the End to Undertake Doctoral Research: Predictable questions as stepping stones. *Higher Education Review*, 35, 1, 31-49. Also available at: http://anglia.academia.edu/VernonTrafford/Papers/1103455/Starting_at_the_end_to_undertake_doctoral_research_predictable_questions_as_stepping_stones

Trafford, V. Leshem, S. and Bitzer, E. (2014) Conclusions Chapters in Doctoral Theses: Some International Findings. *Higher Education Review*. 46,3, 52 – 81. Also available at: https://www.researchgate.net/publication/272775961_Conclusion_chapters_in_doctoral_theses_some_international_findings

Trotter, R. T. (2012) Qualitative research sample design and sample size: Resolving and unresolved issues and inferential imperatives. *Preventive Medicine*. 55, 398–400.

Trow, M. (1970) Reflections on the Transition from Mass to Universal Higher Education. *Daedalus*, 90, 1-42.

Trowler, P. & Trowler, V. (2010) *Frameworks for Action II: Guidance for policy makers on student engagement.* York: Higher Education Academy. Available at: https://www.academia.edu/10276127/Student_Engagement_Framework_for_Action_for_Policy_Makers

Trowler, P. (1997) *From Technological Somnambulism to Epistemological Awareness: Reflections on the impact of computer-aided qualitative data analysis.* Available at: https://www.academia.edu/12432374/From_Technological_Somnambulism_to_Epistemological_Awareness_reflections_on_the_impact_of_computer-aided_qualitative_data_analysis

Trowler, P. (1998) *Academics Responding to Change.* London: Open University Press/SRHE.

Trowler, P. (2001) Captured by the Discourse? The socially constitutive power of new higher education discourse in the UK. *Organization,* 8, 2, 183-201.

Trowler, P., Saunders, M. and Bamber, V. (eds.) (2012) *Tribes and Territories in Higher Education: Practices in the 21st Century.* London: Routledge.

Trowler, P. (2008) *Cultures and Change in Higher Education: Theories and practices.* London: Palgrave Macmillan.

Trowler, P. (2012a) Wicked Issues in Situating Theory in Close Up Research. *Higher Education Research and Development.* 31, 3, 273-284.

Trowler, P. (2012b) *Doing Insider Research in Universities.* Amazon Kindle edition. http://www.amazon.com/dp/B006JI3SGK

Trowler, P. (2012c) *Doctoral Research into Higher Education: Thesis structure, content and completion.* Amazon Kindle edition.

Trowler, P. (2012d) *Doctoral Research into Higher Education: Making Theory Work.* Amazon Kindle edition.

Trowler, P. and Wareham, T. (2007) Reconceptualising the 'Teaching-Research Nexus'. In proceedings of the annual HERDSA Conference 2007: *Enhancing Higher Education Theory and Scholarship.* 8-11 July 2007, Adelaide Australia. https://www.academia.edu/10276020/Reconceptualising_the_Teaching-Research_Nexus

Trowler, P. and Wareham, T. (2008) *Tribes, Territories, Research and Teaching: Enhancing the teaching-research nexus.* Available at: https://www.academia.edu/10276007/Tribes_Territories_Research_and_Teaching_Enhancing_the_Teaching-Research_Nexus

Trowler, V. (2009) *Locating 'Knowledge Workers' In South African Universities Within Changing Dynamics Of Class: A case study of selected strata of 'non-academic' workers at UCT.* Unpublished Med Thesis, University of the Western Cape, South Africa.

Trowler, V. (2010) *Student Engagement Literature Review*. York: Higher Education Academy. Available online: http://www.heacademy.ac.uk/assets/York/documents/ourwork/studentengagement/StudentEngagementLiteratureReview.pdf

Troyna, B. (1994) Reforms, Research and Being Reflexive About Being Reflective. In Halpin, D. (ed.) *Researching Education Policy: Ethical and Methodological Issues*. London: RoutledgeFalmer. pp1-12. See http://tinyurl.com/ndsjlbf

Turner, S. (1994) *The Social Theory of Practices: Tradition, tacit knowledge and presuppositions*. Cambridge: Polity Press; Chicago: University of Chicago Press.

University of Strathclyde: *Theory in Qualitative Educational Research*. http://www.strath.ac.uk/aer/materials/6furtherqualitativeresearchdesignandanalysis/unit2/

Walford, G. (1994) *Researching the Powerful in Education*. London: UCL press.

Walker, P., Thomson, M., and Walker, M. (2010) *The Routledge Doctoral Student's Companion: Getting to grips with research in education and the social sciences*. London: Taylor & Francis.

Warde, A. (2005) Consumption and Theories of Practice. *Journal of Consumer Culture*, 5, 2, 131-153.

Webb, A. (1991) Co-ordination: A problem in public sector management. *Policy and Politics*, 19, 4, 221-41.

Whitehead, J. (1989) Creating A Living Educational Theory From Questions Of The Kind, 'How Do I Improve My Practice?'. *Cambridge Journal of Education*, 19, 1, 41-52.

Whyte, W. F. (1943) *Street Corner Society: The social structure of an Italian slum*. Chicago: University of Chicago Press.

Williams, G. L. (1996) *Paying for Education Beyond Eighteen: An examination of issues and options*. London: The Council for Industry and Higher Education.

Williams, P. (1996) *Letter to Vice Chancellor [name deleted] Regarding Quality Audit Report: Collaborative provision*. 11 January. Gloucester: Higher Education Quality Council.

Winberg, C. (2003) Language, Content and Context in the Education of Architects. In R. Wilkinson (ed) *Integrating Content and Language: Meeting the challenge of multilingual higher education.* Maastricht: University of Maastricht Press. 320-332.

Wolfe, S. And Flewitt, R. (2010) New Technologies, New Multimodal Literacy Practices and Young Children's Metacognitive Development. *Cambridge Journal of Education.* 40, 4, 387-399.

Ybema, S., Yanow, D., Wels, H. and Kamsteeg, F. H. (eds) (2009) *Organizational Ethnography: Studying the complexity of everyday life.* London: Sage.

Yin, R. (2009 4e) *Case Study Research: Design and methods.* Thousand Oaks: Sage.

Glossary

'So What?' question: The question which runs: "So what is the wider significance of this research to the academic community generally and/or to the economy, society or culture?" A doctoral thesis needs to make an original contribution to knowledge and so this question is a very significant one for doctoral candidates.

Academic register: A register is a particular tone and use of words that are appropriate to a given social setting. So academic register is one used in the context of writing academic books, articles or a doctorate. It is formal, tends to use Latinate words, uses compound nouns, passive voice and so on.

Action research: A cyclical process of collecting and analysing data, reflection and taking or amending action in order to bring about enhancement in practices and outcomes in the area being researched.

Advance organizer: "An advance organizer is information that is presented prior to learning and that can be used by the learner to organize and interpret new incoming information" (Mayer, 2007).

Assumptive world: A cluster of values, attitudes, assumptions, ways of categorising, sets of meaning-attribution and precepts for action that are shared by a social group.

Axiological: Concerning the attribution of value. Axiological assumptions are preconceptions about the value of different things.

Cherry picking: In this context, being consistently selective about the data or literature used in order to substantiate an argument already formulated.

Cognitive closure/Conceptual closure: The situation in which analytical possibilities have been foreclosed, meaning that the person analysing the data sees only one way of interpreting them and begins to 'miss' aspects of data which could suggest alternatives. Deciding too early about the conclusions that can be derived from the data, and so ignoring evidence which contradicts those.

Critical discourse analysis: an approach to the study of the production and effects of texts of all sorts. It sees text (language and other forms of communication) as both shaped by and shaping the social world. It focuses particularly on inequitable social, economic and power structures which are sustained by discourse.

Discursive repertoires: Recurrently-used phrases, words, images or metaphors which situate the world in specific ways.

Elite policy study: A research project which studies top-level policy-makers or those who implement policy.

Emic accounts: depictions of the social world derived from data generated within a culture and presented to an audience in such a way as to provide an understanding of the meanings and frames of reference in that culture.

Empirical: Using primary data, collecting evidence from the world or observing it.

Empiricism: An approach to research which focuses on factual data without explicit or acknowledged use of theory, usually adopting a foundationalist position (see below).

Endogenous Research: the study of social institutions by those who are actors in them.

Epistemology: Theories of knowledge and what can be known.

Essentialism: An approach to understanding something which believes that thing to have characteristic properties which must be present for it to be itself, distinct from other things, and that those properties have effects beyond the thing itself.

Ethnography: A research approach which draws on multiple data sources to provide a detailed account of a cultural field.

Etic accounts: culturally neutral depictions of the social world, describing behaviours.

Foundationalism: An ontological position which holds that external reality exists independent from humans' apprehension of it.

Grounded Theory: An approach to research which begins with data collection and from that process generates a series of concepts which have explanatory power. It is an inductive approach rather than the more usual hypothetico-deductive one. The latter begins with hypotheses and theory and tests them against data using a design which arises from the logic of the hypothesis.

Hermeneutics: the art and science of interpretation, leading to explanatory theories. While phenomenology tends to be descriptive of lived experience and perception, hermeneutics is explanatory in nature.

Hidden Transcripts: the occluded articulations of power relations within organizations

Hypothetico-deductive tradition: the approach to research which involves formulating an hypothesis and then testing it with a view to refuting it. Hypotheses which consistently withstand attempts to test them to destruction may eventually be seen as scientific 'laws', though Popper's work warns us that refutation may occur at any time in the future so even laws should be seen as provisional.

Incommensurability: A situation in which theoretical positions are adopted which take such different ontological and epistemological standpoints that they are not comparable with each other, leaving no grounds for determining which is the most accurate.

Insider research: The study of social institutions by those who are actors in them. See Trowler (2012a) for more information on doing insider research.

Instrumentalism: Ideas guided by a desire for practical application, their value being measured by the success of the outcomes of that action.

Interpretivism: An approach to social science which stresses the importance of, and the importance of studying, subjects' interpretations of the world rather than or in significant addition to the world itself.

Methodology: In research, refers to the set of principles and conventions which set out how research should be done and what it can achieve and therefore guides research planning.

Methods: In research, includes the specific techniques used to gather data or to analyse them.

Monism: The opposite of dualism, which sees the world as divided into 'reality' and 'perceptions of reality'. Monism does not make such a distinction: the world is significant only as it is understood.

Naturalistic data: Records of activities that are neither elicited nor affected by the actions of social researchers.

New Paradigm Research: research which combines phenomenological insights with a 'systematic and rigorous search for truth' (Reason and Rowan, 1991).

Nomothetic approaches: Ways of depicting the social world in research which categorises aspects of it and sees those categories as amenable to scientific study and as operating in ways which can be captured in generalised ways.

Normative: Taking a committed stance about preferred present or future situations.

Ontology: Theory of the nature of 'reality', for example realist or social constructionist.

Operationalisation: The process of defining the elements of a concept in order to make its characteristics more capable of being researched or measured.

Outcome space: A term from phenomenography describing a framework of different types of perceptions about a phenomenon among a social group which emerge from the data and are organized into specific categories of description.

Phenomenography: phenomenography is a method of research rooted in phenomenological assumptions. Its focus is on variation in ways of seeing something – the categories of description found among a social group. The usual technique in phenomenographic analysis is interviewing and then careful analysis of transcripts to identify the outcome space.

Phenomenology: Phenomenology is a philosophical school which originates in the work of Edmund Husserl, further developed by Alfred Schutz. In brief it explores the way people make sense of the world – the ways in which their consciousness organizes and classifies it. The aim of studies based in phenomenology is to understand the meaning of things as seen through the eyes and mind of particular groups or individuals.

Phronesis: an Aristotelian term meaning the ability to interpret, assess and appropriately apply knowledge based on the wisdom gained through experience.

Policy trajectory study: A research project which follows a particular policy area from its inception through the various phases of implementation and finally collects data on the outcomes it has brought about, if any.

Positivism: An approach to social science which attempts to uncover regularities and eventually establish laws (or at least strong theories) of causality (predominantly of the form 'if X then Y'), usually through the scientific method, random controlled trials, quantitative approaches and the hypothetico-deductive approach.

Prescriptive: Giving directions about what to do.

Propositional knowledge: knowledge *that*, descriptive knowledge, as opposed to knowledge *how*.

Rational-purposive approach: An approach to management, policy-making and policy implementation which stresses the importance of making plans, devising fully outlined schemes for implementation with milestones, communicating these to those on the ground and moving in stages to planned objectives.

Realism: an ontological position which holds that external reality exists independent from humans' apprehension of it.

Re-speaking: This is the process in which one person listens to natural speech through headphones and almost simultaneously speaks the same words more slowly and distinctly into a microphone in order to get an accurate textual transcription using voice recognition software. It is a technique used for television subtitling and can be valuable for interview transcription.

Restricted Code: textual production which conveys rich meaning in few words, relying on correct interpretation by others in an interpretive community. It contrasts with 'elaborated code' in which text is fully articulated to allow interpretation regardless of context or audience.

Second Record: the underlying meanings of statements made in person or in print.

Shadowed data: By 'shadowed data' Morse refers to the data from interviewees that speak for *other* people: "information that participants give us about the types, characteristics, and dimensions of concepts, perceptions, behaviors, and opinions of others" (Morse, 2001, p. 291).

So What? Question: The question which runs: "So what is the wider significance of this research to the academic community generally and/or to the economy, society or culture?"

Totalising: making statements about phenomena which ignores nuanced differences between them but rather considers them to be one category.

Truth claims: In this context this refers to the claims made for the outcomes of the research in terms of how and where they can be applied, how robust they are and what the limits are of the claims made.

Index

Abstract
  for analysis, 215
  writing, 123
Action Research, 20, 253
Bibliography
  writing, 36
Borderlands, 228
Case Study Sites, 308
Conclusions Chapter, 148
Contextualising the Study, 132
Data Analysis, 146, 269
Data Collection, 331
Data Presentation, 146
Design Alignment, 168
  achieving, 201
Design Misalignment, 169
Discursive Repertoires, *12, 23, 110, 256, 378*
Documentary Evidence, 266
Emancipatory Research, 27
Emic Accounts, 241, 378
Epistemological Position, 178, 289, 318
Ethics and Politics
  insider research, 277
Etic Accounts, 242, 379

Evaluative research, 20, 254
Generalisability, 273, 305, 313, 319
Grand theory, 88
Hidden Transcripts, 241, 309
Hybridity, 228
Hypothesis Testing, 25, 258
Impact, 213
Insider Doctrine, 240
Insider Research, 239
  and theory, 26
Inspiration
  finding, 36
Institutional ethnography, 22, 255
Interviews, 334
  ideal number, 305
Introductory Chapter, 126
Literature Review, 137, 178, 324
Method/ology Chapter, 143
Micro-theory, 88
Middle-range theory, 88
Mixed Methods, 310
New Paradigm Research, 240

Observant Participation, 265
Ontological Position, 177, 289, 318
Outsider Doctrine, 240
Phronesis, 245
Polyocularity, 243
Predatory Publishers, 353
Research Design, 290
Research Questions, 11, 127, 211, 298
Resources for Insider Research, 293
Resources for Thesis Writing, 160
Robustness of Research, 271, 347
Sample Size, 305
   resources, 307
Saturation
   of data, 333
Second Record, 241, 272, 309, *See*
Seven Deadly Sins
   concluding, 150
   contextualising the study, 135
   data chapters, 147
   misalignment, 173
   research design, 30

   research questions, 14, 130
   theory, 101
Significance of Research, 31, 211, 271, 312
Single and Multi-Site Studies, 18, 251
Social Practice Theory, 107, 283
Social reconstructionist theory, 92
Standpoint Theory, 28, 29, 261, 341
Submission of Thesis, 344
Teleoaffectivity, 111
Theory and Research, 133, 180, 336
   and insider research, 259
   nature of, 87
Truth Claims, 123, 124, 126, 129, 130, 145, 148, 150, 185, 186, 255, 383, *See*
Validity and Reliability, 348
Valuable Virtues for Doctoral Success, 158
Viva Examination, 351
Workable Proposal
   finding, 41

About Paul Trowler

Paul is Professor of Higher Education, Lancaster University and Research Director of here@lancaster (the higher education research and evaluation centre). He has research interests which include: academic 'tribes' and their disciplinary territories; higher education policy-making and environmental change; cultures in universities; enhancing student engagement; planning and managing change in universities; the implementation of planned change particularly related to the enhancement of the curriculum, teaching, learning and assessment; and approaches to research and evaluation. Paul also engages in research, evaluation and development work with universities and higher education funding and policy bodies across the world, most recently in South Africa, Sweden, Chile, Italy, Norway, Australia and Ireland. Paul has published a large number of book, chapters, articles and reports both physical and electronic form.

You can connect with Paul in the following ways:

Amazon author's page: http://www.amazon.co.uk/-/e/B001HQ35TY

Email: p.trowler [at] gmail.com

Youtube channel: https://www.youtube.com/channel/UCp8o0sXsbkwRyl4JPad2SFA

Visit my website for a full list of all my physically published books, articles, chapters and reports at: www.paul-trowler.weebly.com

Copyright 2016 Paul Trowler. All rights reserved.

Printed in Great Britain
by Amazon